ACKNOWLEDGEMENTS

First, I would like to thank all at Gill Books for the opportunity to go on the wonderful journey that writing this book has taken me. At every turn they respected the difficult spaces I found myself in as I relived the traumas of my life. I would also like to thank Brian Langan, who made the editing process so much easier than I thought it would be.

Trinity and my community have supported me at every inch of my journey so far and I am proud to be a Tallaght woman, and honoured to be part of the Trinity College community.

None of this book would have been possible without the trust of my friends and the families of the friends I have lost. They have trusted me to tell parts of their lives and the lives of their deceased loved ones, and their trust in me has been a huge part of my healing at this juncture of my life. I think it is important to acknowledge and remember the precious lives of those who will never get the opportunity to live it. I am lucky to be alive and I remember them daily. They are part of why I fought so hard to survive.

Twitter and social media can be a tough place sometimes but I would like to acknowledge the huge amount of love and support I receive on a weekly basis on social media. It has picked me up on some very tough days in my political life so far. Strangers young and old from all around the country write to me to share their own struggles and to encourage me to keep going. I would like to thank them for that.

I have so many supports in my life but it has to be said that Seb McAteer, who was my campaign manager and now manages my office, has become one of the most important people in my life. He is indispensable and I would not be as successful in my job without him. I owe him so much.

I would also like to thank my counsellor Tommy Deegan, who on and off for nearly fifteen years has facilitated me through some tough times, often for free as I sometimes wasn't in a position to pay him for his time.

It is also important to thank my hairdresser and friend Amy Cummins. Amy has been my friend since we were very young, and she has done my hair for nearly twenty years. Every month when she did my hair she talked about how I should write a book someday. She believed in my ability before I realised it.

I would like to thank my family, both immediate and extended. I am very lucky to have such a supportive structure. I would like to extend my gratitude to my daughters' families, both the Wallaces and the Joneses, and all my daughters' siblings. I consider my girls' families to be part of my family.

I would especially like to thank Alan (Jordanne's da), because to tell my life, I had to tell parts of his, and it cannot have been easy to allow me to do that.

Thanks to my boyfriend Rónán, who wasn't there during the difficult times of my life but was a constant source of love as I found myself back in the pain of my past. He played a crucial role in getting me through the heartache I felt for the past year as I wrote each painful memory, and as I felt the pain of each word as if it were happening now.

My brother, Jay, sister-in-law, Laura, and nephew, Caiden, have given me 100 per cent support throughout the process. Even though my brother rings me constantly to tell me how proud he is off me, I will never tire of hearing that.

Most importantly, my ma is a source of strength that I have tapped into my whole life. She is my hero.

My wonderful daughters have come on a very bumpy ride through my life but stood strong by my side all the way. They have allowed me to talk about our lives and I hope I have done them proud, because they make me proud every second of every day. I love them with every part of who I am and I look forward to the rest of our lives together.

PEOPLE LIKE ME

LYNN RUANE

Gill Books

In memory of my da, John Ruane

Lynn Ruane is a social activist and politician who has served as a member of Seanad Éireann since April 2016. Independent of party affiliation, she is a prominent advocate of numerous progressive causes, including the reform and modernisation of Ireland's drug treatment and counselling infrastructure, universal access to education, women's reproductive rights, and LGBTQ rights. She is a graduate of Trinity College Dublin and has two daughters, the eldest of whom, Jordanne, is a DFCC-award-winning and IFTA-nominated actress.

CONTENTS

Part Two: Educating Lynn

PROLOGUE:
DEAR SANTA

It was Christmas morning, 1994. I was ten years old. I was sitting underneath the pine tree staring in awe at the letter left in the brand new typewriter. The rest of the world might as well have not existed.

> Dear Lynn,
> We hope you like your typewriter and enjoy writing your book. Well done for being such a good girl all year.
> Love, Santa

Christmas really was my favourite time of year. My da would get the records out and we would dance to 'White Christmas'. The record sleeve was beautiful, with a pop-up Christmas scene in the centre, all snow-capped trees and Mrs Claus's cute little cottage. I can almost smell Ma's Christmas puddings baking as I think back on childhood Christmas fun. She would make the puddings and my aunty Christine would make the Christmas cake. Later, we would go to Christmas Eve mass in our pyjamas and, back home, my brother and I would sit up chatting late in bed, hoping Santa would give us everything on our lists.

I can picture my da sneaking down first to make sure the coast is clear, checking to see that the milk and the cookies have been eaten and that Santa is nowhere to be seen.

I was so excited that year. The typewriter was at the top of my list, above the Christmas clothes and surprises. You see, I'd decided I was going to be an author. My parents bought me countless books, which I read morning, noon and night.

I loved Enid Blyton and A. A. Milne. That year, I'd even written to Enid Blyton for advice, not realising that she had died in the 1960s. I'd accidentally joined her fan club. I would read every sentence of every book as if the author was speaking straight to me and only to me. *"You can't stay in your corner of the Forest waiting for others to come to you. You have to go to them sometimes."* It took me a while to grasp what A. A. Milne was trying to say to me, but I think I understand now. At the time though, my little corner of the forest was sweet, innocent and safe. Sometimes I wish I'd stayed there.

I had asked Santa for everything I might need to be a writer. But I never really got the hang of typing then and I never wrote back to Santa. My life took off in a very different direction. So I am pretty excited, and also pretty scared, that after all those years, after how much I let that ten-year-old girl down, I am now finally writing my book. If I were to write back to Santa now, this is what I would say:

Well Santa,
It took a while to write my book but so many things got in the way. It is now 2018 and while I enjoyed the typewriter and tried to write many books, stuck together with Sellotape, I never really did manage to complete one in full.

This book will be very different to the one I might have written then. My book won't be like a Famous Five adventure, or about trips to the Antarctic and encounters with woolly mammoths like I promised, but it will take me to many cliff edges – psychological ones. These pages will be filled with extremes, from deep grief to limitless love. It will be about my life, my family and my community, and it will be as honest a reflection as it can be. I can only tell this story through my eyes. So I am sure many will disagree with what I have to say and that others from my community have lived very different lives to mine. But this is my history, my reality, how I experienced the world.

There will be stories and reflections in this book that those I love will be hearing for the first time – assaults I endured, sadnesses I kept to myself, my deepest thoughts on what my life was like as a child and teenager.

The pages of this book that might have been filled with magic and wonder instead tell of struggle and teenage motherhood – but also determination and triumph. My story is filled with as much life as death.

I have an amazing life. I have laughed a lot, and with the support of my loving family and close-knit community I have come out the other side of trauma – a little bashed, a little scarred, but I have taken that trauma and transformed it until I found my power.

The funny thing about human experience is that it is both individual and collective and these things don't always fit neatly together. I have lived my life through conflict, a conflict of heart and mind and a conflict of what I should do and what I want to do.

Back to Enid Blyton. One of my favourite lines comes from *Mr Galliano's Circus*: "The best way to treat obstacles is to use them as stepping-stones. Laugh at them, tread on them, and let them lead you to something better." This book, Santa, is a book about overcoming obstacles, whether they are self- or state-imposed. Overcoming obstacles takes more than just the self; it relies on others who have stepped on the stones ahead of you, smoothing the path, always ready to put their hand out and help you jump. So, before I take you through my life, be sure that I recognise all of those who stood on those stones and helped me to jump my way to safety, and I thank them for it. I also know that there are people in my life who may be triggered by some of the events described, because they lived through them alongside me; they lost their friends too.

Finally, Santa (Ma and Da), thank you for being you and for never judging me, rejecting me or turning away from me, even when I was at my darkest. Ma, I know this book will be hard for you to read, but please know that I wouldn't be who I am now if you hadn't put the right foundations in place. I came back to the safe embrace of your love and it was never your fault that I strayed so far away. I only survived life because of you.

There are many things I hope people get from this book. I hope some can relate to it and know that they are worth more than they think. I hope people see that politicians are just humans and life throws us all around a little. I hope my community knows that this is not how it is meant to be; we should not die so young.

All I can do is be honest, because in honesty I can find my most vulnerable self. My only request of readers is that they understand that on the other side of these pages lie real lives, and that we are all human. I may finish this book as an author and fulfil the dream of that ten-year-old girl, but I never, for a moment, thought my book would be what it is. That ten-year-old girl is still in me, but it has taken me a long time to find her, and to tell her everything will be OK.

Love, Lynn

PART ONE:
THE PLAN AND THE PATH

CHAPTER 1:
A KIND OF MAGIC

"Look, Ma – what's wrong with that bird?"

It was a sparrow, hopping around beside the bus shelter, one wing fluttering. The other was at a funny angle.

Ma shifted her shopping bags around. "Aw, the poor thing. I think its wing must be broken."

I bent down and lifted the sparrow gently, trying not to hurt the damaged wing.

"Can I take it home? I can put a splint on it."

Ma looked at me and sighed. She knew I'd sulk if she said no. "You'll have to ask the bus driver."

Of course, when the bus arrived, the driver wouldn't let me take the injured sparrow on. I turned to Ma again. "Can we walk home?"

"Ah, Lynn, not with all this shopping. It's too far."

Tears in my eyes, I placed the little injured sparrow under some bushes behind the bus shelter. All the way home on the bus, I prayed and prayed that it would heal and fly to safety.

I was obsessed with animals and felt I had a connection with them. I used to rush home from school every day to get a fix of *The Jungle Book*. I envied Mowgli's life in the jungle.

As well as an author, I wanted to be a vet. Not just any vet: one of those park rangers in Africa, or maybe a zoologist travelling the world with David Attenborough. Maybe I could have done both. I would sit in silence for hours watching David Attenborough on TV. I dreamt that one day I would get to see the Big Five – lions, elephants, rhinos, leopards and buffalo. I would picture myself in safari clothes, driving an open-top Land Rover across the African plains. I hoped that one day I could walk through the bush and that I would be at one with the lions; they would accept me as family. I wanted to see the saltwater crocodiles of Mexico, and I wanted to stand in the centre of the great migration, close my eyes and hope I didn't get trampled by the herds of wildebeest. For now, though, I had to stick with the smaller animals.

My friend Robo taught me how to skate. I loved speeding around the road, but that changed when I ran over a nest of woodlice. I felt awful that I'd destroyed their home, so I made a little house out of a pile of Kellogg's cereal boxes. It took me days. Staples and Sellotape everywhere. Then I pulled up all the grass verges and carried hundreds of woodlice to my bedroom in several trips. I went to bed happy that night knowing that they were safe in their new home, free from the danger of skates. Needless to say, there was not a single woodlouse left in the box the next morning.

My middle name is Bernadette, after my mother. Ma sometimes thinks she's dyslexic. She's not; she just can't spell, probably because she left school when she was fourteen. Of course, she'd been going on the hop for years. She would go straight across the road and spend the day at her friend's house, which was right next door to Brendan O'Carroll's house.

She began work straight away in Gaye Girls Dresses in Moore Lane, and she has worked from that day on, only changing jobs twice. She has been working in the same factory since 1994. She doesn't speak much about her life, and I usually have to probe her to get even a hint of a story from her. It's not because she had a childhood she would like to forget. She had a loving family; she's very much like her own mother, my nanny, who is still alive. Ma isn't much of a storyteller and never places herself at the centre of a story. She is a listener, and a bloody good one.

My grand-uncle Paddy Losty's face was everywhere a few years ago. He was one of the "pintmen" whose photo was used in a book on Dublin pubs. Somebody stuck his face into an internet meme and soon it went viral. I showed some of these memes to Ma, and while we found the funny side to some of them, it felt a little unfair that this man's face was being used to take the piss.

Ma said Paddy was a cattle man like her own da. They were hard workers. She would grimace when she talked about the stench they used to bring home with them.

Like any child, Ma loved playing on swings, or skipping with her friends. Once she started working, she would go swimming every night. By the time her sisters Rita and Christine were heading off to the local disco, my ma would already have done a few lengths of the pool and headed home. She was shy and had very little confidence. She never wore make-up or did anything that would make her stand out. And that was her life until she was twenty, when she started going out with my da, Johnny Ruane. I have a few memories of the factory where they met in Moore Lane. I used to love when Da brought me. I remember the old-style elevator that looked like a cage.

Most of what I know about my da comes from my uncle Noel, a great storyteller. Da was the second of four boys. They grew up in a one-room tenement on Usher's Quay with their parents – my nanny Minnie and Granda Michael, though they later moved to Ballyfermot. Granda Michael was from Mayo and my nanny Minnie, who was born at the end of the 1800s, was a strong Dublin woman who worked hard when she could find work. My granda was a keeper in

Dublin Zoo. I never got to know my Ruane grandparents, but I like to think my dream of being a zoologist came from Granda Michael. According to my uncle Noel, Granda was once attacked by a bear at the zoo, but Granda fought him off with a sweeping brush.

Da was a very handsome, dark-haired young man, with lots of potential both in sport and school. Noel jokes about it now, but I think he feels guilty that he may have got in the way of Da's schooling. Noel was badly injured in an accident on the Quays and suffered permanent damage to his leg. He spent a lot of time in hospital and never went to secondary school. Da spent a lot of time caring for him. They couldn't afford a wheelchair so Da wheeled Noel around in a baby's buggy, which led to a lot of slagging from the local lads.

Da was close to all his brothers. I still love seeing Noel and their youngest brother, Michael. It's like spending a little time with a piece of my da. They are all good humoured and tell similar stories, like collecting jam jars so they could pay into the cinema, or going to school with beer mats in their shoes to block the holes. They often went for penny dinners in what is now known as Little Flower Penny Dinners on Meath Street. The way they described it, they were like characters straight out of *Oliver Twist*.

I'm never sure how many of these stories I should believe. Like the time Da was coming home from school and spotted his older brother Barney floating down the Liffey in a rubber ring. My da jumped in and swam after him. Barney was laughing but Da panicked. As Da told me this story, I was unsure why he was so scared for Barney, as they swam in the Liffey all the time. He laughed at the end and said Barney couldn't swim.

Da used to tell us random things about himself. He once told us he could speak French. He hadn't a word but apparently the name Ruane is of French origin, which meant we probably at least had some French blood.

Da didn't even drink regularly; I don't think he had his first drink until he was forty or so. He would encourage us not to drink and only ever do things in moderation. After he retired, he would go to Killinarden House, the local, for one pint and a bet. He never bet more than a euro.

I wish I knew more about my da's life before I was part of it, but I don't. It is as though he and my ma created a life where only the four of us existed. It was safe in there all the same, as a kid growing up. My da was a good man and he was loving. I miss lying in his arms with my head on his chest, listening to Willie Nelson or watching a black-and-white movie.

My ma and da used to tell me all about my arrival into the world. A taxi dropped my parents to the Rotunda Hospital, where I was born at 10.55 a.m. on 20 October 1984, a Saturday morning. Ma looked at me and thought I had a face full of freckles, until the doctor told her they were bruises, from my top lip right up to my forehead, from the cord being wrapped around my neck. My toes looked a little funny too, my baby toe wrapped over my next toe on both feet, but they fixed this with a little operation.

My mother was twenty-three years old. My brother Jason was two years old. We lived in a one-bedroom flat in a seven-story block in Ballymun. My ma enjoyed living in Ballymun. She felt close to her sister Christine, who lived in the next block up, and her sister-in-law Ann Wright, who lived in one of the towers.

I have no memories of the flats as I was still a baby when my parents were offered a council house in a little cul-de-sac in Killinarden in Tallaght. Ma missed her family when she moved to Tallaght, and she used to cry her eyes out on the bus home from the northside. It felt like she was miles away from everything she knew.

My earliest memories of home life in Killinarden are of a perfect family. The team effort of my parents' relationship was present as long as I can remember. My ma worked on her sewing machine in the kitchen when we were young. My da would cycle in and out of Moore Lane clothing factory every day and bring my ma's work to and from the factory in big black bags strapped onto the back of his bike. When Ma wasn't on the sewing machine, she was knitting jumpers. I thought I was great dropping around to see my friend Jennifer Mealy in my new "Forever Friends" jumper, only to find her in an identical one. Turns out my ma and Jennifer's ma shared knitting patterns. I wasn't impressed.

I love to sit with Ma looking back at photos of those early days. We did everything as a family. In every family picture, we're at a carnival, on the beach, or playing with conkers in the grass in the Phoenix Park. Some of my favourite pictures are of walks in Albert Park. Da looks so handsome in them all, his hair still dark, which is not how I remember him. I can't help but notice just how much I stare up at my da, the biggest of smiles on my face, which is framed by blonde curls.

Saturday nights were my favourite. TV shows such as *Blind Date*, *Catchphrase* and *A Question of Sport* kept us all entertained as we tried to outdo each other to be the first to guess the correct answers. Da always won *A Question of Sport*. His knowledge of soccer was endless. He watched every league match, not just the League of Ireland and the Premiership but any soccer from around Europe. He was a Leeds United supporter, a referee, and in his younger days he even did stints with Bray Wanderers, Sligo Rovers and St Pats. He had also been a champion boxer when he was in the army. He was an amazing sportsman.

Aunty Ann was a huge support to my ma and would babysit regularly. I sometimes spent the night in Ann's with my two cousins, Liza and Suzanne. I was petrified of Ann. She was a powerful force, with a strong Dublin accent, and she was loud, unlike my ma. I would later grow to respect her. I learned as I matured that she was a strong woman who herself fought for many years to provide services to drug users in Blanchardstown.

My parents stayed strong on everything together and there was no room to play them off each other, which wasn't ideal for the mischief-maker in me. I was, apparently, a pet as a toddler – until you pissed me off. According to my ma – and my school reports – I was a good kid, but I was very opinionated and extremely headstrong.

One day in playschool, I went for a boy when he wouldn't let me play with his tractor. So my ma brought me to a different playschool. On the first day, I begged her to allow me to bring my teddy. He looked like the TV puppet Sooty. Ma warned me that it was not a good idea, but I was adamant. She was right; at the end of the day, I couldn't find Sooty. My beloved companion was gone.

I remember feeling sad and confused as I strolled home from school hand-in-hand with my mother. How could Sooty just disappear? Someone must have taken him. When we got home, Ma smiled at me and said, "I have a surprise for you. Come upstairs". And there it was: a brand-new teddy, a panda. Ma must have put it aside as a present for me, and decided to give it to me early because I was so upset. I soon forgot about Sooty. I held that panda so tightly with one hand and held onto my ma with the other. I loved my little baby panda bear in an instant and I vowed never to lose him. I kept that promise and, to this day, this baby panda bear sits on the top of my wardrobe, along with a mammy bear and daddy bear. Baby bear is a little worn; one eye is missing and his fur is in bad condition. He lost his stuffing in 1990. I remember the year because I used Italia '90 flags to fill him up. But they sit there now, the perfect little panda family.

While I had a few negative experiences with teachers over the years, I adored my very first teacher at the Sacred Heart primary school, Marie Tuohy. She was amazing, always encouraging, always praising me for my reading. She would get me, at four years old, to read to the class. She also allowed me to read my own, more advanced, books along with my friend, Sinead Redmond. We would sit together, lost in adventures, while the rest of the class were still on *Ann and Barry*. I was lucky to have this wonderful woman for my first two years in primary school.

But things changed in first class. The teacher was scary and stern, and seemed only interested in bullying and frightening children. She made school a nightmare, and she almost stole my love of learning. Even back then, it wasn't in my nature to let people in authority mistreat me. So, if she grabbed my arm too tightly or shouted at me for no reason, I would speak up. She didn't like this. She would get her revenge.

One day, the film producers and crew from *School Around the Corner* visited our school, chatting to kids and observing classrooms to get a sense of which kids would work well on the show. I knew I would be good. I let them know I wanted to be part of the show. But it seems the teacher decided that my TV debut wouldn't happen under her watch. She told the crew that I was a bold kid who had run out of school early the day before. This was news to me. I was six years old; where would I have run to?

I'd had enough of this woman. I cried all the way home from school that day, frightened that she would tell the principal and my ma the same lie she'd told the TV crew. I told Ma what had happened, and she believed me. She promised that she would sort it out first thing in the morning. I was so relieved, and proud of Ma.

The next morning, Ma asked to see the principal. Ma asked her one simple question: "Why didn't someone alert me to the fact that my child ran out of school?"

The principal looked blankly at Ma. It was clear she hadn't the foggiest what she was talking about.

Ma didn't let up. "If a six-year-old leaves your school without permission, surely you'd phone a parent or the police? Anything could have happened to Lynn – if," she held up her hand, "IF the story is true."

My ma was always a timid woman, never raising her voice or temper, but she was my hero that day.

Happily, they removed me from that class and I felt safe again with the lovely Ms Hazel Browne. My teacher the following year, Ms O'Grady, would become very important to me. She developed my love of music; learning the tin-whistle was a real bonus for me. I loved learning new things.

Down the years, I always stood up for myself. Why should I just be quiet and get on with my work, forget about having a voice? Much later I would realise that it was only standing up for myself that would keep me moving forward in life. Once, Ms O'Grady blamed me for breaking something, and, much as I denied it, she wouldn't take my word. This was a big no for me, a massive trigger for anger, and I made a complaint to the principal, but I quickly forgave Ms O'Grady.

I also sang in the choir under Sister Bridget. She was no pushover and, while we would clash over the years, she was a good, strong woman. I loved going to church and I skipped down the road every Sunday morning to sing. Fr Pat was a lovely priest and I liked him very much. He always had great prizes for the winner of the colouring competition, which kept us kids busy during mass – usually a giant bag of sweets, more than my ma would ever be willing to buy me.

After months of begging Fr Jim and Fr Pat to be an altar server, I was allowed to be "one of the boys". I felt special being the only girl on the altar, glad that I would stand out.

I hated wearing dresses. As soon as I put on my Communion dress, I went out to the coal bunker to wreck it, and I played with the oily chain off a bike hoping my dress would become so grubby Ma would eventually take it off me. Ma never raised her voice, she just took it and did her best to wash out the stains. Later that day I also tipped a glass of fizzy orange over it while we were visiting Ma's friend, Anna Bowden. They tried to make it look as clean as possible before we moved on to visit the next house.

I loved being one of the boys. They seemed more fun to me. We all knew each other so well and there were so many kids on our street. We would play queenie-i-o, rounders and bulldogs' charge. In sports, too, I would always sweep up in medals and trophies at the Community Games and sports days. Even though I loved sports I wasn't naturally talented at anything. I would have to put in hours and hours of work. I despised boys telling me I couldn't play because I was a girl. Just like on the altar, I wanted to own my space amongst the boys on the football pitch. Looking back, I wish that I had instead fought for the right for all girls to participate but I was usually driven by my own desire to not be excluded because I was a girl.

I went to the local youth club too. One day, I was watching two older lads, Dicko and Sundy, playing table tennis.

"Here, give us a shot," I said.

They laughed, and one of them said, "No, you wouldn't be good enough."

They were both decent players and it's likely, looking back, that they had no interest in wasting their time playing me. That drove me mad, and I vowed, "I will fucking show them."

From then on, I'd make sure to get there early. I'd push the table up against the wall and play against myself. They were right, I was no good; but I persisted. My parents got me my own bat, a really good one, and I was delighted. I can still smell the rubber. Now I didn't have to wait until youth club nights; I could practise for hours in the kitchen.

As soon as I felt confident that I was good enough, I went back to Dicko and Sundy and asked for a game, but they still found ways to keep me out. I can't recall when they finally let me play but once they did, that was it; I was welcomed in.

I played for a while, and even attended two big competitions. The first one was in a community hall in Cabra. It was full of kids of various other nationalities, mostly Chinese. I took one look at the Chinese kids playing and knew that Sundy, Dicko and I were all crap.

For the most part my childhood was happy, full of fun and laughter. Some of the best years I had were in the summer projects and youth club, trips to Cavan and camping in forests. I wish I had known then what I know now and maybe I would have appreciated those days and friendships more. My early childhood was beautiful.

Friendship in Killinarden was a collective thing. If you were friends with one person, it was usually because whole families were friends with families in every house in the street. There was always more than one kid in the house and we all mixed together. Our road was tight and we made lots of fun memories, from water fights in the summer to sitting on the big step chatting in the evenings.

I never really felt like I had a best friend. I always wanted to be surrounded by people but I often felt that I was the second choice, that they had best friends and I was just "a friend". Before my teens, I spent most of my time with Niamh, who was a little older. I looked up to her as she would refuse to do anything she didn't want to do.

The first friend I made on our estate was Jennifer Mealy, who was sweet and giddy. We remained friends throughout our school life. We even had our first kisses at the same time – I was kissing Reds, a boy off our road, and Jenny was kissing my brother. The kiss was a street affair and all the kids gathered around to watch. It was democratically agreed that twenty seconds was an appropriate length of time for a kiss. So the four of us kissed to the accompaniment of a crowd of kids counting: *1…2…3…*

The laneways were my favourite place, maybe because my ma always told me to stay away from them. If they weren't being used for kissing boys, they were a place of spirits and Ouija boards. We spent one entire summer obsessed with calling people back from the dead, frightening the shite out of ourselves. Once we even convinced ourselves that one girl, Laura, had been marked by the devil. A council worker cutting the grass in the field had looked at us and we convinced ourselves that his eyes turned red. The next morning, when we knocked for Laura, she was in tears. She turned to the side and lifted her hair, and we all gasped. Two rows of square marks were imprinted on her neck. The devil had bitten her! Looking back now, she'd probably slept on some patterned object.

My friends and I all dressed the same. I loved to put a bun in my hair with about twenty bobbins and scrunchies holding it in place, even though it would hurt my head. We spent a summer wearing what I can only describe as plastic rave soothers. We hadn't yet discovered raves but we somehow discovered the colourful soothers, which we wore around our necks.

We followed every passing fashion trend, from NAF NAF jackets and X-Worx jeans to carpet shirts with red tab Levi's. Our mas started to buy us brand-name clothes for our Christmas presents, as most of us couldn't afford them all year round. I think Ma knew that other kids got them and, at that age, we just wanted to fit in. The very first pair of "real" runners Ma got me were Asics Gels, white leather with orange logos. These were followed by a pair of British Knights and then Reebok Classics. I was so happy to get them I would sleep in them.

My friends' parents often gave out to me. I was cheeky and always stood up to them. I never allowed anyone other than my parents to raise their voices at me. Standing up for myself got me in even deeper trouble, but I couldn't help it. I had a compulsion to tell people they were wrong or that they'd no right to speak to me if they came out shouting. But if they sat me down calmly and asked, "Lynn, my kid said you hit them. Is this true?", I'd answer them honestly.

I had a short fuse, which came in handy at times, but it meant I was testing the boundaries of adults when I was way too young. I soon came to realise that they weren't that scary at all. Nothing really happened if I gave them a mouthful, apart from Ma being disappointed and grounding me.

My brother Jay was more popular than I was. Jay and I were very different as kids. He was less intense than me and made friends more easily. He was smart and good in school. He just seemed to be better than me at most things. He didn't get grounded every two minutes like I did. He was innocent and I had an edge about me. Those roles may have reversed somewhat over the years.

I would never have admitted it at the time, but I loved him so much. When we were kids, he had bunk beds in his room. Ma had given me the biggest room because I had so many Barbies and every holiday home, horse and carriage, and wardrobe a Barbie could possibly need. I even had a mini grow-house where I grew cacti and my walls were covered with posters of Roy Keane, Andrei Kanchelskis, Lee Sharpe and Eric Cantona. I collected rubber ping-pong balls too – never played with them, just kept them in empty Chupa Chups containers.

I'd sneak out of my bed at night to sleep in Jay's room. I would have swapped all the Barbies, ping-pong balls and cacti in the world just to share a room with him. I envied my friends who shared with their siblings, even when my ma told me how squashed they all were growing up in her house with ten kids. Safety in numbers.

Jay was obsessed with Dublin Bus when he was little and still today he can tell the route of every bus number. He used to call the Local Link bus the "Local Stink". My poor parents used to have to take buses everywhere on weekends to keep him happy. They'd have to ask any passengers sitting on the front seats of the top deck to move so he could sit there. And God forbid if the bus driver didn't give him a roll of tickets as he got off. He would scream his head off. As a teenager, I once spent a drunken hour twisting a bus stop out of the tarmac to plant in our garden so Jay could open his curtains and see this bus stop standing in front of his bedroom window.

Jay was a brilliant footballer, following in Da's footsteps. I could see the pride on Da's face as he watched him play. My envy of their bond set in when I was very young, so much so that I often felt like

Jay was his favourite. In fact, I suspect I only learned sports so Da would not spend every weekend at Jay's matches and would have to choose whose match he would go to. I grew to believe that I had to be good at something, talented or a little more like Jay for Da to love me as much as he loved him. It took me a long time – too long – to realise I just needed to be me.

More and more, I seemed to be getting the blame for things I did not do. Maybe it was because I was loud and a little rebellious, but when I was not believed, it sparked an anger in me. I still very much carry that with me today. Maybe that is why I am so forthcoming and speak with honesty and truth about my life. I am petrified of being known as dishonest.

One day Ma came charging up the stairs, waving a soaking roll of toilet paper, shouting at me for throwing it out the window. I had no clue what she was talking about, but she blamed me anyway. It was hardly Jay, the golden boy, was it? He later admitted to me he had dropped it down the toilet by accident, then thrown it out the window so Ma wouldn't know. I resented Ma for this. Why didn't she believe me?

This sort of small, meaningless situation shaped my thinking as I grew towards my teenage years. Why be good? Why tell the truth? No-one will believe you anyway. What is it about me that makes me seem like a liar? Why is Jay assumed to always be telling the truth? I loved Jay, but sometimes I hated him.

One winter day when I was about seven or eight, Da brought home a magic wand. I loved magic. He got us all to sit on the sitting-room carpet.

"This is a special wand," he told us. "It has two wishes left. One for you, Lynn, and one for you, Jason."

We were both excited, but then Da handed the wand to Jay. I folded my arms in a huff.

"Why does he always get to go first?"

"Because he's the oldest," said Da.

Curiosity got the better of me when Da put a hat on the floor.

Jay was anxious, shuffling about uncomfortably. "What'll I wish for?"

Ma made a suggestion. "How about a new button for your duffel coat?"

Jay closed his eyes and waved the wand. "Abracadabra, hocus pocus, alakazam alakazoo. I wish for a duffel button."

I could not believe my ears. The dope! He had one wish, any wish, and he asked for a fucking button. I wasn't going to be fooled like that.

Then, lo and behold, Da pulled two duffel buttons from the hat. I was fairly shocked. It worked!

My turn. I wouldn't be as stupid with my wish. I waved the wand. "I wish for a puppy."

As you can imagine, the wand didn't work on my turn. Jay had his bleeding duffel buttons and I had feck-all but a broken wand.

I was disgusted. I wasn't sure magic was real anymore. And if magic wasn't real, then what was real?

We did eventually get a dog, but even that became a source of conflict. For several months, I held it against my parents that they allowed Jay to name our dog, Toby. I got no choice, even though I was the one who had sat up with him all through his first night in his new home. I even performed a DIY christening, sneaking into the church and filling up an old Cadet bottle with as much holy water as I could. Back home, I sprinkled the dog, chanting "I christen you Toby Rex Ruane". In this way, I took back control of the dog's naming.

Through all those amazing years of family life, full of potential and love, of games of Scrabble, of swimming lessons and magic tricks, a sense would creep into my mind, a sense of something being missing or a feeling of not belonging. My family was loving, we were a unit, my parents never fought and my brother was my best friend. But I had started to snoop around, full of suspicion, trying to find something, determined to uncover what was hidden beneath the smiles, rooting in every drawer in the house. But for what?

Over time, the feeling that something was wrong grew, and this was confirmed for me when a secret would emerge that shattered everything I knew to be true, turned my world upside down and shaped a huge part of who I am.

I would soon be left with more than a disbelief in magic and a broken wand.

CHAPTER 2:
TA DAH!

One day, when I was about nine years old, I was playing outside the local shop. There were bars on the shop windows that we'd sit on and hold onto to do tumbles. My friend Jessie told me it was her parents' anniversary. I stopped mid-tumble.

"Anniversary? What's that?"

"How long me ma and da are married," she said.

"What do ya mean, married?" I asked her.

She looked at me like I had two heads. I felt really stupid that I didn't know what she was talking about. I also knew I had found my first clue.

This was the beginning of a two-year search. It was time to put everything I'd learned from those Enid Blyton mysteries to work on a real-life investigation. From here on in, whenever I was in the homes of my friends and family, I'd take mental notes of the wedding pictures hanging from walls. They were everywhere, the white dresses and sharp suits, some in black-and-white and others with bad eighties hairdos.

Of course, our home was filled with photographs too. Christmas mornings, Communions, holidays to Tramore. We had loads of

Halloween pictures, usually me and my brother with white bedsheets over our heads or black bags with holes cut for our eyes. There was even one of Jay wearing my school uniform. We looked like the happiest kids you could imagine, big smiles in every picture, apart from the communion photos – I don't look very happy in either Jay's one or my own.

So where were the wedding photos? Why were there none of my ma in a white dress, or my da in a sharp suit? What was wrong with us?

When my parents were in work I would raid their room in such a hurry that I would scare myself. I convinced myself I would find some evidence at the top of their wardrobe so I pulled down all the biscuit tins of pictures. Surely I would find what I was looking for in all these photographs? There were more happy family photos but they weren't what I was looking for. I almost shit myself trying to squash everything back into the tins, frightened my parents would cop that someone had been at them.

I was becoming agitated, convinced that someone wasn't telling me something. I could never bring myself to ask. Maybe I was afraid of what the answer would be. One time, when Ma and Da had grounded me to my room, I drew a picture of a wedding, ran down the stairs and slipped it under the sitting-room door, but they never mentioned it.

There was so much I didn't understand. Like why Gary on our road used to annoy Jay by singing some nonsense song with the words, "Losty, got lost on the moon on Christmas night". I learned that my name used to be Lynn Losty when I first moved to Tallaght from Ballymun. Why was my surname Losty and when did it become Ruane?

I started to suspect I was adopted. I would analyse every groove on my face and compare it to my parents. I had blonde, curly hair as a child; they all had dark hair. I became obsessed with a bump on my nose. Neither Ma nor Da had a bump. My poor mind was tortured. Over the course of two years, I went from feeling safe and loved within my own home to thinking something really awful must have happened here. Of course, life went on and sometimes I managed to put it out of my mind.

It all came out in the most unexpected way, and not on my terms. It was my da's birthday. We always had sponge cake with candles in it. Da would come in from work and we would hide in the house until he found us. When he did we'd sing "Happy Birthday".

That year, I asked Ma, "How old is Da?"

"He's forty," said Aunty Rita. Ma exchanged looks with her sister.

Something was wrong. "He can't be forty," I insisted. "You told me he was forty last year."

They laughed it off, but I knew by the way they looked at each other that something was going on and Rita knew too but I was not in the loop.

Some days later we were called in off the street and sat down on the sofa.

I think Ma did most of the talking. "Jason, Lynn, there's something we need to tell you. We think you're old enough now. You're ready to hear this." Ma took a deep breath. "Your da isn't forty. He's sixty-three."

You'd imagine after all my snooping into their lives that I would be ready, but I wasn't. *Sixty-fucking-three? Da is an old man. He is going to die soon. You have taken twenty-three years away from me. I had twenty-three extra years with my da two minutes ago and now I have twenty-three years less. You, you two in front of me have taken twenty-three years away from me.* That was all swirling around in my head, and over the years that followed I'd say all of this – and more – to them.

And that was just the start of it. Ma hadn't finished.

"Your da and I never married. In fact, he was married before, and still is. He has two grown-up children, a boy and a girl."

That was that: mystery solved. My da was an old man, and I was no longer his only daughter.

A few other parts of the puzzle began to fit together then. I never got to meet my grandparents. I remembered my cousin David talking about his Granda Ruane living with them before he died. If David had met Granda, why couldn't I?

When it came out, this secret, I didn't know who I was anymore and I hated my parents for it. Maybe it seemed reasonable for them to wait until we were old enough to understand. But all I could think of was that my parents, the people who loved me, had lied to me.

This would fester in me over my pre-teen years until it turned into rage. A rage that would create a wedge between me and my da that, sadly, I would not fix in time to enjoy the healthy years he had left. I would pay emotionally for this in later life. Even now, it is difficult to think about him and to write about him, because I know how hurt I will feel. Hurt because I missed out on so much with him, because of my selfish, skewed view of what was to come when they told me the secret I so wanted to know.

Why would something that happened before I was born so completely change how I viewed my whole life? I don't have an answer for that.

Every time I allowed myself to think about Da I switched between hating him for having me and hating myself for being born. I hated that I was part of a second family and that I could not also be part of his first family. I wanted to reverse the clock, to never be born. I wanted my da to be with his other daughter.

It didn't matter that this other family were grown up now. It didn't matter that my da loved us. It didn't matter that my parents had fallen in love, stayed in love and were good parents. It didn't matter that they loved me. All that mattered was that I wanted everyone to go away and for me not to exist.

I no longer felt whole. I felt that there was a part of me out there in the world that I couldn't connect with – my siblings. I asked many questions about them. *What do they look like? Where do they live? When can I meet them?* Questions were always met with half-answers. I searched the phone directory, running my finger down the list of Ruanes, hoping I could find them. I would later learn that magically gaining a sister and a brother was about as likely as that magic wand producing a puppy for me.

Everywhere I looked I was reminded of what I felt was a rejection. Every time my friends complained about babysitting for their younger siblings I felt envious. Every time siblings argued and fell out I was quick to judge their pettiness. If only I knew my brother and sister, I would never take them for granted. When other kids were mean to me I imagined my older, unknown brother protecting me. I fantasised about him teaching me how to play football better or how to beat Da at gameshows. I didn't think of my sister as much. I had never had a sister so I had nothing to compare it with. It was also difficult for me to think of her as Da's "other daughter". I pined for my siblings but I hated my parents.

An anger towards my parents grew inside me that just would not subside. I allowed this anger to grip me in a way that would change the course of my life. I allowed myself to be bitter and I dedicated years of my life to making them pay.

I went from being a boisterous, giddy and hard-working kid with a love of animals and people to a more hardened version of myself. The harder I was, the more I could punish them. The less I loved them, the more I could blame them. The more I rejected my father, the easier it would be when he died. And when I peel it all back now to bare emotion, that was my biggest fear. *Da is going to die. It is just a matter of time now.*

There were two Lynns living at the same time – the same person but with alternate realities. One moment I was a paper girl, happily doing my rounds, earning some pocket money, listening to No Doubt and the Spice Girls, playing for hours on the street. The other Lynn was a deep well of anger and hate. A Lynn that didn't give a shit. A Lynn that was tough, didn't cry and didn't take direction from anyone.

I held on to my parents for a couple more years, in the sense that I allowed them to parent me. Something in me was cracking, though.

My childhood innocence was leaving me but normal teenage arguments were not what awaited me on the other side of naivety. I was never girly but I became more boyish, or what I thought was boyish, as I moved towards teenage life. I mimicked how boys walked, talked and dressed. I saw anything feminine as a weakness. It is as though I packed away everything about my true identity.

Every time they tried to ground me or give out to me, I would run out of the house screaming about how much I hated them, sending a barrage of abuse their way about Da's age and their big lie. I remember once my da came running after me, but I sped away through the laneways with my friend Grace Byrne, who lived at the back of Killinarden. I always remember the shocked looks on my friends' faces when they heard how I spoke to my parents.

From a distance, choices look simple, but I don't actually ever remember making a choice to be the bitter, angry daughter from hell.

One summer I was selling newspapers, taking my responsibility very seriously, loving my job. The next summer I was faking robberies and ripping off my trusted employer – two of my mates robbed the paper round money off me and we shared it later.

The most frightening experiences were yet to come. The loss I felt over siblings I had never met would come to seem like a walk in the park compared to the grief I was about to face.

CHAPTER 3:
GRIEF DOES NOT CHANGE YOU, IT REVEALS YOU

There's a line in John Green's *The Fault in Our Stars*: *"Grief does not change you, it reveals you."* I remember hearing this line and knowing this could not be true. Grief does change you: it batters you, hardens you and strips you raw to the core of everything you once knew. Grief comes with so many layers and, yes, it reveals your strengths or your ability to continue living even in the face of grief. But it *does* change you, until you become unrecognisable to yourself. There will always be a little piece of your soul missing.

The thing that hurts me most about my life and the impact of living in an area oppressed by deprivation is the loss that everyone feels. It is never just one loss but multiple losses. Every year in our community, if we manage to make it to the summer without a funeral, part of me will wonder why no one has died yet.

Up until I was twelve my parents only ever had to look out the window to know where I was. Myself and my friend Niamh would sometimes call for our friends Jenny and Amanda, who lived in Donamore, but that would be as far as we would go.

Jenny Hoban was such a sweet kid. She had brown frizzy hair and a kind smile. Jenny taught me how to do a fishbone plait. I am no good at plaits, something my daughters give out about, but the one plait I could do with pride was the fishbone Jenny showed me.

One day when I was about eleven, I sat in my porch with Niamh and Jenny, a little tub of Indian ink beside us. I think I was about eleven. I had robbed a sewing needle from my house and we were determined to tattoo ourselves. We quickly put the tip of the needle in the ink and onto our fingers. We had to be quick in case anyone caught us. We figured we could cover up the Indian ink on our fingers with our rings. After lots of jabbing, it worked and we had little dots, the three of us, on our ring fingers. After all these years, mine is still there. Later, in my teenage years, I began to get proper tattoos, but I kept this little dot. It lets me think of Jenny every time I look at my finger.

We were just little kids when we held Jenny's slumber party in my house. She had brothers and sisters so there wasn't much room at hers. I wrote about the slumber party in my diary. Jenny spotted that I'd written about her sneaking off with the boys. She sulked for a while, but we were soon in fits of laughter when Niamh got sick over her shoes.

But I was quickly outgrowing the safety of my little cul-de-sac. It no longer felt like it fit me. Within a short time of this slumber party, our group of friends expanded massively. We drifted away from Killinarden Estate and ventured past the church where I had once spent all my Sunday mornings singing hymns. We swapped the Spice Girls for reggae. We swapped games of kick-the-can with the Redmonds and the Andersons for sitting on a wall in Cushlawn with a group of girls from that part of Killinarden. It felt more exciting, it was new and I always welcomed a place I could reinvent myself.

On a cold November night in 1997, I was in a house in Killinarden with a group of lads, when some of the Cushlawn girls knocked for me. Jenny was with them. We walked to the Kusanta snooker hall and bought Monster Munch and Tangle Twisters. We left together, seven girls building new friendships and getting to know one another. We walked in twos and threes.

I question my memories often. So much about that night is so vivid and so much is so blurry. I think the road was wet; it might have been drizzling that night. I had just stepped on to the grass verge when a bus came around the bend at quite a speed. Some of us hurried on to the grass but Jenny and another friend were only halfway across the road. Jenny seemed to panic and started to run back. I honestly can't be sure, but I don't think the bus even slowed. I'm not even sure how I knew it was Jenny. Maybe somebody screamed her name.

I was shaken to my core. My heart was beating so fast, it was as though it was exploding in my ears. Even now, writing this, my heart is racing. My instinct was to run to the nearest house. I didn't even look back; my body just bolted forward. I wanted to keep running until I could run no more, but I knew that I needed to get help. I banged and banged frantically on the door but no one answered. I didn't want to waste time so I ran next door and they came out to help straight away.

An ambulance arrived. I went to run to Jenny but a woman held me back. I think she was trying to protect me. I was so frightened that Jenny was dead, but somebody said that one of the ambulance men asked Jenny to squeeze his hand if she could hear him and she did. Jenny was taken away in the ambulance and the woman who was holding me took me home to my parents. I fell into their arms. I had never felt such a wave of emotion before. I rocked myself to sleep that night.

At seven o'clock the next morning, Ma opened the bedroom door. I leaped from the bed on high alert. I knew. I knew as soon as

I looked at Ma's face that Jenny was gone. Ma stood at the end of the bed but she couldn't get the words out. A surge of grief rose up through me, hurting me physically. This beautiful, kind-hearted, giddy little girl was gone.

Jenny was an amazing kid, always looking out for others. Her older brother was struggling with addiction and she once asked us to sneak into town with her to find him and make sure that he was OK. She was always so patient with her little sisters when she was babysitting them.

I remember she would ask me every day if she could wear my dolphin clip and my Umbro bottoms in exchange for her tracksuit top. I remember talking about what Christmas clothes she wanted that year. I remember her smile.

I hold all my treasured memories not only in my heart but in a Lion King box that I still have: the Umbro bottoms, the diary entries, the dolphin hair clip, even the pyjamas Jenny wore on the sleepover.

I remember so much about her but very little about the days and weeks following her death. It's as though I vanished from the world for those weeks.

For a long time after, I would lie in bed at night afraid to sleep. I would close my eyes and hear those screams and I would relive those moments over and over. I wondered if the rest of the girls did too, but I was always afraid to ask. I am not sure why. I was in my first year in Killinarden Community School and I could not get my head around the fact that everyone was just getting on with their school day. The world and life goes on and you're expected to go on with it. But I was frozen, stuck in that night. I had nightmares that my beautiful friend was buried alive, while I tried desperately to convince people to help me get her out.

I would lie in bed blaming myself, hating myself for staying in Killinarden that night. If I had gone to Cushlawn, the others wouldn't have had to come to me, we wouldn't have been on that road. If, if, if . . .

My waking hours weren't much easier. Every time I stood at a traffic light or had to cross a road I would have flashbacks. I would see the blur of a bus flashing past my eyes. I knew it wasn't real but I couldn't stop it, and I couldn't tell anyone. Who was I to suffer? I was only a friend, I wasn't part of her family. What right did I have to grieve for Jenny?

One summer day, Jenny had written out the words for Bette Midler's beautiful song "The Rose", and told me and Niamh that if she ever died to make sure we had it played at her funeral. I obviously thought that this was a ridiculous thing for someone our age to say. Little did we think we would be keeping our promise to her so soon.

If grief reveals you rather than changes you, then what was revealed in me was despair, pain and years of destruction. Jenny's death and my anger with my parents over my da's age stand as two of the most defining moments in my young life.

This part of my life, this chapter in my book, feels wrong somehow. Jenny's death will never be just a chapter of my life; it would eventually become my driving force for living. Knowing that Jenny never got that chance would leave me fighting for my chances. The words of "The Rose" would play endlessly in my head:

> It's the one who won't be taken, who cannot seem to give
> And the soul afraid of dying, that never learns to live.

Throughout my early teens I felt as though I was dying, but that line "the soul afraid of dying, that never learns to live" would serve as a reminder to me to live.

It's as if from the moment we are born we start the process of dying, and the fear of dying has never been far from my mind.

My soul was afraid of dying and with every death that followed, my soul would die a little more. I knew that deep inside me I needed to fight, but not just yet. I needed to live, but it would take me almost two decades to learn how. My life would take many twists and turns before I felt deserving of love and life. I would experience huge loss and watch painful events unfold in my community before I would stop taking risks with my life and look to living as an alternative to dying, not just its inevitable outcome. Grief didn't only reveal me; it changed me.

CHAPTER 4:
THAT'S JUST THE WAY IT IS

"That's just the way it is, things will never be the same" –
Tupac Shakur

That's just the way it is. My da was an old man and I was not his only little girl. *That's just the way it is.* Jenny was gone and soon more would follow. *That's just the way it is.* We were drug users and some of us alcoholics at the age of twelve. *That's just the way it is.* Some of my friend's families had very little money to survive. *That's just the way it is.* Some of my friends had been sexually abused. *That's just the way it is.* Some of the families in our community had buried multiple children before their time. *That's just the way it is.* We stab each other, shoot each other and batter the life out of each other. It's the fate of our births, our location, our demographics. How can this be just the way it is? What if it is not meant to be like this? We are not born violent or stupid or useless.

I had no answers to these questions.

I was introduced to Tupac by my two pals, Bernie and Tracy. They were inseparable and behaved like sisters. Both had perms and were always in their Levi's. I loved being in their company. Their giddiness was infectious, and I felt protected when I was with them.

We would sit in my house after my parents had left for work, smoking hash and listening to Tupac. Tracy would bounce around singing every song, word for word, as if she was Cushlawn's very own Tupac. One day, the sight of Tracy singing, "I see no changes, wake up in the morning and I ask myself, 'Is life worth living? Should I blast myself?'" was too much for me. I began to choke on the smoke from a bong. Of course, Tracy and Bernie thought this was hilarious. I thought I was going choke to death while those two fuckers just pointed and laughed their heads off. But it didn't take long for me to catch my breath and join in the laughter.

When I began to listen more closely to Tupac's lyrics, I started to wonder about the struggle of the black community in America. It was my first introduction to race oppression and I wondered if other groups felt like that too. I began to open my eyes to inequality in the world, and especially the deprivation around me.

Some of my friends wore clothes that didn't fit them, hand-me-downs from friends or older siblings. Many families in West Tallaght didn't have very much, and although no-one really talked about it, bills weren't paid, rent to the council was in arrears, kids had no school books and often there was very little food in the house. Everyone worked with what they had and looked out for each other as best they could. I'd never experienced that level of deprivation in my own household and it made me more generous and understanding towards those who struggled much more than I did.

After Jenny died, I made a plan, just in case I figured out some other way to live.

My bedroom hadn't yet caught up with my teenage self. It was still filled with everything I used to be: Ladybird books, animal-shaped soaps and boxes of fancy paper. I decided to write my plan on some of this fancy paper. I had changed so quickly from being a little girl to being a teenager, experiencing life in a way that I shouldn't have. I lay on the floor, my back against the bed, wearing my Green Air Max and Paco jumper, jewellery dripping off me, big gold clown pendant hanging from my neck, earrings the size of apples in my ears. I was evolving into the typical Tallaght West girl, but I was still a kid.

I wrote down the words that had been going round and round my head: "If nothing really matters and you are going to die soon anyway, do whatever the fuck you wanna do." Stage one of the plan. I wrote a number of other scenarios, such as if you live a bit longer you can get a job and have a family, but for now, it was a case of "fuck it, fuck it all". *Whatever comes your way, do it*: that became my mantra.

While this seems like an impulsive decision to throw caution to the wind and succumb to all that was available on the street corners of Tallaght, it wasn't really. I had been inching my way towards chaos for a number of years. First went the respect for my parents when they lied to me. With their authority over me now broken, it was easier for me to channel the trauma from Jenny's death in a hugely negative way.

I believed in Santa until I was ten. I played the tin whistle until I was eleven. Sister Bridget awarded me "Pupil of the Year" when I was twelve. Now I was thirteen and the next few years seemed quite unbelievable.

My ma says that I was a little pet, then I was using drugs. It seemed so sudden. She is right: on the outside, it was sudden. But my emotional wellbeing and safety had been struggling long before I displayed it outwardly. It wasn't long before I was robbing gas bottles from the local shop instead of fizzy strawberries. I start blowing gas every day for that few seconds of buzz. Other kids were blowing deodorants, but they weren't strong enough for me. I went from playing tin whistle to inhaling solvents so quickly, nobody could have caught it.

Drugs came to us first in the safety of our cul-de-sac. A lot of the lads in Killinarden had started smoking hash. Before Jenny died I was already drinking and smoking hash but my drug use and any plans I had for life would change drastically in the years that followed. The next few years would take me places I never thought I would go.

For all the shit I put myself through, I am thankful to the teenage girl I was. Even in the depths of despair, I resourced myself in a way that got me to where I am now. I hurt myself and others deeply along the way, but I got here. I didn't always do the right thing but I've no option but to love who I was.

No matter what happened, my friends and I all understood each other's pain because we shared in it. We didn't always speak about it and we couldn't always make sense of it but we were in it together and they've given me some of the best times of my life during some of the worst years of my life. Communities like ours experience things collectively and I found my collective in my friends and peers, rather than in my parents, during this time.

I was unleashing anger on any adult who attempted to interfere with anything I wanted to do. I was beginning to feel more content in the company of friends than family and I had a lust for danger. It's as though fear and caution had subsided and being a risk-taker was the new me. Anything goes when you feel like you have nothing to lose.

By now I was doing very little at school and they were doing very little for me. Some teachers no longer asked me for homework. I had mastered parents' signatures on absence notes. I was usually stoned in school and I ensured the teachers knew I had no respect for them or their authority. Some of this I regret and some I don't. I still feel a little failed by most of the teachers, apart from the guidance counsellor, Eamonn Nolan, and the music teacher, Sister Angela, whom I adored. She was a formidable woman and she cared deeply for her students. She taught me how to read music and moved me on from the tin whistle to the organ. I'll always regret that I didn't continue with music, because I loved it.

I do regret the way I treated those who tried to reach out and intervene. In my skewed view, every adult in my life either failed to notice I was freefalling through my teenage years or they didn't care. That's what I thought anyway, but I was wrong. My parents noticed – how could they not? – but having never experienced drugs, crime or chaos, they hadn't a clue what they were meant to do.

I didn't really care anyway. I was enjoying my new lifestyle and I quickly learned how to lie and manipulate so that my family never really knew the full scale of everything I was doing. I had given up my childhood desire to be the most honest person on the planet. I became a schemer.

I remember the first drug I took that was not hash. I was thirteen. I was babysitting one night with my friends for one of their cousins. My friend's cousin said I could borrow some holiday clothes for a trip to the Canaries I was going on with my parents a few weeks later. She told me they were in the back bedroom in her wardrobe. As I raided the wardrobe I found a small zip-seal bag of tablets. I grabbed the bag, ran downstairs and said to the girls, "Here, do ya reckon these are drugs or just painkillers? Will we take them and find out?" We had a brief discussion on how many we should take and what they might be but it didn't take us long to swallow them.

I was barely thirteen years old and I had no fear of what I was putting inside me. I was glad I didn't because for the first time in months I felt some sort of equilibrium. I felt alive, and as my pain fell away, love soared to the surface. I could feel warmth and a sudden rush for how amazing life was. With my senses heightened I was convinced I could hear people talking at the other end of the street. The patterns on the walls and floors transformed from being a normal Jobstown council house to a work of art. Everything about it was beautiful. I held onto the feeling that night gave me and I chased it at every chance I got.

Incidentally, that trip to the Canaries was as weird and messed up as most things in my teenage years. It started with me putting a half-ounce of hash in my unsuspecting brother's Brylcreem. My poor brother had no interest in the life I was living and would never dream of smoking hash and here I was implicating him in carrying illegal drugs out of the country.

I began taking ecstasy weekly, sometimes daily. But even as a teenager, I analysed and absorbed most things going on around me and I knew that the beauty in life that seemed to exist only when I took drugs, and somehow evaporated when I had none, was a false sense of life for me. I wasn't taking drugs for enjoyment or in a safe way. I was running away from the emptiness I felt, and I was using drugs to run.

I felt there was a family missing, a family I'd never met. I felt rejected. Hanging around with my new friends eased this rejection. When I took drugs, I could forget that, in my mind, I didn't deserve a father. If my half-siblings couldn't have him, then I didn't want him either. But when I took drugs I just wanted to go home, hug him and tell him I was sorry. Love buzz.

Between the years of thirteen and fifteen I took an array of substances, each of them giving me a different memory and different experience of who I was. But taking drugs was not enough for me, and soon I was selling E and speed to friends. I can't even remember how I made this decision. I was failing in maths at school, but measuring out and selling drugs made me feel like less of a failure. I felt I had a skill. I would sit in the kitchen when my parents were working, Tupac playing in the background, cuttings bars of hash into ounces and bagging up eighths of speed without a weighing scales, thinking to myself, "That Mr Mulhare fella in school is just a shit maths teacher. Sure I'm great at this." I felt I had some responsibility selling drugs and I could take my profit in drugs, rather than cash. My drug-dealing career was short-lived, though, as I didn't like collecting money.

Our lives were full of extremes and often days of laughter would become nights of fear. I was at my happiest at raves and parties, even when the smiles faded as you began to scag as the sun came up. Every session had an unpredictability. There would be rooms full of people with their hands in the air, "Beachball" or "Brave Heart" bringing everyone together in an E-induced love fest. Right up to this day, when certain dance tunes begin to kick in, I can feel the nostalgia like a chemical flowing through me. The uncertainty of the night was never too far away.

We had a rave one night in the priest's gaff. I have no idea where the priest was but he missed out on the best rave there ever was in Killinarden. Trevor Corr got wind that there was security looking after the house while the priest was away, and they had let some people into the house to have a few cans. Trevor decided to announce this over the intercom in the snooker hall, where on any given night there could be well over a hundred people. Everyone cleared out and headed straight to the priest's gaff, leaving the snooker hall staff in peace for the night. When I got there, it was in full swing. I had double-dropped some E and, like every other weekend, I would push the limits of my tolerance way too far, sometimes taking anywhere up to ten Es in one night. There was a DJ set up in the sitting room, sounds were pumping and I had butterflies at the sights around me. There were hundreds of people in the house. All the different groups had come together – the lads from the Avenue, all of us who hung around in Cushlawn and several groups of friends from Knockmore. Everyone. I was buzzing with the energy in the house.

I was dancing in the sitting room and could hear others dancing in the room above us. Just as I located where the thumping feet were coming from, they were – quite literally – in my face. These two legs in a pair of tracksuit bottoms were dangling from the ceiling. Some lad had danced so hard he'd broken through the upper floor. He didn't seem too fazed and continued dancing, half of him upstairs and half of him downstairs, his legs still moving to the sounds of *Last Night of the Ormond*, as if there was still ground beneath his feet. I moved on to the kitchen to see if I knew any more faces. I walked straight into a bloke who I'm pretty sure was naked and wrapped in cling film. I nudged a friend and asked them, "Do you see that too, or am I trippin'?"

Then the night took a turn that I didn't like. Some blokes were shouting at another mate. "What the fuck did you do that for?" They were all animated and I was curious as to what had happened. Someone else shouted, "He stabbed a fucking dog!"

I felt sick. Part of me wanted to run out the back to check the dog. The other part of me just wanted to run home. I was too out of my face to go home and too scared to help the dog.

A few minutes later the Gardaí arrived and ran us all from the house. I was glad they did. Unpredictability had risen its head and I wasn't able for that. It was always only one or two people out of dozens who would change the dynamic of a room or a party, but it could lead to some really fucked-up situations. Sometimes it would be the hallucinations or paranoia that would steer situations in a certain direction. Sometimes funny, but sometimes very fucking scary.

I never experienced hallucinations in a negative way. For the most part, it was fun. But of course, this was not the case for everyone and I have seen people do some mad shit tripping out of their heads. For the most part, I think I was lucky in my drug use. I really believe that. What else can it be? Some friends – too many friends – ended up dead because of drugs. Others ended up in a constant state of psychosis, their drug states becoming their permanent states.

I remember my first time hallucinating from magic mushrooms. The day I first took mushies, shortly before my fourteenth birthday, I had stolen Levi's, Lynx and multipacks of Wrigley's. I swapped some Lynx and Wrigley's packs for a bag of mushrooms. I made the first batch in the kettle, as someone had told me I should drink them in a cup of tea. I always wonder if my parents got a funny buzz from their tea over the next few days. I decided the LSD from the mushrooms wasn't getting into me fast enough so I began to swallow them whole. They were slimy and disgusting but it worked. I looked in the mirror: I had a rabbit's face. I stood there gazing at my new face but began to feel a deep sadness as the rabbit began to morph into my da's face. There he was, looking straight back at me through my own eyes. I concentrated really hard, willing the rabbit's face to come back. It didn't. So off I went to explore Killinarden through the eyes of LSD.

I was walking up Donamore Crescent with my friend, Sinead. I don't think she had taken anything. I was staring at her and she was getting freaked out.

"What the fuck are you looking at, Lynn?"

"Sinead, you're getting older." I kept repeating over and over to her.

She was half laughing and half annoyed. "What the fuck are you talking about?"

It was true; with every step she took she aged another couple of years. When we'd first stepped onto the Crescent she was fourteen. By the time we got to the end she looked about eighty, all wrinkled up and hunched over.

I quickly forgot Sinead ageing when I realised I had a tail. A gang of girls were walking behind me; I was fighting with one of them and I was worried she might see my tail.

"Sinead, Sinead – can they see my tail?"

The simplest things amazed us when we were in these states. I remember one afternoon in Cushlawn, Kim pointed at our friend Pheno's feet and said, "Look at the size of his feet." We all laughed for a good twenty minutes at Pheno's perfectly normal feet.

But it wasn't always this amusing. One night in Killinarden, after we had been to the mushy fields, everyone seemed to go on a bad trip

– one fella especially. Imagine spending an hour trying to convince your friend he is not dead. Everyone sat him down and told him he was alive and that he was sitting here talking; surely that was enough evidence of his existence? I never saw such fear on someone's face. He insisted on going home to tell his ma that he was dead.

I think it is easy for me to look back and find funny stories from these times, but that is because I got out in time.

So many of us wanted to escape reality, even to the point of knocking ourselves out of reality. Literally. I remember one sunny day I was walking up through Cushlawn and a young fella said to me, "Here, do you wanna buy one of these?"

"What are they?" I asked. The little tablets had a series of numbers and letters on them.

"Heavy duty," he told me. "These'd knock a horse out."

I bought them straight away. Myself and a friend sat ourselves down on the grass, the Killinarden Ring Road to our right. It is a busy road and it was early in the day. We chose this spot without discussion but I think we both knew why. Someone would see us and help us if anything went wrong. We were slightly giddy and slightly scared, but never considered that we should *not* take this unknown tablet. I rolled a joint and we sat and chatted. Then we swallowed our tablets.

When we opened our eyes again it was dark. The streetlights had come on. We'd taken the tablets on a warm summer's morning and woken up in the same spot on a chilly night. I spent weeks trying to get another one of those tablets.

I didn't want to die. I just wanted to be temporarily knocked out of life. I feel incredibly sad for myself now looking back, but I didn't connect with myself then, I was reacting all the time. I know I am lucky to be alive and I wish I could go back and hug her. Hug Lynn.

After being suspended from school for the umpteenth time, at the age of fourteen I decided I'd had enough and wouldn't bother returning. My parents weren't too happy, but I didn't care.

I had become an accomplished shoplifter by this time, taking stacks of Levi's off shelves and selling them. I discovered that the security tags in most shops were duds and didn't set the alarm off. Then I started making tinfoil bags to block any alarms that did work. I would get long bags designed to hold rolls of wallpaper from Wigoders hardware shop. At home I would layer each bag up with tinfoil, followed by a layer of masking tape. Then I'd place the tinfoil bag inside another bag and off I would go, fleecing shops of their red tab Levi's. This would mean less time in the shop removing bugs – I could do that at my leisure at home. I almost felt proud of this talent I had discovered. I grew more and more brazen by the week. Some younger lads even asked me how to make the bags. I only ever showed a couple of them as I didn't want to do myself out of business.

I finally got caught robbing perfume and a pair of trousers. The guards were called and I was charged. Being caught didn't deter me, however, not in the slightest. By the next day I was walking out of Argos with my friend Duggner, both of us pushing trolleys full of goods.

How we fitted so much into a short space of time I will never know. When I think back on those days, I can still feel the freedom of running around the streets, radio in one hand, taking drugs and drinking cans of White Lightning or flagons of cider. I miss those days. I miss the recklessness, which seems odd to say, but it's true.

I often try to marry this feeling with the many painful realities of those times. I experienced some of the worst days of my life back then, but I think it's the collective sense of togetherness, this belonging to a tribe, that keeps me linked to it, pining for those days. We were all there, in the shit, together. We lost our friends together and only we could understand each other's pain. We *got* each other. We stuck through it, and those of us left still stick together. Much more loosely maybe, but when it boils down to it, we know we can call on each other. We know we still carry a collective sense of guilt, pain and sometimes shame. Yet we remember the experiences so fondly. Maybe we have to remember them this way just to survive. So that we can feel OK about our histories and the choices we made.

I feel at my most comfortable when I sit with my childhood pals, like when I have a catch-up with my friend, Val. She had older brothers who would have gone mental if she'd done half the stuff I did. I wish I'd had something to stop me. Something I could place between me and the pit I was willingly falling into.

I was running out of steam. I had exhausted myself with constant highs and very dark lows. I hate to admit it, even now, but I was pretty fucked up. I was depressed, desperate and very lonely.

If I was to look at it honestly, I abused myself, I frightened my parents beyond belief and I hurt and attacked anyone who stood in my way. It doesn't matter that I felt I was, at heart, a good person, because my actions spoke louder. I was violent and I was angry. Yet I would stand strongly over my belief that I was vulnerable and not to blame, not completely anyway. I inhabited those two identical, yet very different, Lynns, co-existing in the one world. I am sure the security guards I would spit at if they tried to throw me out of the Square would find it hard to imagine that same person crying herself to sleep that night, her baby panda bear pulled closely to her chest.

I made so many mistakes in such a short space of time. Maybe I was looking to fight the world, looking for ways I could express the anger inside. I was doing so many things that I knew were not who I was inside. I was not a fighter but I kept fighting. I was repeatedly harming myself through my actions. I was so confused. I enjoyed the drugs but not everything else that they brought. The absence of control and the loose inhibitions, the feeling of having no power over my own mind and my own body.

I can see my mother's face, how she must have looked those worrying nights when I didn't come home. She'd aged a little around the eyes. She was clearly in shock and every time I went missing it must have been a new trauma.

I knew this, yet I did it anyway. I lied almost hourly about where I was going. Putting her off the scent, knowing she would be out looking for me later on. I would be in a field somewhere laughing with excitement as I was flung around the back of a robbed car doing 360s.

Ma's nights weren't so exciting. It was never exciting for my parents. Most nights they spent going door-to-door – the Joyces, the Grocotts – asking if anyone knew where I was. When I went AWOL, Da would drive the streets. I am pretty sure they didn't sleep much for two years.

I knew when I walked through the door on those mornings that they wanted to hug me and punch me all at once. My brother often ignored me. I could tell he was becoming angrier with me for what I was putting them all through.

Luckily, for them, my days of being missing in action would soon come to an end, but I am sure they thought it would never end. I was only fourteen. Surely I had years left in me to keep fucking up their lives?

I can't ever remember my ma crying then. I know she did, but I was too consumed with myself, with my needs and with my destructive agenda. I see her cry now, though, twenty years later. She sobs as I revisit those nights with her for this book. She is sad because she thinks she failed me. I hope she knows now that it was her who saved me. She may not have found me on the streets at night; she may not have been able to get between me and my craving for drugs; but she stayed consistent in her love for me. She showed me what a mother is. Soon after my days full of speed and scrapes, I would do everything I could to be her.

CHAPTER 5:
SCARS

I remember the first time I went joyriding. There were six of us squashed into a stolen Opel Vectra. I was one of only two girls in the car. We were both really nervous as neither of us had done this before. But I got such a buzz from it, I wanted to do it again and again. I was even allowed to drive the odd car – not very well, mind you.

I loved the thrill of the chase. I placed full trust in our drivers to keep us alive and get us away from the garda, never once thinking that I could die, or get arrested. I certainly never spared a thought for the person who had worked hard to pay for the car. We'd developed our own twisted moral code, setting out with the idea that we'd look after the cars we stole, that the owners would get them back the next morning and all would be fine. Of course this was not always the case.

One night a group of us were driving a car through Rathfarnham. We were running low on petrol and it was my turn to do the fill-up. As we sped away from the petrol pump with a full tank, an unmarked car came from nowhere. The lad who was driving took off down a lane so narrow I was sure there'd be no doors left on the car. There was a sudden crash and we were all thrown around. We had driven head-on into a tree. The driver shouted for us to run. He was gone like Linford Christie, disappearing into the night. I jumped out the back of the car and began to run, but didn't get far. I was wearing my Spice Girls boots with platform soles.

The detective pulled a gun and, like some American cop show, shouted, "Stop or I will shoot!" I stopped, not because I thought he would shoot, but because I thought it was hilarious: this big man pointing a gun at a seven-stone girl in a pair of Spice Girls boots. I was laughing so hard I couldn't run. I also knew the odds of getting away were stacked against me.

He grabbed me and dragged me after him as he attempted to catch the others. I became a dead weight in his arms so my friends could keep going. The driver got away but, like a pair of saps, two of my friends had rolled under a bush in a nearby garden. The detective began to kick one of them so hard she leaped out from under the bush. He must have realised by now that we were only kids and not violent, but his violence towards us would only escalate.

There we were, three kids in the back of an unmarked detective's car. There was a second detective in the car, but I have no memory of him. Maybe that's because he was not a violent bully. The experience of the next hour would feed into a hate for police that would take me decades to undo.

We didn't put up a fight. We allowed ourselves to be handcuffed to each other. My friend started moaning; her handcuffs were so tight. We spat on her wrists, trying to lubricate them.

"Here, will ya loosen the cuffs?" I asked, nodding at her wrists. "Look, her fingers are going blue."

He turned around in the car and looked my friend in the eye. "What's your name?"

She gave the detective her first name.

He leaned right in to her face. "I said, what is your fucking name?"

Not quite understanding him, she gave the detective her first name again.

With that this big detective swung his arm and gave her such a backhander I could almost feel it myself. "Your full name," he shouted.

My other friend reached out, trying to intervene, but the detective responded by striking him, this time with the gun, which he was still holding. I was horrified as the blood streamed down my friend's face.

We were taken to Tallaght garda station and placed in separate cells. I had done it again: I had forced my parents into a situation they never thought they would be in. When they picked me up, I tried to convince them that I hadn't been in a stolen car, but then I just looked at their worried faces and I got in the back of their car and sat in silence.

That was the first time I experienced such violence from a garda, but it wouldn't be the last. I understand that we robbed a car and deserved to be arrested, but we didn't deserve such violent treatment. All it did was drive me deeper into drug use and crime, and fuelled my hatred of authority.

I grew up in a passive household. My da had been a champion boxer in the army but never threw a punch outside of the ring. He would boast about this fact. He taught me that not using your fists is something to be proud of, but that didn't stop me from throwing my fists when I needed to.

Like my da, my brother was full of a sense of sportsmanship and always looked to resolve disputes with words rather than with fists. Jay would get lots of stick for this and his pals would joke with him that he would have to get his little sister to fight his battles for him. Jay was not afraid of people; he was just not willing to fight for the hell of it. People liked and respected him anyway so he rarely had any need to fight.

I was with my brother one night at the Spawell in Templeogue. We went to hail a taxi on the Tallaght bypass when a group of young fellas walked passed. Recognising one, I said hello, but for no apparent reason, two of the others started laying punches into me. I fought back, and Jay was behind me fighting others off. Somebody hit him with a concrete block, and when I turned to look for him, he was lying unconscious on the road, people starting to gather around him. I thought he was dead. I ran to him and tried to wake him, but he was unresponsive, blood pouring from his mouth. I crumpled up into a ball beside him, screaming. I could hear an ambulance in the distance. I thought it was happening again, like with Jenny. I was convinced he had some internal bleeding and was going to die. Thankfully, he came around, but his poor face was unrecognisable the next day.

It's scary how quickly I became acclimatised to violence. One time a man followed Da home in a car. When Da got out, this big man came charging at him, his face a furious red, saying he had cut him off on the bypass. I saw my da try to reason with him, but the man got right up into Da's face. I'd been watching from a window, so I grabbed a baseball bat and came charging for him, screaming and swinging like a lunatic. The man retreated to his car and drove off as I bounced the bat off his roof. If I'd hit him, I felt I would have been fully justified in doing so. I turned back to my da feeling proud for defending him against this big bad man. But my face fell when I saw the way he was looking at me. "I can't believe my daughter would hit someone with that," he said, his voice shaking. Later, I found him crying alone in his room, and knew he was disappointed in me.

Moments like this always made me feel like an outcast in my family. I still don't understand why I was different to them. My perspective on life was so different to theirs. Instead of bringing us closer, episodes like this pushed me further away from them.

When I was fourteen, something happened that made me distance myself from the streets of Cushlawn. I got in a fight that ended with me being sliced in the face with a Stanley blade. I nearly lost my eye.

I will never forget my ma's face that night in the Accident and Emergency room. She was clearly distraught and scared, yet I was screaming like a mad thing at the doctors and at my family to get the fuck away from me. My anger was too big to handle, so much bigger than any rationality my parents could use to persuade me to calm down.

I woke the next morning in the children's ward with my face all bandaged up. My first thought was how I could get out of there. I was being watched by everyone. A security guard followed me to the hospital shop and told me I wasn't allowed leave the ward. I looked at him as if he was mad. I was in a hospital gown and wheeling the machine for the drip in my arm. I wasn't going to run away like this, was I? In reality, I just wanted everything to go away, to go home and forget this awful event happened.

I was ready to be discharged but Ma and Da pleaded with the hospital to admit me for longer. They were so frightened. Nothing they had done to date had worked. They had tried it all; they had contacted social workers, the gardaí and psychiatrists. Throughout those years, they sought help in all the places they could think of. The stress was clear on their pained faces. I was almost happy that they were refusing to take me home. Even though I could never show it, I was ashamed. I felt huge guilt for what I was putting my parents through. I wondered what it must have been like for them, gardaí arriving at the door to tell them my face had been cut open, my ma taken to the hospital in the back of a garda car. She was told I'd been stabbed, and she didn't know if I would be alive or dead by the time she got to the hospital.

A few lads came up to visit me. I was trying to act cool, like I wasn't bothered by what had happened to me. In the middle of my real-life theatre piece, a clown came in asking if I wanted a balloon animal. A fucking balloon animal! Could he not see I wasn't a balloon animal type of kid? I was mortified. How could I pretend to be one of the lads and this dope is trying to make me a fucking balloon giraffe? There I was, thinking I was real cool, stitches in my face and my own security, when I was suddenly reminded I was just a kid.

I laughed at this later on as I retold it to my family. I could be angry with everyone, especially my family, but when we laughed we usually laughed together. Though we had grown distant from each other, we were still able to connect through humour. I will always love that my family can use laughter at the times we should laugh the least. It became the only thing I would share with them for those couple of years.

A couple of weeks later, as the doctor removed the stitches running from my forehead, down through my eyelid and under my eye, he bluntly told me that if I had not blinked as the blade made contact with my face, I would have lost my eye. As it is, it left a scar that's there to this day.

At the end of their tether, my parents sent me to a psychiatrist. I must have wanted help on some level or I'd never have agreed to sit in that room having my mental state assessed. It was not easy for adults to get me to do something that I did not want to do. I was upfront and told this psychiatrist everything; I prided myself on being honest when asked direct questions, a legacy of my experience of dealing with the revelations about my da. I told her about all the drugs I was using.

At the end of the session she whipped out a urine sample container and said, "Your parents are worried that you might be taking drugs and we would like to sample your urine." *Is she for fucking real?* I had just opened up to her, told her outright which drugs I was taking. What the fuck was this doctor doing when she was meant to be listening to me? I took the bottle and said, "Yeah, sure." I never returned to her.

I knew that day that, at some stage in my life, I wanted to have a job like hers, and that I would do a better job than she ever would. I would listen. My real engagement with therapy would come a couple of years later but, for now, I was on my own.

After weeks of dodging weapons and carrying my own, I finally started to question who I was and where this lifestyle was taking me. I knew I was not invisible but I had mastered the pretence that I was somehow not affected by my own behaviour. I was out of control.

At ten o'clock one morning, I found myself sitting in the visitors' room at Wheatfield Prison, out of my face, my eyes rolling into the back of my head from ecstasy, struggling not to swallow the drugs hidden in my mouth. One of the female screws was watching me. The lad I was visiting came in, and I kissed him over the counter. That was it; I had passed the dropsy, my only reason for being there. We chatted for a few minutes, for appearance's sake. But when I turned to go, the screw who had been watching me grabbed my arm. "I hope he swallows them," she told me. "I hope he swallows them whole and I hope he chokes on them."

She didn't frighten me – I was done being frightened of people – but the thought of swallowing those drugs into my system terrified the shite out of me. I could have died, but I also realised in that moment that I must want to live. But it would take me a while to settle into the thought of living beyond my fifteenth birthday. Of feeling connected to the world again.

CHAPTER 6:
VIGIS

One summer's day in 1998, at least fifty of us gathered around one of the vigi huts on a field in Cushlawn. These metal cabins had been erected all over the estates. There were no vigilantes in it anymore, as a few people had already gone on a spree, burning them out. I was happy about this. Vigis out at last.

For months and months, it had felt as though a war had broken out. It was a different sort of war; it wasn't between gangs of kids, or even between the gardaí and us. It was between the adults in the estate and anyone that they felt should be put under their control to keep our community safe.

In the 1990s there had been huge concern about the level of drug use and robberies in the communities in West Tallaght. Local communities set up meetings for concerned residents and also parents worried about their own children getting caught up in the drug scene that was emerging. I can imagine it being quite a scary time for parents faced with the reality that they knew very little about heroin and had little insight into how it might impact the lives of their loved ones.

Heroin first hit the streets of Dublin in the 1970s but it would take a bit longer for it to find its way to suburbs such as Tallaght. At one of the early meetings in Killinarden, a local drug user produced a list of those using drugs, and I remember being told that it was then that the extent of the problem really hit home. People wanted to do something about their kids on drugs, and with that in mind, Tallaght Against Drug Dealers (TADD) was set up.

Apparently, a similar effort had been made in Killinarden in the 1980s when it was discovered there was one man selling drugs from Killinarden Estate. He was run from his home. I have no memory of this but later became aware of it through my time working in the services. Now, in the mid-nineties, the same tactic of intimidation was going to be used on the houses of young people across the estates.

I remember the first march, the chants, over and over. That one was about joyriders. "What do we want? Joyriders out! When do we want it? Now!" They moved from house to house, anywhere there was a young person known for robbing cars. This seemed absurd to me.

For the most part, they marched on houses where they knew there were kids who robbed cars or who sold small quantities of drugs to feed their own habits. In a few cases, they marched on the houses of families whose kids weren't even under the roof anymore; often they were being held at St Patrick's Institution. When they marched on my friends' houses, I found it odd that they went by the name of Tallaght Against Drug Dealers as surely those fifteen-year-olds were also victims of the drug culture. They were drug users, not drug dealers – easy targets for the marchers.

I was then and will always be against the marches that happened in the late 1990s in Killinarden. Yet I understand why people were frightened and angry and wanted action. I get that many people thought that fighting fire with fire would chase drugs out of Tallaght, and that it would frighten young people out of criminality. But, at least in my eyes, this was a completely flawed thought process.

There were genuine men and women on those marches who thought they were taking a stand against the dealing in their communities. There were lots of good people who wanted to take action to make their communities safe. But their efforts would be drowned out by the more sinister fringe of the vigi movement – men who used violence to assert control over the estates. It became a mob, a mob of adults. Those legitimately concerned community residents or families were becoming overshadowed by a violent section of the marchers.

I would stand watching dozens of people assembling outside people's homes until I realised that those watching the vigi marches made the crowd look bigger, so I decided to stand back. I didn't want to be part of this. This was violence, a violence not directed at the state, but at us. I will always remember one friend breathlessly telling us that the vigis had just poured petrol on him and threatened to set him alight.

I became part of the mob on one occasion – when they marched on a known paedophile's house on the road behind ours. I shouted as loud as anyone. "What do we want? Paedos out!" This was the only time I agreed with their choice. Beyond that, I had nothing but questions about their tactics. Who decided what house to march on?

Once they marched on the family home of three young people with a heroin addiction. I stood there, barely in my teens, wondering how their mother felt, sitting terrified in that house, watching her kids fall further into addiction, and knowing that her own community saw them only as outcasts. These were the kids she had so many hopes and dreams for, the kids she brought to football training only a few years earlier, the kids she dressed neatly in their school uniforms and sent off in the mornings with a wave from the door.

Could the mob outside her door now not think of her, of the turmoil that heroin was causing in her home? Instead of aggression and rejection, why not offer her empathy and help. Can you imagine how much more of an impact that would have had on the community?

What parent brings a kid into the world and chooses a life of addiction for them? When people asked me, as a young child, what I wanted to be when I grew up, I would tell them I wanted to be a vet. What child would say they wanted to be a heroin addict or a criminal? Those kids standing in their gardens feeling guilt and shame for what they had brought to their mothers' doors, facing this angry mob – what did they want to be when they were small?

Of course, between that march and the next I was happy enough to smoke blow in my ma's house while she worked.

We had no understanding of drugs. When I began to move away from drugs I would become a support to those who were still using drugs and I have spent way too many days and nights in hospitals and on psychiatric wards as many of my friends' long-term chaotic drug use took its toll.

Outsiders always assumed that drug use and crime were the causes of deprivation. Just like the vigilantes, they hadn't yet begun to understand that problem drug use and crime were the symptoms of deprivation.

By the time the next vigilante march rolled around the penny still hadn't dropped. This whole community was experiencing trauma and deprivation together. Why were we fighting against each other with these stupid huts and marches?

Like an army they came towards Cushlawn. This march was bigger than the last.

It was clear to me that there were now gangs of men from outside our community fronting this whole thing and their aggression was obvious to see. They rained blows down on anyone who challenged their self-appointed authority as they roamed the streets at night.

For weeks, huge numbers of cars had been lining up outside the community centre for the vigi meetings. Where did all those cars come from? Most people from the area lived within walking distance of the centre, and not that many owned cars anyway. They must be coming from other places.

The community centre was a place for the community, a safe space in my childhood. Now it was becoming a hive of planning and plotting against us. I found this so hard to digest. I knew the people who worked there and they were good people. They provided me with some of my best childhood memories. I am sure they would have a different perspective on the vigi era but I can only account for how I experienced it.

The community centre is where I went to my first disco. It was summer time and my dress had a cartoon camel on it. My friend Curly's da sat in the chair keeping an eye on the disco shop where we bought our Cadet lemonade. A single father of two boys, a father who needed support and encouragement, but would later have to face that mob outside his house too.

The community centre is where I signed up to the summer project every year, projects that gave me the best summers of my childhood in Annamoe, Brittas Bay and Clara Lara.

The community centre is where I learned how to play table tennis and where I met some of my closest friends. Now the community centre had men piling out of it, leading the charge on the very homes that needed the community centre the most.

On one occasion, as the crowds marched like soldiers, some of my friends decided to organise and run from house to house to stand with the families being bullied from their homes. I cannot remember who got the power hose ready but I remember laughing as the marchers were drenched in water.

That same night they marched on the home of a young man who was in prison. Myself and some friends stood silently on a garden wall. One young fella bravely spoke up. "He's in prison, leave his family alone. They didn't fucking do anything." The mob quickly turned on us, grown men throwing kicks and fists at anyone who attempted to challenge their authority. They started punching one young fella heavily in the face, and myself and Tracy tried to intervene. I was a young teenage girl but they didn't seem to mind giving me the full force of their fists.

There would only be pockets of violence like this in the community but I seemed drawn to those pockets, and for the most part those who shouted loudest and who fought the most seemed to get hurt the most. This level of violence was new to me.

As kids, we couldn't grasp why all this violence was happening. I know people now look back on movements like this with different perspectives and some believe they were examples of positive action, but I disagree. They weren't marching on some big international drug dealer's door, they went for low-hanging fruit. A young man once said to me that violence is the only way to survive. If you are not willing to protect yourself or stand up for yourself, then you will be walked all over.

I watched the vigilantes and the gardaí use violence and began to wonder where it all began and where it would all end. My da respected the institutions that were meant to protect us. He taught me to trust them. And yes, using force and fists was not a new thing; I saw it across the generations. But people were now swapping their fists for weapons in some cases.

Why on earth did we need to protect ourselves from each other? Who was our enemy? Our neighbours? Our friends? It did not make sense. We were kids. We should have been battling on GAA pitches and in the local boxing clubs – and some people were. But there is something fundamentally wrong when so many of us had to roam the streets with weapons in our pockets. It's as though we knew we had little chance of exerting power in society, so we would find ways to exert power over each other, too young to realise we were all in this situation together.

I was happy to see the back of this time in Tallaght. It was scary and it didn't stop the drug-dealing and joyriding. I am thankful that the community centre reclaimed the space for its youth population and has gone on to play a crucial role in providing services to the community.

CHAPTER 7:
LOVE IS NOT ALWAYS A
SUBSTITUTE FOR HEROIN

When I was about fourteen, I watched a fella I was seeing injecting himself with heroin. I watched his eyes roll as he slowly, seductively slid down the wall until he was slumped on the floor. He looked lost in happiness. I wanted to feel whatever it was he was feeling. It excited me.

I was being drawn to the lure of heroin, unaware of the void it drags you down into, but I also had something in me that was pulling me back from that void. I had my plan, the one I wrote when Jenny died.

One night outside the Kusanta snooker hall, I asked a young fella, who was out of his face, if I could buy a score bag from him. I sat in my bedroom for hours that night with the little bag in my hand. I thought about taking it on my own and never telling anyone. Sure I will never get strung out, I convinced myself. I hid the score bag in my shoe and fell asleep. The next day I went to the library and began my reading.

I spent hours that week reading books about heroin. I read about heroin and where it came from. I read about methadone and its purposes. I read about the history of opium. I read about the Vietnam veterans who came back from war with a heroin addiction. I read about Richard Nixon's belief that he could declare a war on drugs and win. I spent hours reading about the effects on the body. I was fascinated with every word I read, though much of it used a type of language that I couldn't understand then. All this reading triggered a little excitement in me.

After that research and reading in the library I felt fulfilled. I was mesmerised by drugs – taking them and reading about them. I was full of intention to do the right thing, but I was also walking towards the romantic call of heroin. Two powerful forces now joined battle in my head. The power of knowledge and the power of heroin. But that week, at least, knowledge won, and I flushed the gear down the toilet. It wasn't easy, and I would spend years ignoring my lust for a drug I had never even taken. If I was lucky enough to live to adulthood, did I really want to be addicted to heroin?

I watched him through a haze of smoke, stoned and giddy. I was in a friend's house in Knockmore, where I spent a couple of evenings a week smoking hash and chatting the night away. He sat on the armchair across from me in his immaculately clean runners, Pringle socks, Pringle jumper and Levi's.

After a couple of years of daily drug use, taking sleeping tablets and buying methadone, I was tired of it. No amount of Reebok tracksuits and green pyramid Es could mask the fact that I was out of my depth. I was looking for a way out – and there he was. Alan Jones, Jonesy, somewhat shy in nature and very handsome. I had never seen him before, although his sisters worked with my ma. His family had moved to Knockmore from the inner city. I knew instantly that he was a good person and I felt safe in his presence. I wanted to meet him again.

Over the next couple of weeks, I learned that Jonesy had been in and out of prison, but he was currently clean from drugs. I naively thought he had permanently kicked the habit. All my reading had given me knowledge about heroin, but, in the real world, I had little understanding of its power. I knew that I managed to flush my heroin down the toilet the summer before I met Jonesy. I knew that some of my friends were becoming dependent on heroin, but Jonesy looked great. He did not look like some of the addicts that I knew. His teeth were whiter than white. I would learn later that during his years of active drug use he carried a toothbrush everywhere with him and would scrub his teeth so the heroin wouldn't stain them. I was convinced that drugs were in his past and that we would live happily ever after together.

I was in love. He became Alan to me and not Jonesy. We quickly became glued at the hip. Being with him was like an adventure, exciting and new.

He had a loving family; none of them had lived a life like Alan's. They were always trying to help him, trying to find a way out of addiction for him. It was clear that he was tortured by who he was and wanted nothing more than to just be Alan. He loved reading and was a big fan of Anne Rice's vampire books. He spoke of his days with Home Farm Football Club and how he had missed his chances of playing professionally.

I felt I could reinvent myself with Alan. I could start again. We went to so many places that I had never been before. He took me to town to meet his friends. In and out of the city centre. I was a stranger in Dublin 1; no one knew my history and I craved this anonymity. Nobody knew I was not tough inside.

Alan knew everyone, greeted them all with the biggest smile of those pearly teeth. He would tell me all the stories of the inner city and the people who lived there. The Northside was an exotic land to me. I was mesmerised by the streets of Summer Hill and all the other flat complexes. I had always been attracted to the flats and used to feel disappointed that we had moved out of Ballymun. It looked like so much more fun. The stairwells weren't a place of syringes and urine-stained walls to me. They were full of character and the unknown.

I loved to hear a townie accent; the more common, the more I'd listen. I loved the buzz of the street selling and the wheeling and dealing. I loved the sense of community. One side to me wanted to settle down and stop the drug-taking and shoplifting, but when I went to town it all seemed so much more sophisticated. They all dressed so much better in town. I never questioned where they got the money to afford it. They weren't robbing Levi's from shops; they were driving cars through the front of shop windows already notorious as the "inner city ram-raiders".

All of this stirred my inner conflict, the angel and devil on my shoulders, pulling me back and forth between who I was and who I wanted to be. Alan had no interest in encouraging me to behave in any way that would get me into trouble. I had just turned fifteen and had already left school, against the wishes of my parents. I was actively pretending to be eighteen years old in the job that I had managed to get at a pharmaceutical company. I believed myself to be an adult, not a kid. I looked older too. I never got refused from bars or off-licenses.

Meeting Alan was the beginning of change for me. I had been struggling for so long to do the right thing, but chaos had always been on the fringes of my life. But finally, from the moment I met Alan, doing the right thing started to get easier.

CHAPTER 8:
I'M PREGNANT

I was sitting in the toilets of McDonald's in the Square and my life had just been turned on its head once again. Outside, kids were enjoying their Happy Meals, but I was sitting in a cubicle staring at a blue line.

I was pregnant.

Like everything in my life, I didn't stop to think; I headed for the nearest payphone to ring my ma. But I hung up immediately. I went into the family planning centre.

"I'm sorry," the receptionist told me. "You'll have to make an appointment."

"Please, I just found out I'm pregnant. Could I please just chat to someone for a moment?"

They were very good; someone came out to chat with me for a few minutes.

Back I went to the payphone. Ma barely had time to say "hello".

"Ma, I'm pregnant."

And I hung up again.

I'm still not sure why but these words felt so good to say. It was as if getting pregnant had been my life's goal. Truth to tell, I hadn't cared if I got pregnant and hadn't done anything to prevent it. I'd decided years earlier that I wanted to be a mother. Maybe I saw it as a way to save myself, to have someone to love.

Maybe it's because I was still angry with my parents for their deceit. I'd closed the door on their love. I was too immature to know that not everything was about me.

I headed home, not knowing what sort of reception I'd get. My gentle da and my problem-solving ma. Would they hate me? Would I have to move out and find somewhere to live? Now that I'd a moment to think, I wasn't sure what was going to happen to me.

I remember nothing of the moment I told them, other than standing in silence in the sitting room, waiting for my da to accept the situation. But he stood up and walked out without a word. I could feel his disappointment.

I'd have preferred if he'd shouted at me. What gave him the right to walk out? He had no right to be angry, I told myself; he didn't have a leg to stand on after the big revelation about his age and his other family. Now here I was, about to bring a new life into the world.

I couldn't help wondering if his other daughter let him down like I did. I wondered if he regretted being my da. At that moment, like many times in my young life, I even wished that I'd never been born. Then I'd never have turned into this messed-up, pregnant teen, who thought she knew it all, who thought she could do what she liked without any consideration of consequences.

I thought about running after him. I wanted to scream at him, to fight with him, to give him an earful of the stuff that tortured my thoughts on a daily basis. I wanted him to know I was still so angry with him.

But I also needed him at that moment. He was an old man and he was going to die anyway and leave me without a father. He would never get to see his grandchild growing up. How dare he just leave the room?

Then the sitting room door opened. He took me in his arms.

"It's OK, love," he said. "I love you. Everything's going to be OK."

And, for that moment, my anger melted in the safety of his arms. I gave in to his embrace and I allowed myself to remember how amazing my parents were. Looking back now, I recognise that some part of me knew that my parents would have my back, no matter what. I had a safety net, and I knew that things would be OK.

But I wouldn't allow him to love me just yet – not completely anyway. It would take a while to get past the idea that if he couldn't share his love with his older children then I didn't deserve his love either. I felt a solidarity to siblings that I never knew.

I had my baby to love now and, knowing that I had my parents' support, I could get excited about the prospect of becoming a mammy.

My ma is practical to the point of always making sure things would just work out. She did this with this news too, but before she could help me make plans, she sat me down and said, "You know you have options, don't you, Lynn? I will support you regardless of what decision you make." *Options? What fucking options?* I looked at her in horror. I could not believe what she was suggesting. *Abortion? How dare she?*

"I want my baby!" I slammed the chair back and ran from the room.

I had planned this. I wanted to be a mammy. Could she not see that I wanted this baby?

I felt supported and loved by Alan but, despite the support they'd shown me, my parents were distraught. This was not part of their plan for my life. They had done everything right when I was a child. They'd read to me, tucked me in at night, grounded me when I was bold, talked me through the values and principles a good person must have to succeed in life. Once, after I'd stolen a pound note from a neighbour, my ma had marched me around to them to make a full confession and repay them. Where did it all go wrong?

But it wasn't long before my parents began to see a silver lining to my situation. The second I walked out of McDonald's toilets with that positive test in my hand, I stopped smoking, drinking and doing drugs. It was easier than I thought, although on rare occasions I still craved a joint. I didn't care too much about not drinking or other drugs. For the first time in years I was completely sober and I felt a tinge of what it would be like to be whole.

I also made the decision to return to school to get my Junior Cert. That was part of the plan I'd made: if you live long enough, get an education. If I wanted to plan for myself and my baby, school was the first thing I knew I needed to re-engage with. I was not forced to, it was my choice and my ma supported me and helped me communicate my seriousness to the school.

Walking to Killinarden Community School that first day, I thought about the other Lynn, the girl I had thought long gone and forgotten. I thought about a world where I wasn't a pregnant teenager, a world where I spent most of my days saving animals, training to be a vet and working on the African plains. I thought about the Lynn who wanted to work with David Attenborough. I promised myself I could still get there, I could save animals, or people, or lives. I could save something, but maybe just saving myself would be enough for now. Saving myself would be a good place to start. I wasn't ready to give up, not all in one go anyway.

This would be my first time in school for a long time and I was petrified as I walked through those gates where most of my anger first began to materialise. The school where teachers had watched me jump out of windows because I'd decided I'd had enough classes for the day. The teachers who had been on the receiving end of the full force of my rage.

So, there I was, waddling through the school concourse, growing belly on display, no longer a tiny eight-stone teen but a fourteen-stone mother-to-be. I was there to learn. Learn something for my baby. At least get a Junior Cert, for all that was worth.

I held my head up high, feeling not an ounce of guilt or shame. If I felt any sense of anxiety, ambivalence or concern for my future, there wasn't a chance in hell I would ever allow this to surface for anyone to see. I always kept those feelings buried so far down inside me, I was not even sure if they existed. I was a brazen, strong and fearless young girl – or at the very least that was the mask I wore, and I wore it well.

But it didn't last. On that very first day in the concourse, a woman who worked in the school told me, "You have wasted your life. You know that, don't you?"

There it was: the judgement, the shaming. A throwaway comment for her, which she most likely doesn't even remember saying. But it has stuck with me all these years. Who the fuck did she think she was? She knew nothing about me. *Wasted?* I couldn't get my head around it. I was fifteen. If I was lucky I could live another sixty years. What would I do in those sixty years? Would I fail at motherhood, at life? Would I just sit at home and never see the light of day again? *Wasted my life.* I hadn't even begun to live my life yet – not my new one, anyway.

I wanted to hurl abuse at her. Get right up in her face and tell her what I thought of what she had just said. My anger sometimes felt completely uncontrollable. Like it wasn't even me, like some demon was rising up inside me and taking me over as soon as someone challenged me or insulted me. But if I learned anything from that day, it was that suppressing that anger, or at least letting it subside, would be a daily fight. Often it would leave me shaking inside. Keeping the anger in seemed as unhealthy and tiresome as letting it out. I lacked the skills to manage difficult situations. On that day, however, I was there for me and I was there for my baby, and not being fucked out of the school on my first day back was more important than this woman's judgemental forecast of my life.

I strolled home from school feeling a little deflated. I had made this huge decision to go back to that school and sit in that classroom, and I felt proud. This was their chance to support me. Show some encouragement and at the very least be able to acknowledge that I had taken a positive step in coming back to school.

I couldn't escape what she had said, though. I wondered if she was right. Had I wasted my life? What was my life anyway? I couldn't have wasted my life. Only months earlier I was consuming silly amounts of drugs and robbing cars and now I was back sitting in a classroom. I felt I was making progress and here was this woman telling me my life was past tense. Talking to me as if I was already history. What did her comment mean for the little girl growing inside me?

As I sat in my bedroom that night I listened to "One in Ten" by UB40. The words "statistical reminder of a world that doesn't care" brought me back to reality. I was not past tense, I was fifteen and I had my whole life ahead of me. The more I processed her comment, the more determined I became, and I vowed to use her disregard for my life to fuel me. I would show her. I refused to be a statistical reminder of an Ireland that didn't care.

My return to school wouldn't be the only time I would feel shame during my pregnancy. On the second occasion, I wasn't upset for me, I was upset for my da.

"Juvenile, juvenile, clear the court," the judge in Tallaght District Court shouted at the top of his voice. I stood up and made my way toward the dock, unsure of what would happen, but hoping that the judge would let me off because I was pregnant. My da stood with me that day, and I was sad he had to see this. I could see the respect he had for the environment he was in, this law-abiding man who, yet again, found himself in a very unfamiliar situation because of his daughter.

I was facing several charges for stealing cars and shoplifting. I was convinced the other people in the court were judging me, thinking that I was stealing cars while I was pregnant. I wanted to shout that

I was going to be a good mammy, and that I wasn't a thief anymore. I wondered if they thought it was funny that the judge was clearing the court for a juvenile who was about to become a mother. A juvenile having a juvenile. But I forgot about what the other people might have been thinking when the judge spoke to my da.

After the charges had been read out (I was given probation), the judge turned his attention on Da. The gist of his words were: "Your daughter is pregnant, Mr Ruane. How did you let this happen? What exactly have you done about this? She is underage and it is against the law for your daughter to have sex at her age." With every word directed at him as a father, I sank deeper into my own guilt because I knew he wasn't to be blamed for how my life was.

In my heart, I wanted to tell the judge that my da was a good man. He drove the streets at night looking for me. He rang the police to help him when I was running wild. He rang social workers and psychiatrists and never gave up trying to reach me. I wanted to tell him how my da taught me how to spell. How he taught me the importance of sharing. How he and my mother brought me to football practice, running training, the girl guides. How they always grounded me when I got out of hand. How they always made me come in when the street lights came on. I wanted to tell them my da taught me the importance of not smoking and set incentives for myself and my brother to make healthy decisions. I wanted to tell the judge how I had found my da crying in his room because he felt like he had failed me. How he didn't know how to fix me.

I wanted to say all of this to the judge, but I couldn't. The words I wanted to say would not come out of my mouth, and not because I felt intimidated by the judge but because I was still a volatile teenager with a lack of respect for the justice system. I knew that if I spoke, all that would have come out was: "Shut the fuck up, you. What the fuck would you know, ya fucking prick?" I knew anything I said would just prove to the judge what he already assumed and that I was standing there, pregnant and facing the possibility of prison, because of my da's parenting. So instead I stayed silent, and I had to watch the judge berating Da, my head bowed in shame and regret for my father. Holding my head up with pride and a "fuck you, world" attitude didn't seem appropriate anymore.

The headline in the *Tallaght Echo* that week read "Dad of pregnant teen criticised in court". They couldn't print my name because I was underage but everyone knew who it was. I wasn't shy about telling people either, waving the paper around as if making it to the court pages of the *Echo* was some sort of achievement. *What the fuck is wrong with me?* I'd think when I was alone. How could I go from feeling sorry for my da to acting as though none of it mattered?

Everything in my life seemed to be going like this – my heart feeling one thing, my physical self acting out differently. I was two completely different people and I didn't know how to reconcile them. There was a war inside me, a raging, violent war. I wanted deep down to be a good mammy and good daughter but I couldn't do this until I healed the hurt inside me. I thought about counselling and anger management but I had little respect for the ability of people working in those spaces, which stemmed from the experience I had with the psychiatrist.

At that time, two things got me through my tears – and I only ever cried alone. I was either alone with my music or alone with my dog, Toby. He would listen to me and lick the tears from my face. He wouldn't judge me. Toby would stay by my side through everything, and there was still so much to come. If UB40 or Tupac didn't bring me back to fight mode, then Toby did. I continued crying alone right up to my thirties. When I put down my weapons and surrendered, when those layers that protected me from the threat of my life were no longer needed, I finally began to cry, out in the open, less from anger, much more from sadness.

CHAPTER 9:
JORDANNE

One night, Alan and I went into town to meet up with a friend of his who had just been released from prison for a robbery. Alan wasn't a big drinker, and of course I was drinking 7Up as I was pregnant. We decided to sleep at his mate's parents' three-storey house in Sheriff Street that night.

It was four or five in the morning. I reached out for Alan in the bed. He was gone. I sat up and wiped my eyes, listening carefully for any sounds. I was scared in this big house. It was dark and I couldn't find the light switch. I felt my way down the stairs. There he was: Alan, with his friend, tinfoil in hand and tooter in his mouth.

I felt my stomach turn. I turned with it and fled. I sat on the bathroom floor, crying and howling as if someone had died. I had been convinced he was clean, that he had kicked the heroin. He didn't know I had seen him; he never wanted anyone who loved him to see him using drugs.

I didn't realise it at the time, but that was the beginning of the end. We had so many good times after that and Alan fought every relapse. The love he had for the child growing inside me was in a full-on battle with his addiction.

This would be the beginning of my education on the power of addiction. I learned that having babies doesn't fix the past; becoming a parent doesn't heal all wounds.

My pregnancy went well for the most part and either Ma or Alan supported me with every hospital visit. I was completely drug-free and alcohol-free and focused on having a healthy pregnancy. I had a positive experience with the Rotunda Hospital as Ma used her health insurance for me to go semi-private. I would watch the long queue of girls in the main public appointments area, thankful that Ma always ensured I was supported as best I could be.

Alan was excited at the prospect of becoming a daddy and we shared so much at that time, chatting endlessly about names, looking at baby clothes and planning all we needed for our little baby. But there was one thing I didn't share with him: the sex of the baby. He didn't want to know and I did. So, I never told him that I knew. I led him to believe he could pick the name if we had a boy (he wanted to call him Roy), when I knew quite well that we were having a girl.

I wasn't scared at the prospect of becoming a mum. I wasn't upset that my life was about to change. I craved that change. My bedroom was filled with the preparations for our new baby. My parents bought everything I could possibly need. Enough nappies to last a year. Everyone just accepted that this was happening and supporting me was the only way my parents could handle it.

It was me and Alan against the world. What else could a baby need apart from us? Sure, as long as we loved her, clothed her, fed her and kept her stocked up in little Nikes, weren't we grand? I never once sat down and thought about the fact that I still had enough anger inside me to fill the whole estate, while Alan was struggling to stay clean. I thought being pregnant would cancel out everything bad in our lives. Alan was gentle and protective and I was strong-willed and somewhat intelligent. Our potential as parents was evident, but opportunity was our obstacle.

I was so excited going into labour. I didn't think I was just a kid; I felt so ready for this. Alan, my ma and da had sat for days at my bedside in the Rotunda. The doctors were deciding whether or not to induce me. A pocket of water had broken but not my main waters and they were not sure what to do.

I knew Alan wanted to play an active role in the birth process. I loved him and didn't want to exclude him, but when I went into labour all I wanted was my ma. I tried to express this but Alan was so excited at the prospect of witnessing the birth of his child that I never asserted myself by insisting I just needed Ma. Alan was supportive and helpful in the labour suite but I was only pretending to be grown-up and I was distraught not to have her holding my hand. I have since learned to put my own needs much higher up the list of priorities but back then I didn't feel I deserved to put myself before anyone.

Alan and I loved Jordanne, but her introduction to the world wasn't exactly the joyous moment we imagined. As soon as she was born, Ma came running in with pink babygros. Alan copped on straight away that I had kept the baby's sex from him. He was furious and I was in floods of tears. Looking back now, I know it should not have been like this. I shouldn't have tricked the father of my child like that; and he shouldn't have let it get in the way, not at that moment. Especially as my traumatic experience in the labour suite hadn't finished. Alan and his hurt feelings would have to wait.

Just after Jordanne was born, I began to bleed excessively. The doctors came rushing in. It seemed to take forever before they told me my womb had been torn inside. The doctor had to put his hands right up inside me to stitch inside my womb but the blood kept coming and I was brought to theatre. Thankfully, they managed to stem the bleeding, but there was some permanent damage.

Alan and I would repair our friction the next day, apologise to one another and move forward.

Our lives weren't steady and we weren't always rational. We had our little girl and we had our ups and downs. But I have to acknowledge that, given the circumstances of our lives at the time, we were good parents. Of course we would have been better parents with stability and security in our lives, but we tried hard to do what we could to be the parents Jordanne needed. Her life was full of obstacles and that was because our lives were full of obstacles. We would go on many an adventure together. And ultimately Jordanne and I would go hand-in-hand on a journey of our own.

Alan was my first love but I was slowly realising that heroin was his. I could never compete with its power. It had taken over his life long before we met. It was not a choice for Alan; he did not choose between his family and heroin. When addiction is at its most powerful, the ability to choose is jeopardised.

I began to battle Alan the addict and love Alan the father at the same time. I would watch as he held Jordanne in his arms, fed her and rocked her to sleep. They were inseparable. He would tell me to go back to sleep in the mornings while they would go off to feed the ducks in the park. He was the proudest father that ever was.

We took the good with the bad. Even at that time, there would be periods when Alan seemed to be doing OK. Often, Jordanne would not leave his side. She had little interest in mammy. Alan was her favourite; she adored him and he adored her. When he was clean, she would stay with him for days on end sometimes. He was an artist and when he was doing well he would spend hours teaching Jordanne how to draw. Every time she sketches now, I am grateful for this gift that he gave her.

Even when heroin won the battle in Alan's head, he would make sure we never had to witness it. For the most part he would take it far away from us, disappearing into town to smoke heroin. Even at his most vulnerable he hid his addiction as best he could. He knew he had to protect me and Jordanne. Especially Jordanne. I believe deep down that Alan knew Jordanne needed one of us to survive. Given my own history with drugs, he ensured he never had drugs in my environment. The only proof I would ever find was in his bedroom in his ma's house. Sometimes there were dozens of Cadbury Turkish Delight bars hidden in drawers. Rumour had it you could only smoke gear off the foil from those bars because they had changed the material used on the other bars.

Thankfully, heroin wasn't a permanent fixture in our young family. Alan could be clean in any given month. We would go to the zoo or take walks in parks. Our parents would babysit so the two of us could get some time to ourselves, go for a meal or a night out. He even proposed and of course I said yes.

Alan had three sisters and lots of nieces and nephews. The whole family were supportive to us and Saturdays in Nanny Jones's would become a permanent fixture in Jordanne's upbringing, right up to today. Coddle was always on the menu, feeding the gangs of Joneses – at least until, at nine years old, Jordanne decided that she could no longer eat anything that once had a face.

There were funny times through those years. One Saturday morning, after my brother and some of his friends had sat drinking all night in my ma's kitchen, I decided to take advantage of their drunken state. I got out Jordanne's fancy dress costumes and persuaded them to put them on. There was a Bugs Bunny, a clown, a princess and, funniest of all, a ballerina – our friend Gareth squeezed his big body into a tiny leotard. It was so tight that his testicles hung outside, looking a little strangled.

I piled Jay and his friends into my car – a little Saxo, my first car – and drove to my ma's factory. Ma herself was away for the weekend. All the Saturday workers were sitting at their stations when all these characters barged in. Gareth did the most perfect pirouette, leaving nothing covered up. The assistant manager, Breda, went on a mad one, while I rolled around outside in a heap of laughter.

When Ma returned, she tried her best to give out to us. "That's my job, you know. Imagine your kids running through your factory dressed as half-naked ballerinas." We knew she didn't mean a word of it, because she couldn't keep a straight face. She found it as funny as we did.

My break-up with Alan, when Jordanne was around two, is all a little blurry. It felt like a long goodbye.

So much had happened between us and we were both messing up all over the place. Our own pasts insisted on seeping into our presents. Through it all, we struggled to create the right environment for Jordanne, even though we were at each other's throats sometimes.

The hardest thing to accept was watching this doting dad turn into Jonesy from the inner city and disappear again. He would run away with his addiction and sometimes I wasn't sure which was worse: his absence or the addiction. Those periods on the missing list were the hardest for Jordanne to take.

I felt really hurt and betrayed when Alan began to use heroin with two of my friends. He would disappear for days with them. I had more tolerance of his addiction than of theirs. I felt more betrayed by them than I did by him, maybe because I had accepted that he had been an addict before I met him, but I had been their friend long before drugs came into our lives. It's not very logical but at the time I was hurt.

So it wasn't a clean break-up. Sometimes I felt like I hated him, felt betrayed. But deep down, I never could hate Alan.

I returned to my own inner battle. My pain came long before Alan was in my life; he was not the source of my battle. He had been a nice distraction for a while from my broken self but it was only in his absence that my battle and subsequent growth would emerge.

Here I was, feeling that anger again, and there he was, fighting with the hunger for heroin. I felt a pull towards just going mental, taking loads of drugs and accepting that that was who I was. I would fantasise about drugs and finding adrenaline in some form, from somewhere.

I was still making the wrong decisions. I hadn't learned to verbalise my pain. I was a kid and I was a mother. Could I really be a mother? Did I really have to do it without Alan? I was feeling more lost now than ever and I didn't know if I was strong enough.

Jordanne Jennifer Jones, blue eyes, black hair and as content as could be, would become the anchor between the world I wanted to be in and the one I was stuck in. My life depended on hers as much as hers depended on mine. Our journey has been special but turbulent and the responsibility we as her parents placed on her shoulders – to save us – would take its toll. I didn't notice this at first and I never really understood that the trauma that existed in our lives shouldn't have to be there. All the painful situations I found myself in didn't seem like big deals at the time. It is as though I had little ability to assess risk, or maybe I diminished the pain so much so I could get through them, make them small enough for me to handle. I have had a number of near-death situations in my life, but I didn't view them as that at the time.

I continued to live with my ma and da for long after Jordanne was born and everyone played a role in helping me raise her. She was sweet and polite and never looked for much. She would draw most of the day and as long as she was kept stocked up on art supplies she was happy. She had very little hair but we still put it in hairbands because they looked cute. I would read my Winnie-the-Pooh books to her and our room was filled with Winnie-the-Pooh – from wallpaper to bedclothes. She loved it. Later we transformed our shared room, painting the ceiling a navy blue with glowing stars and planets everywhere.

I would have loved a family unit with mammy and daddy under one roof, but that wasn't to be. Both Alan and I tried our very best to put a protective shield around Jordanne. Up to the time that Alan went to prison when Jordanne was about five, we would still do Santy together so that on Christmas morning Jordanne had both parents with her. I wanted Alan to be there every Christmas morning, just as my da had been, tip-toeing down the stairs to see if Santa was still there. I never expected not to get the fairy tale.

The scale of the impact of our lives on Jordanne's life would only become evident as she grew up. I would spend years trying to pick up the pieces. The hidden harm of addiction would impact on her in more ways than I could have imagined. I was a broken young girl trying to be a mother and Alan was addicted to heroin and trying to be a father. For all the effort that we took to protect her from Alan's heroin use and my own battles, we could never protect her from the pain she would feel from not having her daddy around.

His time in prison tore chunks out of our daughter's emotions and how she viewed herself, and neither of us ever really knew how to fix it. We made up every excuse for Alan, but every time I tried to justify myself, I hurt her even more.

From the outside I had started making some of the right choices, but on another level I was failing. I put very little value on myself. Jordanne became my reason to live. But she was just a little growing human, and giving a child that level of responsibility is not how parenting should be. I made just as many bad parenting decisions as I did good ones and this inconsistency confused us all.

The biggest lesson I had to learn was that Jordanne was entitled to be angry with us, and it hurts. She was and still is a kid, and no amount of education on addiction, teen pregnancy, social deprivation and criminality was going to help her understand our lives. And of course, she did understand those things; she just didn't understand why she deserved better. I would spend my life trying to show her that it was we who didn't deserve her.

It was not safe or secure enough for any of us, but I kept fighting through the insecurity and imperfections and knew I had a goal in life, and that was to succeed, somehow, as a mother and as a woman. We had some tough times ahead, but as represented by the phoenix tattooed on my leg, we rose from the ashes time and time again, until we found our footing.

My life will forever be intertwined with Alan's. I will always champion him in his search for recovery. I know with the right intervention and the right mindset Alan will master his recovery from drug abuse.

We are still learning how to accept our circumstances. Jordanne is still finding ways to grieve for the years that she can't get back. She shares this grief with her da's parents and siblings, but in a very different way.

Alan was and still is a gentle soul, until he has to defend himself. He has had a fair few scrapes along the way and, like me, has fought, lied and manipulated when he had to, but at heart, Alan is a good person and I believe he will keep fighting his addiction. It is for him and for all my friends who battle their addiction daily that I chose my career in developing addiction programmes.

Alan hasn't yet found his peace but I got a glimpse of mine at the age of sixteen in the form of An Cosán.

CHAPTER 10:
THE PATH

It wasn't easy learning that my da was an old man. It wasn't easy watching a bus hit my friend. It wasn't easy becoming a mother at fifteen. It wasn't easy watching my friends giving in to addiction and dying around me. But saving myself would prove to be one of the most difficult tasks I would have to face.

Saving myself would become a daily struggle, a struggle that has lasted over seventeen years, but as I removed each layer that I had wrapped around myself, I healed a little more. There are layers made up of the stories I tell myself to survive, layers of pain and rejection and fear, and any other possible layer you can think of. I love what the writer Gail Sheehy said: "Growth demands a temporary surrender of security." My layers of security are shrouded in anger, pretending I didn't care, pretending I was tough and possibly invincible. To surrender this security meant showing the world who I was, showing them that I was dying inside, showing them that I was lonely, hurt and afraid of dying.

The biggest challenge through every event in my life has been in how I chose to respond. Sometimes I would get it bang on the button and do the right thing. Other times I would be so hurt I would lash out at the ones I loved most, the ones who deserved my vengeance the least. When I gave in to the anger, I would scream and shout and hurl all sorts of abuse before slamming my bedroom door and telling everyone to fuck off. I would hold Jordanne tight in my arms and cry myself to sleep, upset that I had lost my cool – again. I was like a big open wound, oozing unresolved pain. All I needed was some healing, and some time to grow. I was on the right path for that, I knew I was, I could feel it. I just needed to keep moving forward.

Slowly, over time, I would learn to harvest the trauma and transform it into energy for the fight ahead. That fight started with learning how to be a mammy to my beautiful Jordanne. I knew that becoming a mammy would not magically absolve me of all my anger. My desire for drink or drugs, my instinct to act out, didn't just dissolve the moment I held her in my arms. But I knew now that I had someone other than myself to fight for.

I had a steep learning curve, coming to understand that I could not control every aspect of my life right down to the tiniest detail. Being the architect of my own life had its limits and I would have to keep strong and keep moving forward. This does not mean that I was not still fucking things up. When I had a night off from being a mammy, my drinking was excessive. *Jordanne is in the Jones's house*, I would tell myself, *and I deserve a night off*. I hadn't developed new social skills that avoided binge drinking and sessions until the early hours of the morning. I was still lashing out at life and I would use my nights off to do that. I was still harming myself and I lacked a level of healing that was necessary to truly be a positive role model for my daughter.

One Saturday night – I was around twenty and Jordanne was at her dad's – I got into a drunken fight at the Spawell after some girls started on my friend, Bridget. I went in, fists flying. Somebody hit me with something – either a knuckle duster or a broken bottle – and it nearly took the tip of my nose clean off. I charged for her. I didn't want to behave like an animal, but I did. Going home that night in a taxi, one of my friends opened the window, and as the wind came rushing through I could see the tip of my nose flapping. Most people would have panicked, but I held the tip of the nose on tightly and went on to a party. The next morning, when I arrived at the hospital, they said they could not glue it as it had already fused with hard blood and begun to scab over.

When I was around 16 and in the middle of a lot of madness, I found An Cosán, an adult education centre in Jobstown in Tallaght, co-founded by Dr Ann Louise Gilligan and Katherine Zappone. I would later learn that, from the meditations to start the day to the smell of home-baked scones wafting from the kitchen, the very core of all that An Cosán strives to achieve is steeped in the gentle and warm nature and the holistic approach of those two wonderful women.

But before the Department of Social Welfare sent me for an interview there for a pilot programme called the Young Mothers Programme, I had never heard of the place. I can't remember the interview, I just remember wanting to go because I could make use of its childcare facility, Rainbow House, if I was accepted on to the course. Jordanne was barely one so it came at a perfect time for both of us.

I remember my first weeks there. I thought it was great. I knew lots of people on the course and I found new friends, especially Aisling, who became a very good friend of mine. I would get up every morning and push Jordanne up the road to An Cosán. It was peaceful and calm. Sharon, who baked the scones, made all the young mothers feel welcome every morning as she handed each of us a cup of tea. Jordanne was downstairs being looked after in Rainbow House while I sat upstairs, finally starting to look after myself.

I was happy to be there and my parents were delighted I was doing something. An Cosán ran courses on everything from computers to public speaking. But it was not the course content that gave me a necessary foundation to create change in my life, it was the environment.

My time in An Cosán was crucial to my life but it wasn't always easy. Nor did I make it easy for others. I was still quite resistant to authority and I would argue back and challenge the facilitators all the time. The difference now was that they were willing to listen and have conversations with me. I was not suspended for being challenging. They dealt with the stuff I brought into the room, which eventually meant I addressed it.

In the early days of my healing, I was still rough around the edges, cheeky and very angry. And I still am to this day; I have just learned to channel it differently. I have always sought validation and praise. I have always had ambition to do well at whatever it was I was doing, whether it was legal or not – whether it was to be a senator or an author or the best shoplifter or the best joyrider in the best cars. Now it was time to be the best mother, to raise my daughter to be better than I was. Without realising it, from this point I set out to live my own life by giving Jordanne the best life I could give her. If she made it smoothly through life then I would know I was doing well.

In the first week, we were introduced to the opening circle. We would all sit around a candle on a purple satin cloth, instrumental music playing softly in the background. I had never listened to meditation music before. We would sit in silence while the facilitator would lead us into a meditation and a visualisation.

I found it difficult. I didn't know how to be still. The silence was painful and, like some of the others, I struggled to hold my laughter in. The facilitator would say, "Now imagine your heart. What does your heart want?" But all I could hear in my head was my own voice saying, "Ah here, would ya fuck off, ya big hippy cunt." This way of being was foreign to me, and I couldn't understand its importance.

But slowly I settled a little more into the circle. I shifted a little less in my seat and I didn't feel compelled to laugh as much. Instead, I would sit in the opening circle, begging the universe to save me.

It was only very recently, when writing a tribute to Dr Ann Louise Gilligan following her death, that I realised that my big breakthrough came about during a day spent in "The Shanty", Ann Louise and Katherine's home in the Wicklow mountains, in 2002 – on a day for participants of An Cosán, known as "Isobella's Day".

I remember so much about that day. I remember the big dog in their garden and the beautiful scenery. I remember hearing sheep baaing in the distance. I remember taking my runners off at the front door and slipping my feet into a pair of cosy wool slippers, smelling the incense and feeling the warmth. I remember laughing as we were encouraged to hug a tree, laughing but loving the idea of it. I remember doing a workshop on animal guides. (My animal guide was a whale.)

I remember feeling at home and realising this was what I wanted in life, to be able to enjoy such simple things and know that I was OK. I knew in that moment I was beginning to heal.

But mostly that day, I remember the meditation, because it was the meditation that would nudge me an inch or two away from the void I felt. The meditation began: "Imagine you are walking in the sand." I concentrated hard. *Sand, Lynn, picture it,* I thought. *Try to imagine a beach you know, that'll help.* I tried to picture Brittas Bay; I have so many lovely memories from there. But I could not stay on that beach for longer than two seconds before my mind would wander. I opened my eyes and looked around the room, at everyone sitting still with their hands in their laps. The smell of cooking chicken wafted through the room. I really wanted to feel the stillness of meditation and I wanted nothing more than to connect with my own skin. I was searching for some inner peace and I felt tormented that I couldn't spend ten minutes following the meditation. However, it was the first time I really began to see the possibilities of this method, even if I still couldn't fully embrace the stillness and silence.

What that day gave me was a determination to reach down inside my core and unpack the peace and stillness I so wanted to feel. I borrowed meditation CDs and books from the library and I began to practise meditation at home. I read up on techniques and spent

82

thirty minutes every night listening to the CDs with Jordanne. One CD encouraged me to imagine a place I felt safe and secure, a place where I could be alone for a while and spend time with my inner child. And finally, a week after that day in "The Shanty", I let go of a part of my resistance and surrendered to the stillness.

Jordanne lay beside me, asleep, her head on our moon-and-stars duvet set. I listened carefully to the voice on the CD, giving me control over where I wanted to bring myself. I ran and ran until I found myself in a field. The grass was so long that even as I ran through the field, it was waving in the wind, far above my head. When I could run no more I dropped down, pulled my knees tight up into my chest and rested my forehead on them. I could feel the security of it, knowing that I had chosen it. I had chosen this field and I could hide here in the long grass in this foetal position, and no one had to see me. Nobody could see that I was just a little kid, choosing to sit on the ground with her head on her knees. Nobody could give out to me here; nobody could see my vulnerability here; nobody would ever have to know. When I chose, I could get up and leave. I could stand tall and be strong again.

Over time, I developed this visualisation more. What worked for me was visualising my plan – the plan I wrote after Jenny died, which was etched in my mind. I was sixteen years old and still alive, and I knew what came next on the list: *If you live long enough, get an education.* So, I began to imagine myself in that field, on a hilltop, but now I was reading the list. I would imagine myself in long blades of grass, the darkest of greens, miles of fields around me. I could see it as clearly as if it were real.

This safe space has stayed with me until this day. I still imagine myself here often, so often it now feels as familiar as home. These days, when I look back at my life or when I am dealing with a difficult situation, I retreat to this place in my head, the list in my hand. When I feel sadness or fear, I go silent and still – and this is where I am gone. My boyfriend tells me that I instantly stop communicating and he doesn't know what is wrong. I can't change this technique and I don't think I want to. It took years to master this great escape into those beautiful green fields. No more drug-induced escapes, instead it's just me, in a field, not a mushy in sight, gathering myself.

Society is obsessed with students learning skills to suit the market, to make them employable, to add skills to their CV. I had left school again for good after completing the Junior Cert. Re-entering education with An Cosán did not give me a skill for the market; it gave me a skill for life, a skill for survival and growth. It taught me how to resource myself in a positive way, using skills to cope that weren't harmful. An Cosán taught me how to be a little more centred, to acknowledge the big gaping hole at the centre of my being, and to give me a foundation that I could build on, so that I could fill that hole with a sense of purpose and confidence.

Success is about learning to love yourself, realising your worth and value and striving for something better than your current situation. We must have our basic needs met before we can truly pursue knowledge. We must access the skills necessary to put knowledge into practice and, most importantly, trauma must be addressed and people must be supported to enter education at whatever level they are at. You can't offer someone a course in something and not have a follow-on avenue for them to pursue. The continuum through all stages of learning must be in place to move people on at the other end. All our paths are different and society must be able to adapt, to accompany each of us on our walk down our individual paths. My path was a battle through pain and a quest for peace and understanding.

An Cosán was the beginning of that journey – level one of my transformation. As I neared the end of my time in An Cosán I wondered what was next for me. I was ready to do something with my life, I just didn't know what that something might be.

I had a long way to go in life and if I was to get there I needed to start. I couldn't sit at home, getting into a rut. During that time, I was working nights in Dunnes Stores while Jordanne slept, then I briefly worked in British Bakeries. Neither of these suited me. I knew this wasn't what I wanted to do with my life. I wanted more for myself and for Jordanne. I'd been working from an early age, from paper girl to working in Burger King at the age of thirteen, pretending as always to be older. I knew I was a terrible employee. My heart was never in those jobs. I was never happy to be there.

I had a sense that I was meant to help people. When I thought about it, the thing that got me most exercised was addiction. I came to realise that I could play a positive role in life through supporting people with addiction.

I had a talent for taking in information on drugs, drink and addiction and the behaviours and trends related to them. I would read something once and remember it. I never experienced this with any other subject and I knew in my heart I could do good, I could help, I could make positive changes for people in addiction. This ambition was spurred on by the fact that so many of my friends were on heroin at the time. My love for them drove my ambition to understand. For the first time in years, learning wasn't a task. I had the vision in my head and I wasn't letting go.

Having witnessed, throughout my teenage years, heroin being used as a painkiller for trauma, it made sense for me to dedicate my life to trying to help people who fell victim to its lure. Deep down, part of me never understood why I wasn't a heroin addict. I often felt like I deserved to suffer in just the same way as everyone else. I even felt guilty for succeeding through all my pain, and to alleviate my guilt I worked to change other people's circumstances. Let's face it, I haven't got the power to change society as a whole, but I will always fuel my efforts on the memories of the lives of those I care about. I will keep talking about drugs, class, trauma and collective pain until I die. The second I stop telling our stories is the day I have removed myself from my history, from my roots and from the reality of those on the fringes.

Becoming a mother and finding An Cosán had allowed me to put some distance between myself and drugs. Now I was at the end of my journey with An Cosán, it felt natural to me that I would return to opium, my long-lost love, but this time it would be to learn more, understand more and hopefully help others in their relationship with it. All these experiences spurred me on to pursue a career in addiction.

A key moment came when I met Tommy Deegan and Eamon White, the founders of SWAN Family Support, set up to support family members of people experiencing addiction. They had been invited to talk about their work. During our final months in An Cosán, we had to source work experience in an area that interested us. I approached Eamon and Tommy after their talk and asked if I could volunteer in SWAN. I took to them straight away; they were as working class as they come and it was clear they had a wealth of real-life experience in addiction. Within a week or so I was taken under their direction and they played an important role in my development.

I was too young for college, I had no money and I was unsure how I was going to enter this work. When it was time to move on from An Cosán, Eamon pointed me in the direction of the addiction studies course at IT Tallaght. Armed with my two years at An Cosán, my ambition and these two mentors who knew their shit, I applied for my place on the addiction studies course.

I was initially knocked back by Fr Liam O'Brien who ran the addiction studies programme in IT Tallaght. He refused me entry on the course, quoting lack of life experience as the reason. He obviously felt I was too young and maybe he felt I wasn't ready. Thankfully, his colleague Alice Murray fought my case and it is due to her that I was accepted onto the course.

I got three things from that course: a chance to prove I could succeed; a job offer later on from Fr Liam to develop a service for teenage heroin users at the Community Addiction Response Programme (CARP); and one of the best friends I would ever have in Debbie Brennan. Debbie was the administrator of CARP and was also doing the course with me. She was a huge support from the moment I met her. Over a decade older than me, she was intelligent, confident and very ambitious, looked after her health, and cycled everywhere. She was the perfect friend for me to have and became part of the new space I was entering.

I was still struggling at that time to stay away from drugs. I thought about them all the time. I still wanted to go out on weekends and get wasted with my pals. Thankfully Debbie, who had no history with drugs, was a lifeline for me, someone I could spend time with who had no connection to all the stuff I was trying to steer away from. I attribute my progression through life to many interventions by a number of people and Debbie is one of those people.

I am sure the other workers at CARP thought Fr Liam was mad to employ me. Nearly nineteen at this stage, they would have had recent memories of me joyriding and drinking in fields. Liam and Debbie stood strong by my side and yet again I got the chance to prove I could do something positive. Over the course of the next four years I worked for Liam and CARP, and also for the Tallaght Cocaine Project, jointly run by St Dominic's Community Response Project and CARP. During that time, I also took a course in behavioural studies at Liberties College, and began my first stint in the homeless sector.

Alongside his work with SWAN, Eamon White was a counsellor and manager at De Paul Ireland. In 2005, he encouraged me to fill out an application to become a relief worker in the Back Lane Hostel. Eamon's confidence in my ability to work in this sort of setting was just the type of support I needed at the time.

Eamon became more than a mentor; he became my counsellor for a number of years before Tommy took over when I was in my twenties (and has been with me until this day). These men came into my life in An Cosán and have never really left.

CHAPTER 11:
I SEE YOU, JAELYNNE

When I was about nineteen, I thought I was so in love. I stayed with this boyfriend for around two years. We were like best pals and we laughed more than I had ever laughed before. We both shared a wicked sense of humour. He was funny and kind and loyal to those he loved. He felt like a big safety blanket wrapped around my vulnerable life. The lack of self-esteem and worth I had developed over the years could hide under this blanket: everyone loved him and so I assumed they loved me too.

I fell in love with his whole family. They had character and wit by the bucketful. They were warm and quirky. Their house was like a treasure trove, every room filled with things they might need one day. If something could be recycled for some other use, then it was. The footstools were milk crates covered in cushions. His dad collected all sorts of useless things – at least you'd think they were useless until a button fell off or your lace snapped. He would disappear briefly and arrive back with bags full of laces or buttons of all colours and sizes.

When I stayed over, I would lie awake at night listening to them talk in their beds until four in the morning. I wondered what his parents still had to say to each other after fifty years together, but they were not short of stories and giggles and I loved it. I had pined for it for my own life. All these years later, I still hold them close in my heart and in friendship.

But at the time, I was a mess. All I could think about was that I wanted to remain in this family, wrapped in this comfort blanket of belonging. I was pathetic in the break-up. I had no sense of dignity and I would sob for hours, calling my ex constantly, trying to convince him he had made a mistake. He didn't make a mistake, but at the time I was distraught, and it took me a number of years to let go. The fear of future heartbreaks stayed with me for much longer though.

I would sit for hours in my porch with my dog, Toby. He loved me and didn't take from me. He never left my side. I would tell Toby about the pain I felt in my heart, always there, as if a piece of me was missing. I would tell Toby about the shame that weighed me down so heavily it felt like I could almost touch it: shame of feeling so weak and pathetic that I wanted a strong man so I could take cover in his strength and confidence. I was aware of the impact the break-up had on me and I knew I needed to mature a little and learn to cope alone. I wanted so much to be loved by a good man, as if that would somehow restore my worth. I sabotaged myself time and time again through my desire to be liked.

Some time after that break-up, I met Joe. I was still very much healing and I wasn't ready to move on. I had been slowly starting to accept that I would need to spend time alone and do a lot of work on my self-esteem and self-worth. I knew it was not healthy to need other people just to feel good. I wanted to feel like I was enough. I knew this would take a very long time to address; as I told my counsellor for many years, "I will be OK when I am thirty-two."

I was drawn to Joe's quick wit. We were only together a couple of months when I learned that I was pregnant. I would be lying if I said I was instantly surprised or upset. If I am honest, I felt a twinge of relief. *Maybe this is what I need to move on with my life*, I thought. *Forget my heartache, start anew.*

During the pregnancy, I took Jordanne on holidays to Mexico, partly to fulfil one childhood dream – to see the saltwater crocodiles. Jordanne was excited and very caring towards me throughout the pregnancy. "Mammy, how is peanut today?" she would ask as we woke in our big fancy bed, or sat at the poolside. At this point, all was fine. I was pregnant. Had it really sunk in? Maybe not.

Then it happened. A few months in, barely out of the first trimester, I felt paralysed with fear. I knew in that moment that I couldn't be with Joe. He was sound and funny, he was a good person, but I wasn't ready for a relationship. I had to look after myself, and maybe deep down I felt this was my chance to prove I could survive alone, to be the strong woman who does what's right for herself and for her future. It was as though, with that one thought, he was gone. I shut him out.

I have always had too much empathy for my own good; now though, I pulled the shutters down around myself and for the first time in my life I felt nothing. Blackness, numbness and emptiness. I liked it a little. Jordanne was my only lasting connection. In one fell swoop, I culled everyone else from my life. I was now shut. I felt like a machine that had just figured out how to sort out all its own malfunctions. Having cut Joe out, he missed experiencing the pregnancy of his first child, but at that point I did not care what that meant for him, no matter how unfair.

I would stare for hours at my growing tummy but I wondered what was in there. I was relieved that I was pregnant as I hadn't been sure, with all my health issues, if I would have been able to have any more. But on the other hand I was frightened as I wasn't prepared for a second baby. I had imagined that, the next time I had a baby, I would be much more stable and secure. To be quite honest, I was scared shitless.

I told the doctor at my hospital check-up, "I feel really scared about becoming a mother again, I feel really disconnected." Before I knew it, I was being sent to the psychiatrist at the Rotunda. I remember nothing about that appointment, but the trip on the number 77 bus to the hospital that day is a vivid memory. I was lonely and frightened and I became more and more irrational as the bus journey went on. I worked myself into a spin. I was frightened about being a mother again and I was frightened to tell the people around me. My ma knew I was pregnant, but I hadn't told her that I was struggling. I wasn't sure I was strong enough to have another baby. I felt shame just for feeling scared.

I remember staring out the top window of the bus at a woman standing at a bus stop below, her baby strapped to her front in a harness. She was gently stroking the baby's little cheek. It looked so perfect; they looked perfect. I almost jumped off the bus to go home in that moment.

How could I be scared of something so beautiful? I bet if I told that woman how I am feeling she would think I am a horrible person. Am I a horrible person? I wish someone would tell me I am not a horrible person. If I admit I am scared of having another baby, does that mean I am a terrible parent? Will the doctors call social workers and take Jordanne away? What if the psychiatrist says I am only imagining the pregnancy? I wasn't sure what all these thoughts meant but I battled them, most of the time not wanting to battle them.

I remember little else of the first two trimesters beyond this emotional confusion. I still haven't forgiven myself for my thoughts and I feel I had some sort of personality change through the whole experience.

But one thing was clear to me: I wanted another girl. I was more worried about raising boys in working-class communities, where young men seem to suffer a little more. So many of my male friends seemed to have it so much harder. I felt I had a slightly better chance of keeping girls off drugs and out of prisons. I was convinced if I had boys they would die younger or experience much greater hardships.

I don't ever remember seeing the psychiatrist again. As quickly as I shut off, I switched back on again. I wish I could explain this in the same way I try to explain and understand every other part of my life, but I can't. Maybe I had a mini-breakdown, like I was crippled with fear, fear for the future. I do not know how, but I temporarily disconnected, disassociated and shut down. However, I do feel I emerged in a much stronger place. I am very lucky to have some of the survival tools I have gained. And I am very lucky to have my amazing mother's support.

I breathe and I accept I am pregnant. I am having a little girl and I know that I am going to call her Jaelynne. My brother is Jay and my name is Lynn. So, Jaelynne. I spelt it so it would match Jordanne; both names have eight letters, start with a J and end with 'nne'. It's perfect. Surely, named for three people who love her, she would never feel left out or unloved?

Before Jaelynne came into the world I began to figure out ways I could make it up to her. To allow her to feel our connection, I decided I would breastfeed. It wasn't something I had planned on doing, nor had I breastfed Jordanne, but this, I felt, would heal us and our rocky start. She would love me and she would never feel that I briefly disconnected from this pregnancy. She would never know that I had a wobble.

The pregnancy seemed so short and, all of a sudden, I was in labour. Ma was by my side. Joe was in the waiting room. The labour was as quick as the pregnancy. Keeping fit paid off. No drugs, no dramas like the first time. A few pains, a few contractions while doing circular motions on an exercise ball, and there she was after a few short hours, already looking like a toddler. All 10lb 2oz of her. It was 26 January 2007, a Friday morning at 9.26 a.m., and she was here.

Jaelynne demanded the room instantly, with her large frame, her cheeks, her cry, her fat knees. I had just managed to appreciate the moment when I looked at Ma's concerned face. It was happening again. The blood pooled under the bed, like someone had taken a hatchet to my uterus. The room was filled almost instantly with concerned midwives. I was losing blood at a rapid rate. I could hear them talking about transfusions. My ma is solid in a crisis but she looked frightened now. *I am going to die,* I thought. I am haemorrhaging but it takes them a while to realise how serious it is. Ma points to the bed and tells them that the floor is covered in blood. Jaelynne is taken from me, I am whisked to theatre and knocked out. My insides have never been the same again; I am full of scar tissue inside and the pain has stayed forever. That day I felt I was going to die before I got to love my little Jaelynne, before I got to meet her properly.

When I woke up, Jaelynne was beside me, this big sturdy newborn. We had to buy her three- to six-month clothes and give away all the newborn stuff. I took her out of her crib beside the bed and laid her on my chest. I stroked her face and told her I was sorry. I held her close for hours and for the first time in ages I felt a sense of contentment. I felt happy again. Lynn, Jordanne and Jaelynne – three girls together. I remember thinking to myself that we would be strong women, and we would stick up for each other, and if someone did something to one of us they would have to deal with the three of us. My tribe. My need to be part of something could start and finish with the three of us. I made so many plans in that moment. My beautiful daughter lay there in my arms with her chubby jaws guzzling on my breast and I promised her we would make it in this world.

Jaelynne's life got off to a good start. She was healthy and we were happy. She had no tear ducts though, and after two years of not being able to shed a tear she was brought in for a little operation. But, before they brought her in to theatre that day, she suddenly began to cry – and the tears flowed and flowed. It was as though she willed the tear ducts to open just so there was no operation.

I wish I had been in a better place with Joe on a personal level so that we could share the parenting more, but I wasn't, and things were often difficult. I needed a lot of support if I was going to be able to return to work. I was lucky to have Donna, my friend, who became the first childminder I ever had.

I found it very difficult to do so much alone. Of course, my parents helped but my ma was in work much of the time and my da was ill by now. But Joe's mother, Jaelynne's granny, was always happy to help if I asked. She and Jaelynne have the most amazing relationship. They are like best friends. It is often very difficult to find a right balance when raising a child when you are not together as parents. Jaelynne's relationship is positive with her dad and his family and she is very like them. Things may not have always been perfect when trying to parent separately, but as the years went on it worked itself out.

CHAPTER 12:
AN CHÉAD STAD EILE AN
CLOIGÍN GORM

In 2007, when Jaelynne was only a few months old, I somehow found myself sitting in Bluebell Community Centre, waiting to be called for an interview for my dream job.

Where the hell is Bluebell? It's as though it only came into existence with the development of the Luas:

Next stop Bluebell. An chéad stad eile An Cloigín Gorm.

This little community sandwiched between Inchicore and Ballyfermot was like the land that everyone forgot. They didn't even have their own doctor. This little community that I'd never heard of would become the heart of one of the most significant times in my life.

On the strength of my experience working for Fr Liam in CARP in Killinarden, I had applied to the Canal Communities Local Drug Task Force for the role of community development drugs worker in Bluebell. I always ignored what might be seen as my shortcomings and pretended that I was the best person for the job. I've always managed to turn fear into confidence and I always held the belief that honesty and willingness to learn would get me everywhere I needed to go.

As the previous interview was running over its allotted time, I sat waiting in this old room in the community centre. The walls were so thin I could hear all the questions they were asking the candidate, so I had time to think about my own answers.

Before they called me in for the interview, they decided it was time for tea and biscuits. I was a bit pissed off as they were already running late, but I put my annoyance aside when I finally sat in the cold chair in front of the panel. I felt intimidated as it was my first time to face more than one interviewer. They introduced themselves: Tony Mac Carthaigh was the coordinator of the Rialto Community Drug Team; John Bissett was the regeneration worker with the Canal Communities Local Drug Task Force; and Cathy Thorpe was the youth worker from Bluebell Youth Project. They were all dressed casually, and John especially, with his flat Dublin accent, sounded tough. I wondered if he was a past service user.

I have very little memory of their questions – apart from one. John asked me something about community development. I hadn't a clue what the question meant. He was clearly from a background like my own, but he had words in his vocabulary that I had never even heard from a teacher. He tried to help by drawing a diagram.

"OK, here's the person," he said, drawing a little circle. "And this is the community." He added a big square around the circle.

I looked him straight in eye. "Ah here, that's a fucking washing machine. Ya drew a washing machine."

Cathy nearly pissed herself laughing and I struggled to hold in the laughter too. But when I left the interview, I was convinced that my honesty had probably cost me the job.

Cathy rang me that evening.

"Lynn, we'd like to offer you the job."

I couldn't believe it. After I'd accepted and thanked her, I went on: "Congratulations on having a service user on the interview panel, by the way."

That infectious laugh came down the phone again. "Lynn, John's not a service user. He's the chair of your new board."

Cathy would go on to be a strong influence in my life.

I was now the community development drugs worker in Bluebell. I was honoured to be in a position to develop the services in this community. Working out of a little flat in Bernard Curtis House, I worked tirelessly in those early days to get to know the community. I visited the other projects and walked the streets night and day doing all the outreach possible before a renovated space was ready in the community centre.

I began to notice something odd about this community. In other communities, heroin use seemed to be a lot more out in the open, but in Bluebell, it seemed either invisible or non-existent, or else it skipped a whole generation. But just because I could not see the addiction instantly did not mean it was not there. Addiction was hidden in Bluebell and it took me a while to figure out why. But before I could do this, I had to build up enough trust to be let in to this tight, close-knit little community. I just had to sit tight and allow Bluebell to accept me enough to let me see it. Once I did, I began to understand the fear that gripped Bluebell.

Bluebell didn't seem to have a population of young teenage heroin users in 2007, but this changed a little as the years went on. In the beginning it was primarily older women who availed of the service, most of whom had been living with addiction for a long time. Some were still actively using heroin, others were on methadone and many had replaced heroin use with alcohol. Many of the people who eventually used our services kept to themselves and there was no sign of groups of drug users on the streets. The location of our centre was probably key in that it allowed for some level of anonymity as it was located on the Old Naas Road rather than centrally in the community where everyone would have been able to see drug users come and go.

I never felt unsafe in Bluebell. My project was safe and over time the community felt enough ownership over it to use it freely. Bluebell was filled with so many amazing young people and its older community was strong and engaged. I loved Bluebell and I inserted myself in the community as if it were my own.

I wanted to create a space for people who were using drugs to feel safe with me. My thinking was that I didn't have to talk to people about their drug use; I just had to create the space for engagement with them. I built up a programme of education, activities and any-thing artistic or creative I could tap into in the community.

I knew in my gut the ones who distrusted me the most – the young men especially. I knew that they needed the space the most. Behind every one of them was a story and behind each story was vulnerability. Behind every "Fuck off and leave me alone" was a young person who, not too long ago, had either been playing football or go-karting with the youth project. The young people of Bluebell had experienced unimaginable trauma over the years, and more was to come.

Bluebell went from appearing like a settled community to a place full of distress and violence. Over the course of the next few years I would watch a community desperately try to hold itself together as it suffered some of its worst blows, experiences that would shape many young people's lives forever and that tore at the very fabric of that small, close-knit community.

In 2008, less than a year into my job, this sleepy estate, which appeared to be the poor cousin in the Canal communities, was devastated by the shooting of a young man. That morning I drove past a scene I was used to from my own life – flashing blue lights and a garda cordon. The community was beginning to gather and we all knew a body had been found by the canal. I could feel the familiar dread of the young people as they all scrambled around, trying to identify who was missing, waiting for the confirmation of which of their friends was gone. Everyone was on the phone, frantically calling the friends they could not account for. Who didn't make it home last night?

Then it happened. A garda answered Darren Guerrine's phone when his brother rang it. I watched helpless as his brother ran across the football pitch trying to get to the big brother he knew was lying dead behind the cordon. One young woman, Joanne Gelston, ran screaming when she realised her friend was dead. (Joanne would go on to be a very important part of my life, and an inspiration. She eventually went on to third-level education to study youth and community and is now a youth worker in her own community.)

I wanted to help, but I couldn't; I wasn't yet part of the community. But the series of events this set off in Bluebell would become the backdrop to the work I did there. Bluebell Youth Project, where Cathy and her wonderful team worked, became a safe haven for young people over the weeks and months following the devastating murder of Darren.

The shooting would set in motion a number of events that would see more people die violently and many turn to drugs to cope. There also seemed to be a rapid increase in weed and benzo use in the community as many of the young people tried to numb out. Sadly, by the time I left Bluebell the drug use would be as plain as day.

Many families have several generations living in Bluebell, and the pain that seeped through this small community will be felt for generations to come. The biggest challenge in Bluebell was that, like all small communities, everything and everyone was intertwined and there was no escaping that pain.

Against this backdrop, the work that went on in that little community centre became vital for the people who engaged with our addiction project. The project was called the Bluebell Addiction Advisory Group – BAAG for short, which always amused us a little, since "bags" is slang for bags of drugs.

I met people in a one-to-one setting and provided various

supports for them. In the beginning it was standard stuff such as harm reduction support. But to truly help and support someone, it is not enough to prescribe some method of recovery. It requires time and patience, and the relationship can go back and forth before you get a whole picture of the person, where they are and where they are coming from. So I spent a lot of time getting to know people, listening to them – sometimes listening to the same thing over and over again, as though by repeating their traumatic experiences, they would become so used to it that it would cease to hurt or affect them. Others were closed books and stayed this way for a long time, especially if they hadn't found many people in life to trust.

That first year was a year of relationship building. I obviously put other supports in place for them as the need arose, whether through housing or support with health-related appointments. I rarely mentioned recovery or getting clean in the first year, unless they led the conversation in that way. You can push people away very easily if you push too hard too quickly, especially if they are frightened.

Some had been in the same cycle for decades. Many were afraid of recovery, afraid of what it would take to get clean, afraid of trying and failing. Getting clean can mean completely changing your life, changing all that you know. The most difficult part of recovery is often the loneliness that goes with it. How does a person in this situation change their environment and their circumstances to match their recovery if they don't have the resources to do so?

So, I would wait and wait for the seeds that we would plant through our open and honest conversations to take root. I worked with people as I wished people had worked with me. Without even realising it at the time, I was creating a vibe in the building that was close to what I had experienced in An Cosán. It was arty and educational, and this was most evident in the women's group we developed.

Ideas often came to me in my sleep and I would wake the next morning buzzing and raring to get to work. I was determined that I would bring together all the different women with whom I'd been working individually, and they, as a group, would become the development workers. I would become the facilitator of their programme. I called in as many of the women as I could get and we began to brainstorm. I asked the group what were the biggest obstacles in their lives. Along with the loneliness, boredom was right up there. When they were using, their lives were extremely busy. They would need to source money, call the dealer, collect the gear, set up the paraphernalia, use – and then repeat this several times throughout the day. All of this required creative thinking to figure out how they would make money, and this kept them busy and occupied. When they stopped using, all of that creativity and busyness disappeared from their lives. Not only were they left with massive gaps in their day to fill, they also had no friends, as all their social contact with people and the outside world came through that same daily ritual.

Another obstacle was that they couldn't gain employment. Many of the women had not worked in years or had never worked at all. An empty CV was no use to a prospective employer. They also felt that being on methadone for years and being tied to a clinic or a pharmacy kept them in the loop of a lifestyle from which they would like to break free.

Then there was their lack of physical and mental wellbeing. Many had harmed their bodies in various ways for many years and felt disconnected from their own skin. Some felt uncomfortable with the weight gain that methadone use causes but at the same time they were cautious about losing too much weight because they associated being thin and frail with being on the gear. So, they wanted a healthy balance.

At the end of our brainstorming session, we summarised it all in one sentence: they wanted to fill the gap in their day that drug use once filled; they wanted employment; and they wanted to improve on their physical and mental health. From that day, the new women's group developed their own programme, which they called "Filling a GAP at BAAG". GAP stood for two things – most obviously, it was the gap, the void, that big empty space in the women's lives that drug use once dominated. It also stood for "Get Active Programme", to capture the physical and mental health aspirations of the group.

What I would witness over the next twelve months will stay with me forever as a marker of the power of women and the importance of education and holistic settings for recovery. Those amazing women had complete ownership over the group, an important part of the process.

The first thing on the agenda was to fill that gap – but with what? One woman, who would emerge as a real leader in this group, suggested that employment would fill that gap. After some hours, we came to the conclusion that we could address almost all obstacles through one action. That action was to create their own employment.

The women decided that they could learn how to cook – not just your average everyday dishes but proper fancy stuff like teriyaki salmon. We hired an amazing French chef, Yves, who brought colour and laughter and plenty of French grumpiness to the group. I suggested that they could develop a cookbook from Yves's course. However, it wouldn't just be any cookbook. It would be targeted at recovery and improving a person's health after years of problem drug use. Each recipe was researched carefully with Yves. We had dishes to kickstart metabolism, dishes to improve the health of hair and nails and, most importantly for some of the women, we had dishes to help repair the liver. The foods were fancy, but we sourced everything cheaply so that all the recipes in the book would be affordable.

Everyone found where their strengths lay and they took on different roles within the group. One of the women became the financial administrator, looking after all the costings and expenditure of the group. Two of the staff, Ger and Liz, were strong women who treated the place like it was their own. Ger grew up in Bluebell and she volunteered on so many occasions to keep the work going smoothly. Liz, as the administrator, quickly became a hit with participants. Hard-working Liz was a wonderful woman who fitted right in to the project. She didn't need training to understand the dynamics. She was naturally tuned in to what was needed from her and she knew when to back off from an issue and direct people to us.

Some days three women might show up; other days thirteen. It didn't matter how many were there; the group was growing with every project we undertook. When the cookbook was finally complete, we decided to take it on tour. We went to all the other projects in the canal communities areas, hosting buffets for their staff and participants. It was a big hit.

We wanted to capture this energy and use it for other projects, and to expand its scope. We weren't sure how to begin to make money for the women, but then things began to come their way, like the Rialto Community Drug Team hiring the women to cater for Tony Mac Carthaigh's retirement party. We also had a Men's Gardening Group, inspired by local resident Derek Glennon, who had a passion for gardening. They had developed a vegetable plot along the side of the centre. We decided to combine forces, and to include the men in the women's venture. The women now bought much of the produce they needed for their catering from the men's group.

It wasn't long before other jobs came in for the women. To add to their culinary skills, we hired a bakery chef who spent a number of months with the group teaching them how to make speciality cakes. They made beautiful christening cakes and even made a cake for Jordanne, shaped like a guitar pick, inspired by the Jack Black music video for the song 'Pick of Destiny'.

For a short time, the women even took up belly-dancing as part of the programme, with the aim of reconnecting with their own bodies and being comfortable in their own skin.

BAAG had become a family project too, with mothers, fathers and kids all becoming involved in positive activity with their loved one who was in recovery or even still struggling with their drug use. We held family days hosted by Artzone, an art school based in Dublin, involving everything from T-shirt making to still-life drawing.

There was no stopping these women. Their professionalism was unquestionable. They were flourishing and I was honoured to be part of it. So much was happening and at such a fast pace. They were all at different stages of their journeys but they helped and supported each other through the process. One woman became methadone-free, another addressed her benzo use and another her alcohol use. It wasn't plain sailing, but through addressing the obstacles they faced they sourced that power inside themselves to push through the hard stuff and fight for a life they deserved. They were beginning to realise their worth and also their ability to succeed.

For me, the idea of drug rehabilitation work could not happen in isolation. The reduction in drug use was happening for some of the individuals naturally as they began to make use of these spaces for healing, bonding and discovering themselves again. The type of drug user was diverse. There was a core group of young men who smoked weed who began attending our men's breakfast morning every Friday. One of them was Darren Cogan, who would arrive with a big grin on his face. All the lads would slag him as they would have been working hard in the vegetable garden all morning, but Darren would show up just in time for the fry. Sadly, Darren was later tragically murdered – another huge blow to the community.

There were some comments that the lads were only there for the fry-up. Well, of course they were, but, I'd explain, the barriers are being broken down. People who once lived in fear as heroin users were now sharing a space openly with a diverse group of Bluebell residents, both young and old. The Friday fry-up was about building trust across the different sectors of Bluebell that once wouldn't have tolerated a minute in each other's company.

The word of BAAG spread much further afield than Bluebell. I sat at my desk one day writing up some notes when a young man came to the door. There were no security cameras or locks on the building, and I didn't want them, as they would have set a distrustful tone. This man came in and looked at me in my office. I had never seen him before and I was pretty sure he was not from the Bluebell area. I knew instantly he was extremely scared. It is not difficult to recognise someone in drug-induced psychosis so I treaded very carefully so as not to scare him off. It was clear that the sounds of the outside world were making him jumpy. He was shivering and struggling to get his words out. I took him to the quiet of the one-to-one room, sat him down, wrapped him in a blanket and asked a co-worker to make a cup of tea.

"What's your name?" I asked him. He told me and I asked, "Are you OK?"

He began to cry uncontrollably so I placed my hand on his shoulder. "You're safe here," I told him.

He said he had been turned away from a number of places in the city centre where he had sought help. "Someone told me to go to Bluebell and ask for Lynn. She won't turn you away, they said. Are you Lynn?"

"Yeah, I'm Lynn. And they're right – I won't turn you away."

With that, he took a deep breath and look directly at me. "Please help me," he said. "I've murdered my daughter." He kept repeating her name, over and over, and breaking down.

I let him gather himself before I gently asked him for more details. "Tell me how this happened. Why do you think you've killed your daughter? It sounds like you love her very much." I asked where he was originally from. "Who does your daughter live with?"

"My ma."

"What's your ma's name?"

All my questions were starting to aggravate him; he was looking for me to console him, not question him. But I needed to ask him one final thing: "Can you give me your ma's phone number?"

He was apprehensive, scared of me contacting his mother. He didn't want her to know that he had been living on the streets and taking dangerous amounts of head shop drugs. One of the head shops had burned down and he had lived in this burnt-out shell, consuming anything he could find, for weeks. He was also terrified that he had killed his daughter and didn't know what would happen if I called his ma.

I got my phone and sat with him. "Listen, you are safe here," I again reassured him. "I don't believe that you've killed your daughter. Do you think it's possible that all the head shop drugs have induced a psychosis? I think your daughter is perfectly safe at home with your mother."

At this, he broke down again. "Are you sure she is? Are you sure?"

"Yes, I'm sure. Will you trust me? Will you let me call your mother?"

He finally allowed me to make the call and, of course, his daughter was safe and well at home.

This was the first encounter of a very special journey for him with BAAG, one that included his whole family. First, though, it took me days to support him out of the drug-induced psychosis. As he slowly recovered from his psychosis, we got to know each other and he soon became part of the BAAG family.

When I began writing this chapter, that same young man contacted me to chat about his recovery and where he was at now in life. We arranged to meet, but weeks passed without it happening. We kept in contact by message and he had great hopes for his future and lots of will to get his life on a steady path. By the time I finished writing this chapter, he had died. We never did get to meet and I hugely regret not dropping everything to get to him.

The sad thing is that amazing groups like BAAG don't survive austerity. As soon as you remove the supports and the structures, without anything to replace them, everything can come tumbling down.

By 2010 tensions were running high at the monthly meetings as budgets got tighter. The pot was shrinking and we were scrapping for crumbs. Years of work by the projects were at the mercy of the government. Would we survive this austerity budget? What group would be cut? I hoped it would not be mine as we were just making headway. Something was going to go, but what? We were turning on each other, all with our eyes on the same funding.

People chose to take wage cuts rather than allowing money to be taken from programme costs. John Bissett was talking political speak that I only vaguely understood. I heard the words "government" and "Cowen" a lot. The news headlines were talking austerity all the time. My political education began in earnest at that time.

Ultimately, Dublin City Council would interfere with the work of BAAG before the economic collapse would. The site that we worked from was DCC land but the community had a ninety-nine-year lease on it, which, in 2011, had a long time left to run. But the council wanted us out so they could demolish the site. They wanted to move us to a shitty little office space in a new multi-purpose community centre. The new centre itself was great for Bluebell – but not for the type of work we were doing. No one in the council seemed to understand the importance of the space we had developed in the old centre, the growth that was happening there. DCC didn't care that they, along with the ABC, the original body which historically held the lease on behalf of the community, were uprooting us. We were safe in a building of our own. The fear and stigma of being a drug user in Bluebell, which I talked about at the start of this chapter, still existed, and the council wanted to dump us right in the centre of this, and without our beautiful garden.

We had spent years fighting and learning about stigma. A few of us were sitting at the kitchen table in BAAG one day when a cat ran past.

"Oh, I hate cats," said one of the women, and a few of the others agreed with her.

"Why don't you like them?" I asked, laughing.

"They're sly," said one.

"They're predators," said another.

Another woman said, "I don't really know. I just don't like them."

This conversation got me thinking.

The next day my administrator Liz got me a little kitten. I took her under my wing and over the coming days introduced her to the people who attended BAAG.

"This is Stigma," I told them. "She is BAAG's newest member. We are all going to get over our prejudices about cats and get to know her."

And that was how I began to work with them about stigma – the stigmas they themselves faced and how people judged them because of their drug use. Stigma, our beautiful grey cat, quickly won their hearts – and I think they got my point.

Sadly, Stigma ran from my house one day and got hit by a car. Our head gardener, Derek, made a beautiful spot for her in our garden. It was all very sad.

Another more personal loss around this time was of my beloved dog, Toby. His death was more difficult for me than I had anticipated. I had a number of hours with him before the vet came to stop him suffering. I cried uncontrollably as I watched him take his last breaths. The worst part was watching him being removed in a bag and taken from the house. I was heartbroken and had to take a couple of days off work.

I was also becoming very unhappy in my job by this time – not with the community or the people I worked with, but with the structures. I felt very alone in the management of the programme. I was devastated that we would lose our centre and I was feeling burnt out. I was also struggling to understand the politics of it all – how, during austerity, decisions could be made in government that had such a negative impact on people in poverty. I didn't have the language to advocate for the vulnerable and stigmatised populations I worked with. I wanted choice in my own life and I wanted an education to change things in the communities I worked with.

With Bluebell falling away from me, I was having panic attacks, crying so much that I felt my lungs would collapse. Although my job was still safe if I had wanted to stay, I knew it was time to go. I just wanted to make real change and stop feeling helpless and hopeless. I wanted to understand, on a deeper level, what drove parts of society to the margins.

Something else was happening, on a personal level, and much more positively, towards the end of my time in Bluebell. A personal journey began for me, inspired by John Bissett, the chair of Bluebell Addiction Advisory Group – the man who had interviewed me, whom I had mistaken for a former service user – and by Fiona O'Reilly, a researcher who came to Bluebell to do an ethnographic study on the changing nature of drug use. Between John, Fiona and my friend Cathy, I was surrounded by strong, articulate and intelligent voices and I loved it. Bluebell opened up my circle of friends forever.

John became my role model, albeit an unwilling one – I don't think he took well to me looking up to him. My da was sick at this time and I felt isolated and lonely in my journey. I looked for John's approval, looked for him to be proud of me, as if he was my father. I would never have considered that I was capable of university without knowing that John had "PhD" beside his name. I knew he was no more special than I was. If John could progress so far in his thinking and understanding, then so could I. He didn't give me motivational speeches or anything; the very fact of his existence in my world, as someone I could relate to, was all I needed. I wished I could meet more people like him so I didn't feel so alone, people who were academic but still rooted in working-class culture. Luckily, as I opened my mind up I realised that there were thousands like John, and that I was the one who needed to expand my horizons a little.

Fiona took me straight under her wing and didn't resist my neediness. The first day I met her was during her research on the changing nature of drug use, later titled "A Dizzying Array of Substances". I was instantly captured by her knowledge and fascinated with the work she was undertaking. She reminded me of Gráinne Mhaol, the Irish pirate queen, with her crazy red hair and alternative dress sense. I heard the words "ethnographic" and "anthropologic" for the first time from Fiona and I knew when I left her that day that I had found a new interest: research.

Fiona nurtured my interest and it wasn't long before she was creating opportunities for me in her very important research, such as our own project, "Drug Dealers' Views on Exit Strategies". A number of years later Fiona employed me to manage a research team and also to analyse data for her research project, "Homelessness: An Unhealthy State". We still challenge each other in our work, our views and our ideas about what needs to be done to make change in society.

The bulk of Fiona's work for decades has been with the most marginalised groups in society and she is currently the head of the Safety Net Services, which works to provide healthcare to those who need it most but are the least likely to access it, such as the long-term homeless and Syrian refugees.

Fiona and I have remained friends and I have had some of the best adventures of my adult life with Fiona. In between all of our very serious work conversations, we managed to find time for the oddest of events, such as the preparation for Fiona's fiftieth birthday. Fiona thought it would be a laugh for us to put on a dance show as a surprise at her party. I reluctantly agreed when she told us the type of dancing she had in mind – pole dancing! Before I knew it, I was in a studio in Sheriff Street with Fiona and her pal Carol getting pole-dancing lessons. We were terrible, and Carol was the worst by far. Needless to say, after a number of failed lessons but lots of laughing, we abandoned the idea of pole dancing for Fiona's fiftieth.

Aisling Holland became another firm friend through my time in Bluebell. Aisling was the co-ordinator of Connect, which at the time was located in Bluebell before moving to Inchicore. Aisling is the most compassionate, understanding and insightful drugs worker I have ever met. It was like we had always known each other and, even though I was leaving Bluebell with a heavy heart, I was comforted knowing that Aisling was now in my life. She is tiny – sometimes I call her a Polly Pocket – and she is the most beautiful person, and seems to have no idea how amazing she is. At every difficult juncture in our lives for the past ten years, we have been each other's support, spending hours every day on the phone, building each other back up. Aisling and Fiona would become the closest friends I have.

I could write a book on Bluebell as a community: the people I met, the friends I made and the new skills I developed, all of which would serve me going forward on my new journey through education.

I now take all that goodness and I hold on to it, but I was bitter leaving. I was beaten, broken and deflated. I had fought as hard as I could but it wasn't enough. We had lost our battle with the council and lost our space. All those who had benefited were just as devastated as I was to lose the project. I was close to giving up, and then I thought of John, with his PhD, and knew I was making the right move. I left Bluebell with a heavy heart.

I still drive past the old building today with sadness as it stands there, derelict, our once lovely garden, and little Stigma's grave, now overgrown with weeds.

For me, it was time to burn another layer to the ground and rise again for the next stage, the next big reveal of who I am and who I am meant to be. I would be going to Trinity College.

CHAPTER 13:
AROUND THE WORLD

*"The world has grown smaller, since a man can now
go around it ten times more quickly than a
hundred years ago." –*
Around the World in Eighty Days

If the world is in fact smaller, could I really bring my girls around it? It certainly didn't seem smaller. With every obstacle that I faced, the world seemed bigger and bigger and Tallaght was too far away from it – from the world, as though they were two separate things. The world is over there somewhere, and I am here, a young mum with little income. Yet I knew that, one day, I would show them the world.

We saved every year to go to Spain. If I got money for Christmas or my birthday I would use it to book some flights. I loved taking Jordanne and later Jaelynne to the sun and allowing them to explore new people and places. I had very little money and travelling alone with young children was sometimes hard. I would wheel the pram with one hand and drag my suitcase behind me with the other. It was always a struggle but our trips became the best part of our lives as a unit. No work, no school, and away from all that was happening in our lives back home. But I was not entirely happy that I was getting to see the world in any kind of meaningful way. I loved water parks and horseback riding in Spanish mountains but there had to be more I could do to show the girls different cultures.

And so we expanded our horizons. Often, I'd be led by them. Like the time Jordanne had to do an art project on Venice, and rather than just googling it, I decided I'd bring them there. It had to be a budget trip, so I stripped back our plans to a bare minimum. No gondolas, no expensive museums. One highlight of the three days was to be a visit to the orchestra, but sadly that was spoiled. We had arrived early so we could sit at the front. Everyone else was dressed to the nines, but we were in our ordinary clothes. During the show a staff member asked us to move; she told me the kids were distracting. I refused, but she persisted until I told her that she and her orchestra could go fuck themselves, and we stormed out.

We made up for this by filling our pockets with bread every day and feeding the thousands of pigeons in St Mark's Square. Jordanne and I spent hours sitting on the ground with crumbs in our hair and on our legs and allowed ourselves to be covered in a blanket of pigeons. It took two days for Jaelynne, who was just a toddler, to find any fun in this. She was petrified of them. Jordanne would throw a crust her way and she would go berserk. We couldn't stop laughing.

There were other trips too – to Rome, Pisa, Paris, and of course to Mexico with Jordanne when I was pregnant with Jaelynne. I could never afford everything they wanted but I wanted them to know that the world was there for them. As Jaelynne says, "Mammy brought me to see the Eiffel Tower, the Leaning Tower of Pisa and the Coliseum, but we just had to look at them from the outside." And Jordanne tells me she hates croissants, because that was all we could afford when we went to Disneyland in Paris – we would fill our bags with them every day at breakfast.

But while most of our trips were for the girls, the biggest one of all was for me. At long last, a couple of years before I started a new phase of my life at Trinity, I would fulfil a childhood dream.

I had got myself to a slightly more secure place financially when I worked in Bluebell so I decided to book a trip to South Africa with Jordanne. Jaelynne was too young for a safari trip so we would have to leave her behind this time. I worked out that I could manage to save €3,000, a huge sum to me. I committed to paying off the trip in instalments for the months leading up to our flight. I wanted to ensure we got to see everything as we were travelling so far to see the Big Five.

The travel agent at Slattery's Travel asked me, "Are you sure you are OK travelling so far with your daughter?" I put her mind at ease, explaining that we travel a lot on our own. This would be a special trip for us, I told her, as we would be celebrating Jordanne's ninth birthday there.

The next day she rang me back to say they had upgraded us to Richard Branson's private game reserve, Ulusaba, for no extra charge. "Tell your daughter happy birthday," she said. I sat in my office chair in Bluebell, filled with excitement and gratitude. I googled our new destination and it was like nothing I had ever seen before. I couldn't believe my luck. I knew I was meant to go to Africa and this was a sign that sometimes dreams do come true.

August arrived, we reluctantly left Jaelynne behind with family, and headed off on our long trip. By the time we got to Johannesburg we were a little tired but the adrenaline kept us alert. Our last flight would take us from Johannesburg to the border with Mozambique. Our excitement was tinged with panic when we saw the plane. It looked ancient, and flimsy as a paper plane. Jordanne held my hand. "Mam, I love Amelia Earhart, but I don't know about getting on the actual plane she flew." But nothing was going to get in our way, so we boarded the plane, squeezed each other's hands and closed our eyes tightly as we took off.

After a few minutes, we gently opened our eyes and gazed out the window. There it was: Africa. I hadn't yet stepped foot in the African bush and I already felt like I was home. The tears fell as I realised we had made it.

Once the plane landed, we were piled into a pick-up and ferried to our destination, a wooden lodge with a straw roof, perched on a mountain top, surrounded by lush green trees. Everything looked so rich in colour. We were met by the friendliest of staff, who brought us to our beautiful room and gave us strict instructions: "Don't leave the room without a guide because animals often make their way through the lodge. And don't leave your door unlocked from the inside because the baboons like to rob all the pretty things from guests' rooms." Jordanne's eyes were wide open and the excitement on her face made my heart skip. I was emotional with gratitude that we could visit such a place. We made our way out on the balcony just in time to watch the sun go down over the plains.

Only a couple of hours later, we would be out on our first trek in the Land Rover.

Every day we went on two trips out into the bush. The first was at four in the morning. This was by far my favourite. Our guides always met us with hot chocolate and fleece ponchos to keep us cozy in the cold night. We hit it off instantly with the team. James, the tracker, sat on a little seat on the front of the jeep. Greg was the ranger and he drove and told us all about the animals, the scenery and the fauna.

Throughout the week we experienced many beautiful things but I will never forget a single detail of one action-packed day. That morning, just after the sun came up, James jumped off the front of the jeep. He had spotted a leopard paw print. He pointed us in the direction it had gone. Leopards are fairly elusive and getting a glimpse of one is always special. Jordanne and I gave each other a squeeze to contain our excitement. We spent two hours tracking the leopard. We wanted to experience every magical moment.

After two hours, we stumbled on a pair of mating lions hidden down in a dried-up river. The lion mounted the lioness and held her down with his jaw, baring his teeth. He roared as though he was attacking her. They mated every few minutes for ages. But what happened next was unexpected and I loved every scary second of it.

Lions usually just ignore the guides and tourists, as long as you don't suddenly change shape by standing up or moving about. But as we watched the lions, the sun had changed position in the sky, creating a long shadow from the jeep. The lion for the first time looked intently at us and began to pace alongside the jeep. He was huge. Greg whispered, "He thinks we moved our jeep because the shade's now on them. He thinks we're trying to get in his way."

Greg had been sitting sideways, so his feet weren't on the pedals but dangled out of the jeep. It was becoming clear to us that the lion was going to make a move on us, but if Greg moved his position to drive, he would surely pounce. So, we sat and waited for Greg to think of a way to get us out of this. The American couple in the jeep with us slowly slid down onto their hunkers, preparing to hide close to the floor. Not us. We whispered to each other as we turned on our cameras as quietly as possible, turned the flash off, and began to take photographs with one and record video on the other. Jordanne and I were scared but we weren't missing a good opportunity to get a record of the lion staring up into our eyes. Jordanne was closer to him than I was, so I told her that if he were to attack I would have to flip her across my body so he would get to me first.

After what seemed like hours but surely must have been only minutes, Greg said he had an idea. He began to move his hand very slowly towards the walkie-talkie. He picked it up, careful not to make any sudden movement, contacted base and asked for a jeep to come to us. Luckily, he was able explain that we were in the river bed and could easily be found by the trackers who knew the bush intimately.

When our rescue jeep arrived, Greg instructed them to park opposite us, almost directly behind the lions, and then to rev their engine. They did, but the lion was too transfixed on us to notice. The rescuers had to up the effort to attract the lion's attention. They began to wheel-spin the jeep, which eventually worked. For no more than a second, the lion looked away to see what was causing the commotion. As soon as the lion turned its head, Greg swivelled his body so he was sitting with his feet on the pedals. We quickly began to move and everyone let out a big sigh of relief. Apart from Jordanne and I; we were drunk with adrenaline. Jordanne was buzzing as we later looked back through the photographs at those piercing eyes staring up at us. We were so excited.

We thought our day couldn't get any better until our evening trek showed us otherwise. That evening we were stopped in our tracks by the largest bull elephant I could ever have imagined. He seemed to appear out of nowhere, walking at a steady pace right in our direction as if he was on a mission. He had no interest in us and walked straight past us. I didn't know something could be so beautiful and so intimidating all at once. He had wet markings on his temples and urine flowed freely down his legs; Greg told us this meant he was "in must".

Moments later, we drove slowly down a hill into a ditch-like forested area, shaped like a V. We spotted the cutest baby elephant you can imagine. He started to mock-charge us. Greg assured us he was just being playful and practising his skills. However, as he charged us he let out a little trumpet sound, and a huge matriarch elephant came thundering down the hill at us. We were trapped in this ditch and she was coming at us head-on. Greg whipped the jeep into reverse and dragged us back up the hill so fast I thought we would crash. Although we were shitting ourselves, Jordanne and I, as always, were ready with cameras in hand.

James the tracker explained everything to us when we reached safety. He told us that male elephants are thrown out of their herds when they reach a certain age and that the bull we had seen minutes earlier would have upset the herd. When those big bulls are in must, they thrash their way through herds trying to mate – basically acting like big bullies. The matriarch was possibly pissed off by the bull so that, by the time we came along, she was already on high alert.

Before going to Africa, I hadn't given a lot of thought to seeing elephants. But, after that encounter, I had nothing but respect for these beautiful giants.

It was not just the animals and the wonderful people we met that changed our lives on that trip. It was also the stars. Richard Branson had built a massive observatory in the bush and it was a real treat to visit it one night. We could see planets and constellations and we didn't have to look into the telescope to appreciate the Milky Way above our heads. We lay there for ages picking out constellations. The world really is a small place when you see it from that angle.

I know how amazing my kids are, but that week with Jordanne allowed me to see her personality develop. We connected even more through our adventures. Jordanne became a vegetarian at the age of nine after that trip to Africa. Her love and respect for the animals allowed her to take this principled decision at such a young age. I watched her be fearless in some scary situations but we always knew we were safe. She tried everything and I love this about her.

As well as treasuring those heart-stopping moments I shared with her, that trip gave us some hilarious memories to share. We had so much fun and I look back now and only wish Jaelynne had been old enough to have shared those experiences with us.

One day James and Greg knocked on our doors and asked if we would like to go on a walking trek. They said it wasn't something they would usually do with a kid but they were so impressed by Jordanne. They could see we were like sponges and weren't just there to spot an animal or two; we wanted to learn and understand every detail about them. We were interested in the birds and the ants and every creature was magnificent to us. We jumped at this chance to walk around the bush. Another couple came with us too.

Newly arrived in Killinarden from Ballymun. I look like the ideal little girl here. (*L to R*) Jay, Da, me, Ma.

Vote Eileen Lemass! Jay and me, *c.*1989. Ma insists she has no idea where the Fianna Fáil stickers came from, but I don't think they're part of the costumes.

Losing Jenny was a defining moment.
When I think of her, this is what I see:
a smile, kindness.

Stef, Curly, Gareth and Christopher on the field at the Grocott's wall. We were
always there.

Ange (*L*) and Val (*R*). I always envied their big families, and if my ma went out looking for me, the first door she'd knock on would be Ange's. I always lied and said I was staying there.

This photo was taken in 1999, shortly after I was released from hospital. To cheer me up, Ma brought me to get my hair done the day the stitches were taken out.

It was Tracy who introduced me to Tupac, and she was inseparable from Bernie (pictured with her little cousin John). They were like two halves of the same personality. When Tracy died, Bernie seemed lost without her. Years later, Bernie would die on the anniversary of Tracy's death, while John died on Tracy's twenty-first birthday.

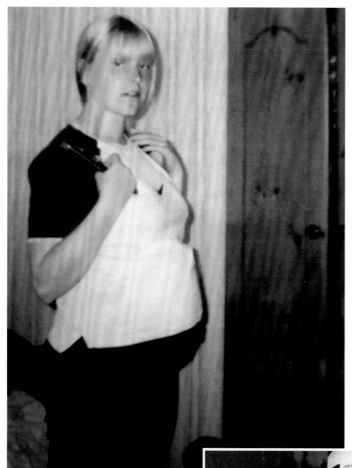

The year 2000. I am fifteen, pregnant and the healthiest I've been in three years. I didn't realise it at the time, but the decisions I'd make in that nine-month spell would shape the course of my life for the next twenty years.

I love this photo. Jordanne was the easiest child, and I loved dressing her up – especially in her Tupac bandana. Maybe the happiest year of my life. The euphoria of her arrival forced everything else into the background.

Me, the consummate teenager, in what still remains my favourite fashion era: tracksuits, jewellery, questionable plaits. I might have had a child of my own, but I was still a kid.

When Ann Louise held your gaze like this, you believed her; you knew it was coming from somewhere special. She did so much to support me over the years. This is the photo that best captures her warmth. I think of her when I think of An Cosán.

With Val (L) and Kim (R). We've been friends for over twenty years, and though life has often taken us in different directions, we've always come back together. These two will always be with me.

Jordanne, Da and Jaelynne, who's probably about two here. Da was unwell by this point but still a hero to the two girls. He was a surrogate parent, the good cop to my bad cop.

In 2010 I left everything behind to spend six weeks tracking wild dogs in the African outback. Here, a lioness, silhouetted against the sunrise, takes a quick break from playing with her two cubs.

With the onset of austerity, my life as a campaigner begins. Here I am on O'Connell Street alongside Joanne from Bluebell.

My first Trinity campaign started small, but soon it began to swell. As it grew, I began to feel more confident; it felt like a validation not only of my ideals but everything I'd been through.

Listening as the results of the Students' Union election are read out. So many thoughts, impulses and emotions seemed to collide in the few seconds after my name was called. A few hours later, I'd be in Sundial House helping a homeless man reorganise his VHS tapes wondering if the election had happened at all. (*Courtesy of Trinity News*)

Hanging with the kids in our front garden.

With the Trinity Students' Union team. They were almost half my age, but I learned so much from them. I hope they learned something from me, too. (*L to R*) Edmund, Molly, Katie, Conor and Aifric.

The kids go viral during the Marriage Referendum. Angered by a few of the posters they'd seen, they decided to make a video highlighting family diversity.

My first day in the new job was a bittersweet occasion. The other new senators had their families with them, but I didn't; I was worried having everyone there would only make Da's absence feel worse. I didn't make a big fuss. (*Sam Boal/RollingNews.ie*)

With Alice Mary Higgins. After realising we shared a lot of views in common, we co-founded the Civil Engagement Group.

All through the various phases of my life, travel has been a constant. The girls and I manage to go somewhere every summer, and I've always tried to share as many new experiences with them as possible. Here, they're getting ready to go snorkelling in the Red Sea.

Included by Joe Caslin in his amazing mural *The Volunteers*, which sat in Trinity's front square. The appearance of the mural coincided with the introduction of my first legislation. I was really fortunate to share the experience with Fiona O'Reilly, who also appears in the mural and has been a mentor to me since my days in Bluebell. (*Courtesy of Joe Caslin*)

Graduation from Trinity! We're doing our best to look serious here, but I couldn't have been more relieved. I sat my finals at the end of my first year in the Seanad.

With Ma at an International Women's Day fundraiser with An Cosán. Later, still glammed up, we'd leave the dinner to head to the Women's March. (*Courtesy of An Cosán*)

With Jordanne, just before we stepped out onstage at the Olympia Theatre for the first Repeal Project event. (© *Conor Horgan*)

The final press conference before ballots were cast. I was nervous, scared and had no idea such a major triumph was looming. (*Brian Lawless/PA Wire/PA Images*)

The nerves of the days and weeks leading up to the ballot gave way to euphoria as the scale of the victory became clear. Here I am, looking much more relaxed, at the RDS on the morning of the count.

Jodi (Val's daughter) and Jaelynne at the Dalkey Book Festival. The story of Yassmin Abdel-Magied, a woman who has made her career on male-dominated oil rigs, really struck a chord with them. With young feminists like this, the future looks bright.

Christmas at the Áras. My family has been the one constant in my life over the past thirty years and, in dark times, so often the difference between life and death. To be able to share special moments like this with them means everything. (*L to R*) Jordanne, Ma, Rónán, Jaelynne, me, Seán, President Michael D. Higgins and Sabina Higgins, Faith, Jay, Caiden and my sister-in-law, Laura.

James led the way and Greg walked behind to ensure we were safe. James had a rifle too, just in case. He reassured Jordanne it was just to let a shot off into the air if something came too close. Jordanne was firing questions at them as always. They showed us trees that the local tribes used for toothpaste, and the tree they used for their toothbrushes. James told us about the village where he grew up and the games they played.

One game involved impala poo. Jordanne was like a poo genius by this time. Greg and James had taught her how to track an animal by their droppings. So, she couldn't resist asking, "Ah, please show us, James."

We walked a bit further until we found some impala droppings. James took a stick and drew a line in the dusty bush floor. He then picked up the impala poo and took a number of steps back from the line. Then he opened his mouth, popped in the poo and spat it. The aim, he had told us, was to spit it further than the line. Without a word Jordanne followed suit. She practically swirled the poo around her mouth, afterwards insisting that she was trying to wet it so it would be heavier and she could spit it further. Then it was my turn. I was surprised to find it was tasteless. James said this was because all impala ate was grass. The couple who had joined us looked on as if we were mad.

On our night treks, we always brought torches and loo roll. When we needed to go to the toilet, James would check that the coast was clear so we could take cover behind a tree. One night, the sky was darker than I had ever seen it as I crouched on my hunkers to pee. Jordanne, video recorder in hand, had followed close behind me and was talking in her "documentary voice".

"So, as we move through the wild African bush, we watch out for—"

Suddenly, she went silent.

"Watch out for what, Jordanne?"

"Hyena, Mam," she whispered.

"Very good," I said. We had tracked Malcolm the hyena the night before.

"No, Mam, really, what is that, just there? Is it a hyena?"

James swung his torch towards us, flooding the scene with light. Jordanne was standing still and then I saw what she was looking at – a big hyena walking close by. As for me, I was crouched down in the full glare of the torchlight, knickers around my ankles, trying not to laugh as this big hunch-shouldered animal walked past and a jeep full of tourists looked on.

That week, we also saw the importance of keeping doors locked. A group of baboons managed to get into a storage room and made off with some huge containers of hot chocolate. A staff member brought us a telescope to show us the baboon gang racing up the mountainside with the hot chocolate containers under their arms. It was such a funny sight.

Jordanne soon became an expert baboon imitator. Like all her acting, she threw herself fully into the role.

I fell so much in love with Africa that I returned the following year as a volunteer on a wildlife reserve. It was a huge decision for me to leave the kids for five weeks. I had to juggle them among different family members and their dads, but I got there. I spent four weeks living in a little wooden hut in Zululand, sharing a room with an amazing Slovenian girl named Alenka, plus one week in Cape Town. Our job was to research the movements of the wild dogs, an endangered species. A litter of ten pups had just been born, and they would move their den a lot to keep the pups away from predators.

I had a second scary encounter with a lion on that trip. For safety reasons at night we were instructed to wear head torches, as they light up the big cats' eyes. I forgot my torch one evening as I left the hut. I heard a lion's roar but assumed it was far away, as sounds can travel a great distance across the bush, so I headed towards the kitchen, which was in a separate building. The loud roar turned into heavy breathing and at that moment I realised the lion was standing beside me. A million things raced through my mind at once. I tried to calm my pounding heart, convinced he could hear it.

Only a few seconds passed before a shot went off into the air and a Land Rover came to my rescue. The rangers had spotted the lion from the watch tower. They drove me in the Land Rover to show me the lion, which hadn't run far. He was one of the biggest lions I had encountered. They told me he was the head of the northern pride. I was exhilarated that I had just been standing by his side and survived it.

I always seem to be searching for knowledge and answers in my life, sometimes not even knowing what the questions are. And sometimes the answers come in the most unexpected places. I learned so much about myself in Africa. I went there to feel grounded, to feel at one with the world and myself. But, during my last week there, which I spent in Cape Town, it took jumping from a plane at 10,000 feet to really ground myself. As I fell through the sky, with Robben Island in the distance far below, I caught a glimpse of my shadow in a cloud. I felt an enormous sense of wonder and life rush through my body as I relished my existence. I am alive, and that is my shadow in the cloud.

Knowing you exist and just existing seem like very different things. It was always hard over the years to listen to some of the people I have worked with – whether a homeless man or a young mother addicted to heroin – saying that they were just existing day-to-day, waiting to die.

As I gazed at that cloud, I realised that, while for a long time I was just existing day-to-day, waiting to die, now I was living, and fully aware of all that life had to offer.

High up in the sky, seeing my shadow on a puffy white cloud, was the moment I decided that things needed to change – for me, for my family, for my community, for those homeless men and those suffering from addiction, who want to live, not just exist. I knew that education would provide me with those answers. I felt happy for myself, but I want everyone else to experience life too, the life they want for themselves. We all should see our existence in the clouds.

PART TWO: EDUCATING LYNN

CHAPTER 14:
SO WHY TRINITY?

It wasn't until 2006 that I stumbled upon Trinity College. How was it that, at the age of twenty-one, I was only stumbling on a massive Irish institution in the middle of town for the first time in my life?

I was an outreach worker developing the Tallaght Cocaine Project at the time, doing one-on-one work with drug users, and pretty much loving my job. One miserable winter's day, while doing a key-working course on Westland Row, someone on the course suggested the grounds of Trinity as a shortcut. As I stepped onto Front Square for the very first time I was stopped in my tracks by a sudden feeling of safety. The harsh January wind calmed and I looked around in awe and thought to myself: *I feel like I am at home.* It felt familiar, like it fitted me somehow, yet I knew nothing of what went on there. But, there and then, I somehow knew I would be back one day to find out.

So, when I made the decision in 2011 to leave Bluebell and return to education, I was asked many times: why Trinity?

I felt completely helpless, voiceless and struggled to articulate the ground-breaking progress and amazing work that was happening on the ground in Bluebell. I didn't have the language to communicate. All that seemed to matter were mountains and mountains of forms and box-ticking exercises to try to justify to a department the value of the work we were doing in the hope that we would survive the dreaded budget cuts. I became angry and grew to realise it didn't matter what work I was doing, who was getting clean, who was making changes in their lives or who were becoming active citizens. I had no power and no platform to make them – the government – hear my pleas.

I remembered the safety I had felt that day in Trinity College in 2006. Now, even though I had not thought about Trinity in years, I felt myself longing to be within those walls, away from the state slaughter of the community sector. I knew at that stage that I was capable of a third-level education.

All my socialist pals told me to stay clear of the place. They wanted me to go to Maynooth. I may not have had much of an education, but my gut told me that sometimes we need to address things from within the system, with everyone in society. How can I educate others about people like me if we all don't get to know one another, understand one another and eventually stand side-by-side with each other? Some would say this is too idealistic, but I won't let go of this vision for unity.

I was unsure at that point what I wanted to study but I did have an interest in philosophy and sociology. When I applied directly for a degree course in Trinity, I was initially refused as I had no Leaving Cert. It was then I found out about the Trinity Access Programme (TAP), a year's pre-degree programme. Derek Glennon from Bluebell kindly rushed me to town with my application with just a few minutes to spare before the deadline. I was so nervous about what was next for me. I needed to get into TAP, I wanted it so much, but I would have to be lucky enough even to get to the interview process, which was not easy as the demand was high. I also had a four-year-old and an eleven-year-old, so I knew that, even if I got into the course, it would be difficult to manage as I was giving up my employment. Becoming a full-time student would mean that money would be really tight and we could potentially be broke for a number of years to come.

I was delighted to find out that I was accepted into TAP. Throughout my time in the access programme, and during the early part of my degree, my father was very ill. I always went home after class to Da and my daughters. It was a lonely time. I wanted nothing more than to experience Trinity like other students, but it was not to be.

Luckily there were other people like me on the access programme: mothers, mature students and early school-leavers. Hitting the freshers nights and becoming active in college societies wasn't really an option for most of us, so I didn't feel too hard done by. Besides, passing maths and economics would become a full-time job if I was to succeed and get myself into my chosen degree, PPES (Philosophy, Politics, Economics and Sociology). I worked so hard and put in so many hours but for the most part I sat in the maths class feeling like a failure. Despite my lack of skill with numbers I wanted to study a degree that required it. I somehow did really well in economics, but all the grinds and support in the world wouldn't improve my ability to do maths. I was disappointed in myself, but I wanted so badly to understand it. I barely got myself over the line in the exam, but thankfully, I did enough to pass.

I've often been asked about fitting in at Trinity. The fact is, I always felt like I belonged there. That doesn't mean it was always easy or that I didn't struggle at times, but I took a deep breath every time I walked under that arch and owned my experience there.

My daughters played their parts in some of my best memories of Trinity – and they made their own mark too. On occasion I would have to bring them to lectures and they were always welcomed. From time to time students would babysit Jaelynne for me, especially during my time in the Students' Union. My friends Damien McClean and Molly Kenny made life as a mammy in Trinity so much easier for me. They would bring Jaelynne to the cinema and would spend time with her even when I didn't need help. The kids were lonely in town in the evening; I had uprooted them from their friends so we could live on campus. So we got a little puppy, Biscuit, to keep them company while we lived there, even though we weren't supposed to keep pets. Trying to keep our Biscuit from barking the place down was a task but we managed to keep the dog under wraps from security.

I loved to watch Jordanne and Jaelynne become part of Trinity life. I wanted it to be so natural for them to be in this environment. Trinity students gave Jordanne grinds throughout both her Junior Cert and Leaving Cert, and Jaelynne strolled around the campus, in and out of people's offices. Everyone knew her by name. On one occasion, up to three hundred students sang "Happy Birthday" to her at Student Council.

My two best moments with the kids in Trinity were at events. The first was when Jordanne attended an event organised by the Historical Society. Australian moral philosopher Peter Singer was speaking on "The How and Why of Effective Altruism". Jordanne disagreed with a point that he made and she was first with her hand up to let him know. He agreed with her and they had an exchange. She was only fourteen and I was so proud to watch this.

My favourite Trinity moment with Jaelynne was in 2016 in the Samuel Beckett Theatre, during Grace Dyas and Barry O'Connor's play *It's Not Over*, an intense, immersive piece about the IRA. There were scenes of violence and nudity, and at one point a dead deer lay in the middle of the room. The audience is very much part of the play and Jaelynne threw herself into it as if she were one of the actors. At this point Jaelynne had starred as Sadie in RTÉ's *Rebellion* and she brought her newfound love of acting from the screen to Theatre Club's performance. She stood behind the bar, which was selling alcohol as part of the instillation, and started refusing euros from the audience. In a spot-on Belfast accent, she began to tell the punters she was only accepting sterling. She walked around the room with a box of King Crisps, flinging them to people, stepping over violent scenes. I remember pubs in the 1980s and 1990s with kids behind the bars or sitting in the corners eating crisps. I imagine in those violent times in the North that kids would have been exposed to violent scenes in pubs. Jaelynne took cover when needed as gunshots rattled people's eardrums, and then carried on as if it were a daily occurrence in her life. In the middle of the play there was a raffle and Jaelynne made her way directly into the middle of the play, without direction, to pull out the raffle tickets. Strangely, she drew my ticket, and of course I refused the prize. It was quite special to watch her assume this role for those three hours, as though she had tuned in instantly to the tone of the play.

One experience I would prefer to forget is too funny not to share. After a wonderful day and night at Katherine Zappone and Ann Louise Gilligan's wedding ceremony in Dublin Castle in January 2016, I arrived back at my accommodation in Trinity. I'd had a fair few drinks. I threw off all my clothes, fell into bed and was asleep instantly. But sometime in the early hours, a loud noise woke me. I got up to go to the toilet and opened what I thought was the bathroom door. As soon as the door closed behind me, I realised it was my apartment door. I was locked out in the hallway of the top floor. And naked, completely naked. I was absolutely mortified. I had to go to the window of the hallway and shout across Front Square to security. They ran across and stood one flight down from me, handing me a key through the banisters. I was scarlet but found the funny side of it with my pals the next day. I emailed the head of security to thank them and ask them to be discreet about my embarrassing event. He was light-hearted about it and even suggested that the Students' Union should invest in onesies rather than hoodies.

I was lonely at points throughout my time in Trinity but the magical moments outweigh this. The students I met inspired me. The campaigns, the creativity and the idealism are exactly what this country needs. So, at every moment when I would feel like I couldn't do something, I would stand back and look at this amazing opportunity I had been given, and I would hold it close. No one, no exam, no doubt in my ability, would get between me and my Trinity experience.

CHAPTER 15:
LOSING DA

Da was diagnosed with Parkinson's disease in 2006. Me and the girls had just come back from a holiday in Disneyland Paris. Our trip had been full of laughter and I was looking forward to sharing our holiday news, but Ma cut me short with the news of Da's diagnosis.

At that time it didn't really seem so bad. We thought we could manage Parkinson's and that medication could keep a tremor from developing. I was naive – we all were – and I never expected the years that followed to roll out as they did. Ma never left Da's side and everything about his life continued to be hers. They were a team through it all.

The first couple of years seemed to be OK. Da tried to keep himself busy around the house. He continued being my da, just a little slower in his pace. A little shuffle of the feet and his hair a little more silver. He began spending a lot of time with Jordanne. The love they had for each other reminded me so much of the love I had had for my father before I rejected him. We never spoke about the way in which I'd treated my parents during my teenage years, which was for the best, as I was not completely ready to let go of my anger. Instead, we met somewhere in the middle.

Da and Jordanne were beautiful together. They would sit out the back for hours and Jordanne would put on her own one-person plays for him, just as she did on Saturdays in her Nanny Jones's house. She was an entertainer and he had so much more patience than the rest of us put together. He would clap and egg her on to do another play, and another, as though he never wanted it to end. Jordanne had his undivided attention. Da was gentle, like Jordanne, and when he was engaged with you nothing else would get in the way. I used to gaze at them from the kitchen window, both envious and thankful that they had each other.

As I look back I realise that Jordanne and I shared similar experiences in how our images of each of our fathers changed – the realisation that your father is only human and they make mistakes too. As we grew we questioned more and we discovered things we wished weren't true. For me, it was finding out my da's age and that I was not his only daughter; for Jordanne, it was her growing under-standing that drugs were part of her da's life. Of course, the circum-stances and impacts of these are different but they both contain elements of loss and what-ifs. What if Jordanne's da had not had to struggle with addiction? What if my da hadn't been an old man? Our heroes looked different through teenage eyes. Our acceptance of who they were was not equal to their acceptance of who we are. I imagine this is pretty normal, because as children we had idolised our fathers. How dare they be human?

I remember a counsellor in a workshop once saying that love flows down, but that it doesn't necessarily flow up. I felt this was a ridiculous statement – of course love flows up, but maybe the expectations are different. We expect our parents not to lie to us, or to put us in harm's way or let us down. The reality is our parents will sometimes let us down in the same way we will let our children down.

I'm not sure at what point I began to notice that Da's illness looked like a little more than Parkinson's.

To begin with, it was as simple as him putting things in the wrong places, like non-food items in the fridge. Sometimes he would forget that I'd told him I would collect Jordanne from school. I would get to the school and feel a little frustrated to find him standing there. He would insist that he had turned up just in case I forgot something. Sometimes I would snipe at him defensively as though he was judging me to be an unreliable mother. He would look at me, with his grey quiff and his black leather jacket, strong and protective, as though his life wasn't slipping away. But then he would realise he was mixing things up and his face would take on a look of sadness and confusion, like a little boy. In a flash I would feel guilty for barking at him. Still, nothing would be said; it was all understood in the silence. Until the moment when we both knew silence was not enough.

That moment came one afternoon. I was still working in Bluebell at the time and I had finished a little early. When I got to my parents' house, there was food all over the kitchen. The floor was carpeted in cereal, bananas mashed into the counter. Da stood in the middle of the wreckage and said, "Lynn, you know if I don't have my mind, there is no point in me living."

I took a deep breath, swallowed the emotion and tried to think of the best thing to say. He was vulnerable and I was so heartbroken. I took him by the hand and said, "We are not there yet, Da, but if the time comes and you want to die, then I will do whatever I need to do."

As I cleaned up the mess around my da, I pretended I wasn't petrified. I kept thinking about the fact that he didn't want to live like that, some version of himself that he couldn't accept. I thought obsessively for weeks about whether I could help him die and convince those of us who loved him that it was the right thing to do. I was scared at how quickly I accepted that if he wanted out of this world, then he had the right to leave. He valued his quality of life, and losing control of his body and mind was not how he wanted to live.

After so many years of my hurt and anger, Da's vulnerability brought a deep change in our relationship. When my brother and I were kids, every night Da would say, "Night night. I love you." I would respond in the same way, until the angry teenage rampage years got in the way. Now we took this old habit up again. We told each other daily that we loved each other.

Da had always been a peacemaker, but there was a change in him as his health deteriorated. His peaceful sleeping hours were now filled with violent nightmares. He would throw punches in his sleep and shout out loud. My da was still my da, but just a little different. He was still a man trying to work, going for walks, being an amazing grandad. But there were now limitations on how long he could do any of these things before becoming confused. He wanted to feel useful, so as a family we would have to work around these confused moments, quietly fixing the little mistakes, like taking his dentures out of the fridge.

But at some point, he began to get hallucinations and delusions, and we could not neatly tidy these up behind his back. They were no longer confined to his sleeping hours; they were now morning, noon and night and they frightened us because that was when we recognised that something was seriously wrong.

One afternoon he was convinced there was a paedophile in the field across the road. He ordered me to get Jordanne in off the street. I did as he said; I had learned not to argue with Da's reality. He wanted to run the man off the road, so I took him by the arm and we went on the hunt for this paedo.

After a few minutes, I knew the delusion was gone when he said, "I think he's gone, Lynn. He knew we were on to him."

"Yeah, I know, Da. Thank God you saw him, I'll tell the guards."

It was easier for both of us just to pretend together.

In December 2008 Da's health rapidly declined. His temperature rocketed, his body began to stiffen up and the hallucinations became more manic. We had to pin him to the bed when he started convulsing. Ma and I had a proper fight to keep him steady as he was physically stronger than the two of us. He hated hospitals, but we had no option but to call an ambulance. Da was left on a trolley in the corridor that night and we were told he had a urinary infection that was causing the temperature and hallucinations. He was admitted for a number of days.

Around this time I began to question the diagnosis of Parkinson's disease. He had not developed a tremor at this point, yet was being medicated for one. The doctors seemed not to recognise that he was hallucinating several times a week, not just on this occasion. We would repeatedly insist over the coming years that his diagnosis was incorrect; it just didn't add up. I began to fight them.

I will always thank my ma for placing her trust in me as I took on the fight about my da's diagnosis. She allowed me to talk to the doctors and gave me the space to observe and record Da's patterns of behaviours. I even began reading medical journals in the hope of finding answers. As with all my reading about heroin addiction as a teenager, real life was what spurred me on to learn more.

I also had wonderful help in my investigations from Fiona O'Reilly, one of the closest friends I had made during my time at Bluebell. Da's symptoms would be our first team effort in relentlessly pursuing answers and demanding better for someone in a vulnerable position. I would do the bulk of the research and would feed my findings to Fiona. We looked at the patterns of Da's behaviours, going back a number of years to look for clues. Fiona had experience with PSP, which is also in the Parkinson's family, and we had accepted that Da showed some similar signs, like reduced mobility and his throat beginning to close. It was clear that Parkinson's featured in his diagnosis, but we were convinced it was not the full picture.

Through all of this, we had many more hospital trips and many more hallucinations. I could handle the hallucinations for two reasons: one was that I had worked in the homeless sector for several years and gained an understanding of various mental health disorders, some of which caused hallucinations. The other reason was that it reminded me of my own acid and mushy trips as a teenager. I decided to accept that my father was on a prolonged acid trip. If we managed it right, it could almost be enjoyable.

He spent some months in hospital. After a visit there one day, I wondered if he had Alzheimer's disease. I always came in with a smile on my face to keep his spirits up. I felt it was important to never appear worried or stressed by his illness. But that day he was worked up and seemed relieved to see me, grabbing me almost violently by the wrist. As I leaned in to hug him he jolted back slightly as though he didn't want me to hug him.

He began to shout, "Please, help me, please, will nobody help me? My kids have gone missing and I can't find them anywhere."

I took a deep breath, inhaling all the hurt that surged up through every fibre of my being. I let my breath go and said, "Yes, of course, John, I'll help you find the kids. I think I saw them playing outside."

I put my da in a wheelchair and brought him around the grounds of the hospital in search of his missing children, scenarios racing through my head. I thought about calling my brother and putting him on the phone to Da to say that the kids were safe at home, but he was too frantic, on a mission to find his kids, and I had to help him. After about thirty minutes, I stopped the wheelchair and kneeled down in front of him, preparing to be a stranger again, but he pulled me into an embrace and said, "Ah, Lynn, I found you, I found you. I've been looking for you everywhere." I began to cry like a child in his arms as though I actually had been lost. And in a sense I was; the moment he didn't recognise me, I was lost. If he doesn't know me, I thought, then he can't love me. I also felt I hadn't made it up to him enough yet for pushing him away, enough to erase the bad years. I needed him to love me and I needed it not to be Alzheimer's. I hated the selfishness often attached to my supposedly heroic efforts.

136

That day, during that frantic search, the thought of helping him die had crept back into my head, but now I knew that he was no longer in the right frame of mind to give a reasonable instruction for me to do so. I knew deep down I couldn't do it, yet I couldn't bear to see him live like this when it was not what he wanted. I wanted him to die with us in his arms, surrounded by love and familiar faces, not by people who had become strangers to him.

That day, the moment he recognised me and his eyes brightened up, I switched back to thinking, as I always do, that I could fix this. I get stuck on things and I refuse to believe I haven't got what it takes to fix them. I still do it now — fix myself, fix the family, fix the stranger I meet on the street, as if everything is a project and I am capable of leaving everyone better than I found them. Usually, though, it leaves me a little worse off.

There were funny moments too. Growing up, Da used to tell us horror stories, though looking back now, they weren't scary at all. One story involved a hairy hand, stealing sausages from a campfire up at the Hellfire Club. Another story was about a banshee sitting on a bridge over the Liffey, combing her hair, scaring Da and his brothers when they were kids. During Da's illness I asked him to tell Jordanne, Jaelynne and my baby nephew Caiden the story of the hairy hand. He started out well but got mixed up, and the banshee ended up combing her hair with a sausage. We all laughed so hard, and Da laughed too, knowing he had got confused. He played along: "Oh yeah — and the banshee had a hairy hand."

I reckon the nurses thought we were all mad. We would gather around Da in a mixture of laughter, song and tears. I was the doting daughter one minute and medical detective the next. I would demand to see the consultant on my mission to find out his real diagnosis. Then suddenly the ward would be transformed into a ballroom in 1949 and all that I needed to do was waltz with my da.

Things would get worse before they improved. After Da was released from hospital, we wanted to be able to care for him at home. Ma did everything in her power to make the house work for him. She got builders in to fit out a downstairs bedroom and bathroom, a walk-in shower with a seat, a hospital bed and orthopaedic chair. The only thing we didn't have was time. Da needed full-time care at this stage, but we couldn't get enough care hours to help us at home. We all worked and, after all the construction, Ma now had a hefty mortgage to pay alone.

We were terrified of him wandering off. Fridays were the worst days as, when he had been fitter, that was when he used to collect his pension and visit the credit union. It always helped him to feel like he was contributing. We had of course started doing this for him, but he wasn't accepting it. One extremely windy Friday, I came home to find he was not in the house. I drove at speed towards the credit union, and I spotted Da standing in the middle of a busy road near the Tallaght bypass, being buffeted by the wind. Coming in the other direction was an articulated truck. Da was about to be mowed down and I had to take a risk to stop the traffic. I put the foot down and swerved my car across to the other side of the road in the hope that the truck driver would see me. Thankfully the truck slowed. I pressed the button for the pedestrian lights and bailed out of the car, shouting at my da to stand still. After I got him safely home I collapsed on the sofa. The adrenalin drained and I began to shake violently. I wanted to scream at my da for being so stupid, but I knew there was no point.

It was such a stressful time. I hated and loved caring for him all at once. I wanted him to both die and live, all in one day. However, I would stay strong and save my tears, to add to the rest of my tears, for when I was alone.

By now he had a catheter bag because of an enlarged prostate. He was always pulling it out and Ma ended up in A&E so often to get this tube refitted or to treat the constant infections he'd get as a result. We asked many times for him to have an operation on his prostate so that he could be rid of that tube, but they wouldn't do it because of his age.

One Friday night, when Ma was at a wedding and the girls were staying with their fathers, I decided I needed a night out. Da had had a good day, had taken his tablets and assured me he would be grand just watching telly for the evening. Before I left, I stuck coloured post-it notes on Da's arms. They read:

> Lynn is only gone out for a few hours
> Don't take the catheter out, Lynn will fucking kill you if
>   you do
> If you are worried about anything knock over to Noel

I came home that night with a bad feeling. Taking off my heels so I wouldn't wake him, I opened his bedroom door. I felt the urine at my bare feet. I didn't care and went straight to him.

"I'm sorry, Lynn," he whispered. "I forgot to read the notes. I thought the tube was a fishing rod and I went fishing." He looked so sad, I could tell he felt like he had let me down or that he had failed in some way.

I sat beside him and held his hand. "What did you catch, Da?"

His face softened. "Nothing, there was no hook on the end of the line."

We smiled and said nothing more. I cleaned everything up and helped him back into bed. I lay in his arms and promised him that I would find a way to help him, and I would start with getting rid of that fucking catheter.

By this time, around 2011, I had established that it was not Alzheimer's disease. Da hadn't shown any more signs of memory loss. But the doctors still wouldn't reassess their diagnosis of Parkinson's. I am sure they were sick of the sight of me, but I knew in my heart that treating him for Parkinson's alone was not enough.

Fiona O'Reilly rang me one evening to tell me to read a journal article about Lewy body dementia. I was awake until all hours that night, reading every line. I was excited: this was the closest I had got in my years of research to something that resembled Da's symptoms. I asked for a case conference with the consultants and Fiona came too. I told them Da possibly could have Lewy body dementia. After going back and forth with the consultants laying out my father's case, they still insisted I was wrong.

However, in a strange twist, they brought me back a few weeks later and told me that, yes, Da had Lewy body dementia. They told me they had reviewed his notes and that this was always the diagnosis. I wanted to call them out on their bullshit, but to be honest I just wanted them to treat him for the hallucinations. I had very little fight in me to take on a battle of misdiagnosis. Anyway, they were all in the same family of diseases.

The consultants went on to say that they had chosen to treat the Parkinson's side of Lewy body because it was difficult to find a combination of medication that would treat both. I could feel my anger rise as they spoke. My da was the patient, we were the family trying to support him, yet they had decided in isolation to treat one part of the disease over the other. Before they could continue I left the room and went to get Da in his wheelchair. I wheeled him before the doctors.

"Listen very carefully," I told them. "Da should be the one to determine what he values more, and what course of treatment he would like to take."

I turned to him. "Da, you know when I bring you up to watch me play a football match? Would you rather walk to the match with me and have no tremor, but when you stand on the sideline you are hallucinating and have no idea who I am or what you are watching; or would you like me to put you in that wheelchair, wheel you up the road, and when you watch the match you would know what it is, enjoy it and could cheer me on?"

It only took Da a couple of seconds to respond. "I would want to watch you play the match. I would prefer to be in the chair."

Da could make the decision, and as soon as he did things started moving for him.

I know doctors are medical professionals, and for the most part Da was treated well. However, sometimes people think that one size fits all, they think they know what's best for the patient, when often the patient is the expert about their own needs. Doctors must create the space to develop care plans in cooperation with the patient and their carers.

Not long after this, Ma had gone away for a day or two when we received a sudden call that a bed had become available for him at Kiltipper Woods nursing home. Ma was so upset that she wasn't there but we had to take the space while it was available. The hardest thing I ever had to do was to pack up his stuff and walk him into the nursing home. We had a long chat beforehand; he was preparing me more than I was comforting him. "Lynn, you know I don't ever want to be a burden," he said, looking me in the eyes. I was blinded by tears.

It was such a hot day that the staff at the home directed us out to the garden area where men and women were gathered around a nun playing the organ. They all had happy smiles and swayed to the music. Some of them seemed so far into dementia and Alzheimer's that I felt my heart racing. *My da doesn't belong here.* "Da, are we doing the wrong thing? Just tell me and we will leave, right now." He held me tightly as I sobbed. He didn't shed a single tear. He was such a hero.

An elderly woman sat opposite us with a doll on her lap. She looked agile and mobile but her mind was in a different decade as she bounced the doll up and down frantically on her knee. I had to turn the tears around. "Here, Da, see her with the baby? Don't get fucking stung babysitting for her, just because you're the newbie." He looked at me and we broke our shite laughing.

I had a conflict of emotions leaving him there that night – relief that we had found him somewhere so close to us and the place looked lovely. The other feeling was one of failure. *I should be looking after him. I should leave my job and take him home.* Looking back now, I don't regret leaving him there and neither does Ma.

Da would spend his last years there. He received a high standard of care and love from the nurses and carers, who made his life as good as it could be. They embraced his love of music and made sure he could sing whenever he wanted. We enjoyed so much of our time with him in those years.

We were five minutes from him and Ma spent much of her time there. She went straight from work every evening, until it was time for him to go to bed. On the weekends she would stay there all day. He had his own room so we filled it daily, watching movies and singing songs. Da and I had long conversations about college and the kids and I curled up with him often in his bed. He had some really hard days but for the most part he kept his spirits up for us. The hallucinations became less severe.

But it was only for such a short time. Da was still strong as an ox but other symptoms began to show, symptoms that would reveal that both I and the doctors were wrong. His throat closed up more and soon his food had to be liquidised. He became quieter in himself and began to stay in bed more.

In April 2013, Ma and I were called in as Da had become unwell. We were taken into a room and told that he had a bleed in his stomach and was unlikely to recover. It would only be a matter of days before he passed. It's strange to feel both relief and grief at the same time.

We were all by his side at the end. I lay beside da, cuddled in like a ten-year-old, catching up on some lost time. I was twenty-eight years old and the time was coming for us to say goodbye.

I am good with death. I've had to learn to be. I am comfortable talking about it and I have come to appreciate the moments I get to say everything that I have to say before they go. I had learned years before that tragedy can take away your chance of reconciliation and sudden death can leave you with years of regrets and what-ifs. I used this time to make sure my da left this earth knowing what he meant to me and knowing my remorse for fucking up during my teenage years.

"Hey Da, guess what? I wrote your funeral speech. Do ya wanna hear it?"

He looked up at me with that distorted grin. "Sure, I'll be kicking the bucket soon, so yeah."

I sat up straight, got out the laptop and began to practise my best funeral voice. No crying, I told myself, be strong, and make sense.

"Ya ready, Da?"

"As I will ever be!"

> I decided to talk today as I felt my da deserves to be remembered for who he was and not the illness he became. Although who he became was still a man filled with love for his family and even in his sickness and pain he continued to fill our days with love and laughter.
>
> Today is a day when people expect us to sit and cry and be filled with regrets or what-ifs. I would rather do as we have done through his illness – that is, to find cause for laughter. Yes, we are heartbroken and will be left with a huge hole in our lives but it's a hole that my da will continue to fill in his absence. He fills this void with the love, memories and stories he left behind.
>
> My da was a gentle, hard-working man who rarely lost his cool and, if he did, it was most likely me who caused it. Da cycled to work for many years into town and back every day, always pedalling away in song. One day when he came home he was singing something very different than his usual Walkman favourites.

"Call him Mr Raider, Call him Mr Wrong" came from this grey-haired, sixty-odd-year-old man as he dismounted his bike. I was in stitches. He had bought this on tape. I continued to play that song for him even in the nursing home.

We had a very happy home with happy parents who were very much in love. I hated it, watching them kiss in the kitchen, snuggling up on the sofa together. The worst was hand-holding in public. I didn't realise how beautiful it was, how beautiful they were, how beautiful they are. We might say goodbye to my da today but my ma will be saying goodbye to a bond that is rarely found, a bond that makes me know I will never settle for anything less than what they have.

My da, the man who taught me how to waltz. Every Sunday morning was a dance class. As certain as Sunday mass, my da would sing me out of my bed. He had so many records and I knew all the words. Our mutual love of the Drifters brought us together in song as he danced me around the room, ferrying me on his feet. I knew all the songs he sang, word for word. I must have been fairly young, maybe seven or eight. I know I was young as I had not yet begun to question his taste in music. My da gave me his beloved Drifters cassette tape after much pleading. My friends were a little confused when I insisted they were listening to the wrong band. "Here, put this on," I said excitedly, as they sang along to Take That. They were a little confused by my music choice. I didn't care what they thought of my music. It was our anthem.

Hand in hand we walk. I am seven years old, anticipating the next word. "Em, let me see . . . spell 'prescription'," he says as he spots the chemists. I get excited as his last word was "subscription". He is making it easy for me. I pause a moment and then spell with confidence. Our matching grins cover our faces. I am happy that spelling these words makes my "dadictionary" proud.

My brother was a talented footballer like my da so I looked for other ways to obtain his approval. Not that I needed my da's approval. I had it, but I still sought it. I would see the look on his face as he watched his talented son, the speedy outside right. The delight on his face as scouts' interests came flooding in. I eventually got that look, although slightly distorted from the Parkinson's and dementia taking hold. The admiration and pride he had in his eyes as I offered to help him die and take him away from the pain and fear he was in.

My da left us with so much. He leaves me with his determination, righteousness and knowing what true love is. He leaves my ma with the years and years of happiness and beautiful memories that they had together (and us of course). And he leaves Jay with the skills and knowledge of what being a good, devoted and loving da is. I know Jay would prefer his head of hair, but hard luck Jay. He left us the biggest piece of him in Jordanne. They both have the most beautiful and pure hearts that make us the luckiest people to have such genuine humanity and love twice in our lifetimes. The saddest thing about my da's death is that Jaelynne's and Caiden's experiences of him are more limited than ours but special all the same. My da would ask for Caiden daily and they would speak in their own language. Jaelynne would make him laugh with her quick wit and her cheeky manner always got him smiling, even on the darkest days.

So when the hole my da leaves is present, we will only have to look at each other to fill it back up again.

"So, da, there ya go. That's it . . . am I missing anything?" I ask him. He held my hand and tried as best he could to speak. I put my ear to his mouth, waiting for him to tell me he either loved the speech, or to rewrite it. Instead, with the loudest roar, he shouted out, "Call him Mr Raider, Call him Mr Wrong". Then he laughed and went quiet again.

He was amazing, my da. Humour was our tool for survival and throughout his illness it was a well-used tool. Humour got us through our darkest days. To us it was a coping mechanism.

The weeks after Da's death are a blur. Ma was strong but lost in his absence. I parked my grief momentarily so that I could sit my summer exams in Trinity. It was really difficult. I cried through every exam and wrote what I could. I was quite shocked to pass. With the exams done I hid myself away in my house, trying to find anything that smelt like him, desperately trying to hold onto anything that remained of him. Darren, my friend and personal trainer, forced himself into my space almost daily during this period, arriving at my house and forcing me to train and to talk. I struggled though, and training around all those people meant I could not cry.

By August of that year I decided to start running, so I could be alone and so I could cry. I started small, just running 3K, but I found it so helpful, some days I just kept running. It was easier to cry while I was running; I could get it out and then return home and be strong for the kids as they were grieving too.

By September I decided I was going to run the Dublin Marathon in aid of the Parkinson's Association of Ireland. Throughout my grieving process, I ran and I ran. I crossed the finishing line in the marathon with a picture of Da held close to my chest. Of course, this didn't remove all the sadness, but it helped. I remember one day I cried so much that a childhood pal took Jaelynne off me, and my friend Aisling brought me to her place. Aisling wrapped me up in a blanket, lit a fire and some candles and just stayed with me, to talk when I felt like it and cry when I wanted.

I can still picture Da so vividly. His handsome, clear face, those beautiful blue eyes and his selfless heart. I am so proud that he was my father.

CHAPTER 16:
PRESIDENT LYNN

In the years after Da died, I had a little more time for college. I became aware that a new position at the Students' Union, Student Parents Officer, was up for grabs. I walked into Student Council where the elections were taking place. I had never been to one before. In fact, I had never engaged with the Students' Union before. I had no idea what I was meant to do, now that I was in the hall. I sat down and tried to figure out what was happening as I observed the confident young students make election speeches for each position.

I noticed that if you were the only candidate, you didn't have to make a speech. I hoped that no one else was running against me. I had never spoken in a public space like this before. I felt inadequate as I listened to the articulate speakers. When the Student Parents Officer position came up, nobody else put their name forward. I asked the young man I was sitting next to, "Do you know what I do here? Do I have to be proposed as a candidate?" He quickly explained the process, and I asked him to second me. I knew no one in this big crowd but that young man, Edmund Heaphy, went on to become a friend. Over the years he has given me great encouragement to write and always helped me tidy up my bad grammar and punctuation.

That was how I was elected as the first ever Student Parents Officer in Trinity College Students' Union. It wasn't long before I became an active part of the team under the presidency of Domhnall McGlacken Byrne. He was something special – intelligent, articulate and deeply aware of privilege and social class. I was instantly drawn to his way of viewing the world. It didn't take him long to understand the reality of my life and the experience I was bringing into the Students' Union. He spent much of his time with me telling me that I would make a great president, that my experience and knowledge were what the student movement needed. He really put the work into making me feel confident and valued and into convincing me that everything I stand for would be a positive for Trinity.

Domhnall planted the seed in me to run for his position the following year, and it is down to him that it was even on my agenda. He helped create the space for me to be part of the union, knowing my differences but celebrating the diversity I brought. This medical student from a privileged background, soon to be a doctor, wanted nothing more than for me to come in and bring something new to the role of president. The rest is history.

The sweat gathered in pools on my palms and my insides shook as though this was a life-and-death situation. I looked around at my team and knew it was small in comparison to the other campaign teams. The other candidates had spent years integrating into college life and had profiles in societies and clubs. I could never compete with this; I had had two kids and a sick father to care for during my first two years in Trinity. I never got to experience college in the same way as they did. We had considerably fewer people, which meant fewer resources and skills. The branding of some of the other candidates' campaigns looked professional. Designing logos, manifestos and T-shirts in such a short space of time was not our forte, but everyone pitched in and we pulled the campaign together.

As I stood in the Students' Union kitchen in that spring of 2015, I looked around at my team: Rob, my right-hand man, had stood by my side since we both entered TAP in 2011; then there was Will, the intellectual scholar with socialist ideals; Oisín, another left-leaning young man with mischief in his bones; Deirdre and Stacy, two very intelligent young women who also began TAP with us; Sean, a mature student, who was so committed to the campaign; Heather, our artistic campaign member; and then there was Jaelynne. My T-shirt hanging below her knees like a dress, she was buzzing with the atmosphere.

There were so few of us in the very first picture of the campaign team, but that was to change over the course of those weeks in ways I never would have imagined. The other teams had almost ten times the numbers we had at the start of their campaigns. It was clear we were the underdogs, but what we didn't have in numbers we had in heart. We believed completely in the principles on which the campaign stood: equality, access and inclusion.

On that first day of the campaign, though, I momentarily forgot who I was as I mimicked the other presidential candidates. I stood before each lecture hall talking policy. I began to realise I sounded no different. I wasn't standing out. I tried to remember Domhnall's advice to me, that I had experience none of the others had, and to make use of that. Jack Cantillon, a Trinity student who had managed campaigns before, gave me the best advice: "Lynn, tell your story, tell them who you are." So I did.

On Jack's advice, Will Foley wrote an article about me: early school-leaver, young mum and working-class mature student challenges for the position of president of Trinity College Students' Union, a position historically held by private-school boys. This was an exercise to get my story out, get people to pay attention to my campaign. Will sent it to a number of newspapers. *The Irish Times* said they would wait to see if I won before they printed anything, but they would be watching with interest. We set the narrative, we drew the attention; now I had to own my story and use it to my advantage. The moment I did, I felt empowered for the first time in this process.

I took the opportunity to bring my story to life on the steps outside the dining hall at the first hustings. I had felt sick going to bed the night before, realising I had been trying to be like everyone else, ignoring my own identity. I looked out at the crowds gathered on that beautiful spring day. The sun was in my eyes, but the air was still crisp. I was shitting myself. I searched my head for some words to amplify across Trinity College's famous Front Square. I could see my manifesto shake like a flimsy piece of paper in my hand. As I stared at it I realised that's all it was: a piece of paper.

"What are you going to say, Lynn?" It was Rob, my campaign manager, looking a little anxious.

"Trust me, Rob. It will come to me. I'm going to be a community worker, and this is a community, after all."

He smiled and said, "You got this, sister."

With that I walked across the steps, took the microphone in my hand and gave the best version of myself: Lynn, from Tallaght, with a passion for making change. I held up the manifesto. "These are just words on a page – pointless, full of promises, just like everyone else's. They stand for nothing unless you have the skill, the experience and the determination to turn them into action." I tore up the manifesto to cheers and promised the students that, like every community, Trinity is a community that should be built on foundations of equality. I made it clear that, while I agreed that plug sockets in the library were a necessity, I would be running on a different platform.

The campaign became real for me in that moment, the very second that I allowed my own personality through. I went from being just another candidate to being a real contender. I took my new-found voice to every lecture hall in every Trinity building and I told everyone who I was and what I stood for. The campaign grew in strength and numbers. Students began peeling off the other candidates' campaign T-shirts and replacing them with mine. By the end of week one we had multiplied, from students living with a disability, TAP students and mature students, into any student who related to my story in some small way. The call for greater inclusion, fairer access and true equality brought people along.

Well, it brought most along. I was quite taken aback by the comments of one student from the campaign team of one of my main competitors at the hustings in Halls, the student accommodation in Dartry, Dublin 6. The room was full, and a question came from the back, something along the lines of: "How are you going to work long hours and represent students when you are a mother?" It sounded like a question from an older Ireland. It was as though everything about me, about women, went completely over this man's head. I went to take the mic to respond but Kieran McNulty, chair of the electoral commission, swiftly intervened to say that I did not have to answer such a question.

After two weeks of campaigning, I was tired but very proud. No matter what happened at the count, which was due to take place in the Davenport Hotel the evening after the election, I felt like a student, finally. I felt part of and supported by a new community of people who valued what I had to say, so much so that many of them had dedicated two weeks of their lives to a stranger. That night was a long one; the elections had been for a number of SU officers, and the presidential count was the last of the races to be counted. I refused to enter the count room, I was so nervous. I sat out in the hotel bar, where the results would be announced, surrounded by my team and my friends. When the results finally came in, and the returning officer said my name, the place erupted. I cried.

I was the new President Elect of Trinity College Dublin Students' Union, the first woman in fourteen years and quite possibly one of the first early school-leavers and teen mothers. One of my first thoughts was for Conor O'Meara, one of the other presidential candidates. If I hadn't entered the race, he probably would have sailed into the position. He is a kind, creative, bright young man and had run a very professional campaign. I felt bad for him in that moment. Before I could celebrate properly, I sought him out and gave him a hug. I hope he looks back and sees the positive impact of me winning this election, the effect it has had, not just on my growth, but also for my children's futures, and for many others like me. Conor was always going to do well at everything he did, but winning that election allowed me to blossom into my own self.

In my new position of TCDSU president that autumn, I was excited by the impressive team I was surrounded by. Aifric Ní Chriodáin, the communications officer, was alternative and very caring, full of empathy for people and passionate about social change. The new welfare officer, Conor Clancy, was seriously impressive from day one. Given my employment background, I thought I would be interfering in his work all the time – not a chance, he was way too quick and tuned in for me to keep up with him. His welfare campaigns were always on point and I had nothing to add to them. Molly Kenny, the education officer, is one of the most ambitious people I have ever met. Her confidence in her ability is something we should all possess as women. She also became a positive influence in Jaelynne's life. Katie Cogan, the ents officer, was like a free-living New Age hippy, and I gave up pretty quickly on the idea of being able to manage her in work. She was a creative free spirit and just did her thing.

Then there was Edmund Heaphy, the young man I had sat beside on that first election, who was elected unopposed as the *University Times* editor. Edmund kept his distance a little from all of us on his mission to hold the Students' Union to account. He is up there with the best of them in the print media. Even in his efforts to remain at a distance, he became my friend, but I also accepted that he felt a duty to report the truth of any story. I just had to hope I would never be the story.

I knew as I looked around at these talented people that I was in for a year of learning in my new role. I would learn from them but they would also learn from me and all the people I was about to bring into their space. The campaigns I would run throughout the year ignited an activism in the Students' Union that was much more representative than before. It was an exciting time for us all.

When I had applied to the Trinity Access Programme in 2011, the task I set myself was to learn the language of those in power, to break down the culture and class barriers so I could receive the education that I deserved. The irony is that it was only when I spoke up in my own voice, using my own language, that I was fully heard. Trinity gave me a chance, a platform and the opportunity to be that voice, not just for myself but for the people and work I had walked away from to go there. I have a voice now and I want to be heard. I want students to be heard. I want the working-class community and homeless sector to be heard. I want the voiceless to be heard.

CHAPTER 17:
HOMELESSNESS AND HUMANNESS

Before I went to Bluebell I had spent a couple of years as a relief worker in the homeless sector and I was determined to return to the hostels after my time in Bluebell. A couple of years into my degree I did and it was the best decision I ever made. As soon as I completed my first shift I would be excited about returning. There is humour, vulnerability and great strength in the homeless community.

The men and women I worked with were in long-term homelessness. They have high needs and their alcohol and drug use is often chaotic. The low threshold hostels were set up to cater for the street drinkers, to keep them safe. It was about harm reduction and improving their health as best we could. The chaotic nature of their lives meant their health took a daily bashing.

This work suited me down to the ground. Chaos, trauma and unpredictability were in my DNA. Many people would be frightened by some of the shit I witnessed and experienced in the hostels. I took it in my stride and responded to it with the best of my ability. In the hostels, I had a philosophy of reaching out and connecting with people who allowed me to. I walked every day into work and strove not to allow people's addictions and behaviours determine my interactions. Instead I took the time to get to know as many of the residents as I could in each of the hostels, always reminding myself that each of them had a story. Some of them want you to know their story and others don't want you anywhere near their pain.

I recently got to share some of my favourite stories in a book called *Looking at the Stars*, the proceeds of which went to the Simon Community. I would like to share their stories again but expand on them here. Sharing my experiences with people is important to me, as I only know who I am through my experiences with the world. These stories tell of beautiful interactions with some amazing men who allowed me into their hearts and allowed me to exist there alongside their trauma.

We all know that every human deserves a place to call home. It is a basic need. However, as a society, we need to nourish the souls of those who have become acclimatised to their own pain, beyond just bricks and mortar. How can we penetrate twenty years of self-medication or child abuse, etched not only into their minds but into the very fibre of their being? We have to try. Having spent half of my life as a community worker with people on the fringes of society, I have learnt that to help them, you have to step into their space, engage with them face-to-face as human beings, and connect.

The residents of the homeless accommodation in which I worked had all experienced pain. Love, caring about being wanted or being attractive all fall down the list of needs as survival takes the top spot. As someone in a position of authority, I constantly thought about how to maintain that authority and maintain boundaries with the residents while also being able to judge a situation. That said, there were rare moments where I was able to connect with them in a way that I'll never forget. It may have been only momentarily, but those moments happened and they have stuck with me to this day.

Love is a burnin' thing
and it makes a fiery ring.
Bound by wild desire,
I fell into a ring of fire.

"Is this music alright, Jim?"

"I know you don't like to be touched, are you OK with me holding you?"

"Do you think there is a heaven?"

"Are you afraid of dying?"

"You know we all love you and will miss you dearly."

"It's OK. I have you. I am not going anywhere."

"Goodbye."

Apart from singing Johnny Cash, those are the only words I spoke to Jim as I held him in his final hours. His answers to my questions were all he said on that last night before his life ended. Jim was a long-time resident of the hostel accommodation and, even though you had to be quick to duck when he swung his fist, he was popular and well liked. Jim was an alcoholic and refused point-blank to see a doctor, no matter how ill he was. "Fuck off!" was the only response to me or anyone else who tried to convince him to do anything he did not want. I would usually answer the same back to him, and he would look up at me with the tiniest hint of a smirk. He seemed to respect me putting it up to him.

Something I learnt quickly about Jim was that he did not like being touched. He wasn't a huge communicator so he never shared why this was – not with me anyway. There could be any number of reasons for it, but it always appeared to be a defence. Maybe years of self-protection on the streets had taught him to get the fists up quick. On many occasions, I forgot the "do not touch" rule. I did sometimes choose to ignore it to catch him from falling. It was never received well. However, this was not the case during those last six hours of his life.

I sat with Jim all night and felt honoured that in his last moments, he agreed to accept human contact. With every exhalation, it felt as if his pain was leaving his soul. With every strained breath, he held my hand a little tighter. He was not afraid to die and believed in God. Death can often be sad and scary, but Jim had lived into his seventies, even after years of alcohol abuse and trauma. I think this is a testament to the incredible work of the staff and services who cater to the long-term homeless who would otherwise, in their absence, simply be street drinkers who die in their forties.

In those last moments it was just me, Jim and Johnny Cash's "Ring of Fire". He said no to playing U2 but smiled for Johnny Cash. It was beautiful. The pain left his face and for the first time in a long time he was held, held with love and care by another human.

Our beautiful moment was quickly tarnished when the ambulance arrived. I had radioed down to the staff on night shift that Jim was gone, that he had passed away peacefully. For the first time a resident had been given permission to die in what was his home. He was linked in with a hospice and there was a "Do Not Resuscitate" instruction in place. I had no idea what to do in this situation. It was obviously too late for an ambulance but I didn't know who should take his body to the morgue. So we had called for an ambulance. When it arrived, the paramedics began to take out their resuscitation equipment. I insisted there was no point, as he had been dead about twenty minutes and he had a DNR. They looked a bit angry with me as they touched his feet to confirm he was going cold. I rang the staff downstairs for the DNR paperwork to be brought up, but they couldn't find it, and as a result, the gardaí were called. The guards asked me for the documentation from the hospice, and I told them I didn't have it.

"Were there any suspicious circumstances?" they asked me.

"No," I said, "unless singing Johnny Cash to Jim while he was dying counts as suspicious."

It was now seven in the morning and residents were waking for their first drink of the day, some of them still pissed from the night before. One of them tried to barge into Jim's room to find out what was going on. I was beginning to panic, not because they might think I had allowed Jim to die but because the residents would soon be up and I was worried about them witnessing a body bag being carted out. After numerous calls to management and the hospice, I was off the hook and they began to zip Jim up into a body bag – an awful sight.

I asked them how they planned to carry him on a stretcher down all those flights of stairs. They said they would have to stand him upright in the lift. By this stage, it was beginning to seem like a comedy sketch. Off they went, poor Jim strapped vertically to the stretcher in the lift. I ran down the stairs, trying to beat them to the ground floor. As the lift opened, one of the other residents was waiting on the other side, small cup of wine in his hand, only barely awake, to be met by paramedics holding on to the body bag. He looked at me and said, "Who the fuck is in the body bag?"

"Ah, don't be minding. You're still drunk," I told him,

"Would ya ever feck off," he said. We laughed a little. Then I told him what had happened. I asked him to keep it quiet until we could tell all the residents. But of course, within half an hour, everybody in the hostel knew.

While Jim never wanted to be touched, he allowed me to hold him in those last moments. He was scared no longer; he was ready to leave this world. Others weren't so eager.

Managing working relationships was often a difficult tightrope to walk as a young woman working in the homeless services. This was especially true when working with men of a similar age who, in any other circumstance, could have belonged to my circle of peers. They would often pass remarks on how I looked, or jokingly suggest a date. It's never really a joke, though. Even though they know it's never going to happen, the human being behind that bravado wants to feel that you might also be attracted to them. It is certainly true that boundaries are crucial in situations like that, but you also need to remain aware that the person you are there to support and to advocate for is vulnerable. The desire to be wanted or to feel attractive can often be seen as a weakness or of lesser intrinsic value than love. I don't accept this. Ensuring that you don't make them feel rejected while also being clear that a line exists that they cannot cross was always difficult. Sometimes, in extremely challenging situations, I felt it was necessary to shift the boundary line. With Noel, it was essential.

"Lynn! Do you like my new tracksuit and my new Liverpool jersey?"

Noel would often go looking for a comment on his appearance. He was in his thirties. He was a non-smoker but he was a chronic alcoholic. His investments in new tracksuits gradually became more and more regular, in a desperate bid to divert from the mustard colour of his skin. We were watching him die in front of us. This young man, who acted like a teenager most days, seemingly just wanted a matriarchal figure to mind him.

Noel would refuse treatment time and time again – eventually choosing death by Budweiser over losing his bed in the homeless system. Noel died because the system failed to ensure that he would be discharged back into safe accommodation if he became sober. He died because he never wanted to sleep on the street again and liver disease seemed like the lesser of two evils. Before his death, he became too ill to stay in the hostel and was transferred to St James's Hospital.

As I slowly entered Noel's hospital room, I prepared myself mentally for the image that awaited me. He was sleeping, he was frail, and he was dying. He would not leave the hospital again and he would die a week later. I sat quietly at his bedside as he slept and rehearsed my facial expression for when he woke, so he would never know I was frightened by how little he looked like himself. If it weren't for his name on the chart at the end of the bed, I wouldn't have known it was him. Finally, he opened his eyes and welcomed me with a smile as big as I'd ever seen. We chatted for a while about life and death and what could have been, but as I reluctantly got up to leave, he grabbed me by the wrist. I could tell he knew this would be our last conversation. He said he didn't want to die so I turned around to face him again. He told me that he had always fancied me and that, if he wasn't dying, homeless or an alcoholic, I would fancy him too. He said that, in another life, I would have gone out with him. He reminded me of a young boy, vulnerable and unsure of himself. So, without any hesitation, knowing that bending the truth didn't matter anymore, I said, "Sure why do you think I'm here? I've always fancied you too." I kissed him on the forehead and gave his hand a squeeze. He smiled, said thanks and I left.

Wanting to be wanted, wanting to feel attractive and wanting to know that you are desirable is something that I always pretend not to care about. But my final experience with Noel brought it back to basics for me. He taught me to embrace the vulnerability in wanting someone to make you feel OK about who you are. He reminded me of the teenage innocence of fancying someone with no motivation or expectation behind it. Just one human saying "I like you" and having that reciprocated. I will remember Noel and his polite, loving manner forever.

Can you imagine what twenty years of dirt looks like on someone's feet? When Patrick finally let me peel the black stockings from his feet I began to appreciate my strong stomach. The elastic of the stockings was so embedded into his legs I really wondered if his feet could fall off with the stockings. His ankles had been so restricted that you might think they belonged to a ten-year-old.

With the basin and the nailbrush in hand, I began to scrub away decades of footsteps and suffocation, and years of dead skin from this embarrassed man's feet.

"You play instruments, don't you, Patrick? I used to play the tin whistle. I was very good, Patrick – I swear. 'Ag Críost an Síol' was my speciality. I used to have to play it for the teachers' masses."

He kept laughing as if I was making it up. I don't think he could imagine this tattooed, mouthy young one playing such a delicate tune. I let him laugh at the idea as it was distracting him from the fact that I was kneeling down with his feet in my hands, something he was clearly uncomfortable with. I just kept rambling on, cracking jokes. I needed the distraction too. He had always refused to allow anyone near his feet. All the counselling training in the world would tell me to respect his wishes never to take his shoes off, but selfishly I had decided I could no longer watch him walk painfully around the hostel. Still, I was not completely prepared for the six-inch toenails that had curled under his toes inside his shoes. The layers of dirt looked like birthmarks or some sort of skin pigmentation. It's as though the dirt seeped into his feet and became part of him. Two hours of washing and scrubbing couldn't completely erase the imprint of his time on the streets.

Patrick was a joker but there was sadness in his eyes about being here in this spot. He would have walked forever in pain rather than allow someone to help. Sometimes when we offer help we can accept the refusal too quickly, reverting to the attitude that "this is not in my job description". It's important when we work with people in vulnerable positions to be mindful that it is just as abnormal for them to have someone wash their feet as it is for us to be washing someone's feet.

Being affectionate, loving and caring may never be written in ink in your job description but being human should never have to be contractual. Every action, every conscious thought and every moment together connects us. There are endless stories of love, laughter and hardship that I could tell about my time in the homeless sector but the ones that always touched me the most on a personal, human existence level, were the ones that were honest. It was these real human interactions that have shaped and moulded me as a person. They define me on a much deeper and more lasting level than other events that have happened in my life, those times when people took a piece of me. Unlike Jim, Noel and Patrick, who all left me a better person than they found me.

On the night I was elected Students' Union president, as I made my way home in the early hours, I got a call from Sundial Hostel. They were short-staffed for the following morning. I would have to be in the hostel in three hours, but I didn't mind. I was too excited to sleep, and I wanted to tell my news to the men in the hostel. Especially one man, who had given me rosary beads for luck in the lead-up to the campaign. I didn't have the heart to tell him that I had no use for Catholic keepsakes. It was his intention that meant the world to me, not what the beads represented. Sitting in his bedroom, the door open to release the cigarette smoke, I relayed the whole campaign and count night to him. His neighbour overheard us talking, and as I said, "President of Trinity College" (but before I could add "Students' Union"), he jumped at me and said, "This is great, Lynn! Me, you and the IRA can now make our way through the underground tunnels and blow Trinity up from the ground." Having heard many of his conspiracies and delusions, I promised him I would find out where they keep the map of the tunnels.

That is what my life had become in a nutshell: sitting on the ground in a cloud of smoke, listening to the stories of the wonderful characters in the homeless community, having spent a night celebrating my election as president of the Students' Union in the most prestigious university in the country. I have lived for several years now in such contrasting spaces.

Sadly, the man who gave me the beads has since passed away, but I still have his gift, draped around the gearstick of my car.

CHAPTER 18:
#METOO

As Jordanne hit certain milestones in her teenage years I would feel anxious about her and boys. She came home one day with skin-tight jeans and I lost the head.

"You are not wearing them. Why did you buy those jeans? So boys could see your arse?"

She looked at me, horrified. She was so upset. I suddenly realised that my shame was becoming her shame. I was projecting all my own shite on to her. I didn't want men looking at her. I somehow internalised the idea that she was the one who had to prevent herself from being targeted by boys.

I went to bed that night and dissected everything I had said to Jordanne. I knew in my heart that it was wrong and that she was not me. I had to be open and honest with her and empower her to love herself. I knew I had to teach her that she is not to blame for others sexualising or objectifying her. I wanted her to have a positive relationship with sex and I wanted her to have someone to talk to when she was in her teenage years. I had never had that.

I was still struggling with the negative relationship I had had with sex from my teenage years, so I would need to try to balance my negative past with being a good role model for Jordanne. This meant being open and honest with her. It meant pushing past my shame and reluctance to talk openly. I spent a good deal of Jordanne's teenage years pretending to be comfortable with the topic of sex – until, eventually, I was.

It was working and Jordanne benefitted massively from this open dialogue, as did I. She was comfortable and confident with talking openly with me. I was still learning how to shed some of the shame I would feel literally moments before I would create the space for Jordanne to ask questions.

It was as though it was a relay race. I would read a book or an article about sexual empowerment, consent and positive, negotiated sex. I would take this baton in my hand, run home to Jordanne and hand her all this new knowledge. Jordanne was unaware that I was empowering myself in the days and minutes before I would share my new-found empowerment with her. I was not the developed, together, confident and sexually open mother that I was portraying to her. The fact is, I still had a fractured relationship with myself, cracks I was filling in at the same time I was handing her the baton in this relay of life and womanhood. Jordanne knew I was wrong to speak to her about the jeans as I had, but it impacted her and it wouldn't be the only thing she would have to contend with.

It all came to a head during my time as president of the Students' Union. The welfare officer Conor Clancy and some of the team were working on consent workshops and the national media was showing interest. These workshops opened up so many conversations about sexual consent. I was learning. I would sit back and soak up my younger team members' confidence and knowledge about sexual consent. Every conversation would answer one of the questions I had been asking myself, filling in another piece of a puzzle that had been rising to the surface for me. And with those answers came the inevitable conclusion I was finally able to articulate: when I was twenty-five I was raped.

The realisation came to me during a conversation with Conor as we sat on a train on our way to USI training. Conor's phone was hopping with requests from the media. We were talking about consent and rape, and it all came together for me. The words were out almost as soon as I'd thought them.

"Conor, I was raped."

"What?"

"Yeah, back in 2010, I think it was. I was raped. I've never told anyone before. I've never really even told myself."

I call it rape now because that is what it was. It was rape. I didn't call it anything back then. I never spoke about it. I never told a single person, not even my counsellor. I had carried it and punished myself for it for years.

I was still working in Bluebell, living with my daughters in an apartment in Deerpark. The kids were in their dads' houses and, after a night out, I had invited people back to my apartment to continue the party. I soon regretted this as I can never stay awake very long past a certain hour. I announced that I was going to bed. I never felt unsafe, not for a moment. Everybody left and I went to bed alone.

It's dark. It's the middle of the night. I am woken by the movement of someone on top of me, inside of me, and I suddenly become aware that I am having sex with someone. Or maybe they are having sex with me. I instantly feel freaked out but also very confused. I struggle to gather my thoughts. Why don't I remember the start of this? Why don't I remember going to bed with someone? I try to figure out what the hell is going on. It feels like ten minutes have passed since I woke, but it must be only seconds.

Now I am fully conscious and remember more clearly going to bed alone. I try to push him off me, still silent, as though I have no voice. It is as if I have forgotten how to speak. I am usually well able to defend myself but I feel paralysed. I push him away in a polite manner. Not using any real force. Just enough pressure for him to know that I want him to get off me. "Ssshhh, it's OK," he whispers in my ear. This time I use much more force and push him off me. He gets up then and runs away, down the stairs and out the front door.

Every time I think back now to that "Ssshhh, it's OK", I feel like I am going to vomit.

He's gone. I lie in the bed and go over and over what has just happened. I check my phone to see if anyone texted me before I went to bed. It's now five o'clock, a good four hours after everyone left.

I don't even cry. I have been woken up by a man in my house, his penis inside me, but I don't cry. I am disgusted and angry, but not at him; rather I am ashamed of myself. I wish I had used all the strength I had to attack him, to pin him to the wall by the throat, turn on the light and see who it was. *Why didn't I lock my door? Why didn't I wake up quickly enough before he could do what he did? Maybe he was really drunk and thought he was at home in his own bed?*

I didn't tell anyone about that night but my behaviours began to change. In the weeks that followed I became silent in myself and to a certain extent I buried what had happened as far back into my head as I could.

The apartment didn't feel like home. I felt trapped, like it was closing in on me. It was already so small, but it felt smaller the more I began to hate my own company. I couldn't escape myself.

I had put so much work into making that apartment a home, especially decorating the kids' room. I'd never liked much about the apartment. I hated that we had no garden. I would watch my kids in their room looking out at the children who lived in the house downstairs play on their swings and trampoline.

I was working but it was still difficult to get everything that I needed and pay rent. I was a single mother of two girls, just about paying the bills each week. It was even harder to pay rent after I was raped in my home. I think I resented the place so much I wanted nothing to do with it.

Now, not even my bed felt like my own. The fact that the kids used to take turns at sleeping in my bed with me deepened my sense of sadness. Jaelynne was only a toddler and she especially loved to get into bed with me. After that night, I would force her to go back to her own bed. She would get upset that Mammy was suddenly changing the rules, but I couldn't have her in that bed with me.

I became emotionally withdrawn from most people who loved me, and wouldn't let others get close. I removed myself from friends. I resorted to my usual way of handling things – working all hours, keeping busy. If someone questioned my mood, I would say, "Ah, I am just stressed from work" or "I am really tired".

I hugged less. Snuggling with the kids for hours watching movies didn't feel as natural as it once felt. I haven't begun to figure this out yet, all these years on. My only guess is that I could still feel him on me, in my hair, on my skin. When I hugged my kids or embraced a friend, he would be there, between us, involved somehow in everything or everyone that I touched. I was even afraid to kiss my kids goodnight in case his lips might have touched mine while I slept.

I struggled most nights to get to sleep. It's not that I was replaying it every night in my head. What kept me awake was this overwhelming sense of being alone. There was a massive hole inside me and the only emotions that seemed real were loneliness and shame. Every struggle I had in my life I shared with someone, but not this one.

I made choices during this time that I don't remember making. Like sleeping on the sofa or spending multiple nights in my old bed in my parents' house, with the girls asleep in Jay's old room. When I did stay in the apartment, I would avoid the bed, sitting up watching lots of comedy DVDs. One night I realised it was five in the morning and I had sat up all night on my own switching between Peter Kay and Des Bishop DVDs. I had drunk ten cans of Budweiser. For someone who doesn't drink either alone or at home, I knew this was not going to go anywhere good if I did not take action.

I did a good job of convincing myself that I had not been raped. I was afraid of the questions. Who was at the party? Did I know who it was? Did I bring him home? Was I drunk? Why didn't I lock the front door? How did I not hear him open the door? I wanted to forget what had happened, not to have to explain it. I wanted to pretend it never happened. So here I was, feeling like a different person, in my own home, in my own skin, because of this thing that happened to me, which, some part of me decided, I was never going to talk about. I didn't want to be judged. I chose to be lonely and I chose to be silent.

Not long after it happened, I went away on a retreat with a friend of mine. He is in Narcotics Anonymous and he and his pals from NA were going to a house in Meath. I don't know why he asked me to go. He is an intuitive guy – you don't spend years dissecting yourself in recovery without picking up good skills at reading feelings and behaviours. Maybe he could see how unhappy I was. I agreed and went with him.

I was taken aback by how much they all hugged each other. One guy came towards me and went straight in for a hug as a greeting. I couldn't even accept a hug. I wanted to tell him to get the fuck off me. It's as though I associated any human touch with a man as some sort of signal that I was willing to sleep with him. That's how messed up my thinking had become.

The main thing I learned from those two days was not that I didn't like hugging a stranger, it was that I had no social skills in this large group of non-drinkers. I didn't drink all the time but it became apparent to me that all my social interactions had been developed around alcohol. Someone put on some dance tunes and everyone bounced up off the sofa, jumping around, dancing, laughing and having fun. I felt like a fish out of water. *Dancing without a drink in me? No fucking way.* I had no skills in a setting like this without alcohol.

.I went to bed that night feeling incredibly sad for myself. I decided that I had two things I needed to address. One was my relationship with drink, and I vowed there and then, at the very least, to learn how to dance without alcohol. The second was that I needed to reconnect with my own skin, my body, who I was as a woman, as a mother and as a human being. I wasn't ready yet to accept that I had been raped, but I recognised how disconnected I had become from my own sense of self. I wanted to feel good enough about who I was so that I could let love back into my life again. Most of all, I wanted to love myself, I wanted to forgive myself and I wanted to be able to bloody well dance to Mark McCabe's "Maniac" without Budweiser in my body. Some part of me knew that, the next time I drank or the next time I was intimate with a man, it was going to be because I chose it, because I wanted it. I wanted the things, the people, the experiences I had in my life to be meaningful but first I must find meaning in me.

It wasn't healthy that I felt I had no real power to walk away from situations that I was not entirely comfortable with, only feeling safe and content when I was in a relationship. In my head, I felt that I was able to stand up for myself. That if someone tried to rape me I would fight them off and then drag them through the courts to pay for what they did. But I didn't do that. I froze and then blamed everything on myself and not on the rapist. Not once saying: *That fucking scumbag raped me.* Even though I blamed myself I knew there was something very wrong with the picture in my head. I had to explore this. I had to feel like I owned my own body again, and I knew I had to come to terms with being raped. It didn't help that I didn't tell anyone. I know now that talking to someone may have stopped me blaming and hating myself for so long.

The next two years I spent alone, refusing any dates or interest from men. I stopped drinking. I learned how to dance and interact with people just as me. Sober, often sad, and celibate.

Even though I began to feel confident again in myself, it took me a while longer to process many of the old wounds that I was just beginning to realise were there – like the marks left by all the lewd comments men would make to me when I was a young girl, barely twelve. I didn't know this stuff was under the surface until Jordanne hit the same age, and that was why I reacted as I did when she bought the jeans.

When I hit thirty, I finally began to realise that what had happened to me was not my fault. The only person to blame for rape is the rapist. I was not confident enough to speak about it just yet, but I was very angry. I had regained ownership of my own body and I had developed a healthier relationship with my body and with sex. I had not, however, dealt with the trauma and I took my fury out on the wrong people – the kids, my ma or even in the form of road rage. I would look for any outlet to have an argument or to give out rather than tell anyone I had been raped.

And that was why sitting on the train that day was the first time I told anybody that I had been raped. Conor was not my family but the truth came out, there and then on the train, almost in the same moment that I finally admitted the truth to myself.

I know now that I was raped. Those were the words that came out of my mouth. In my head I still expressed it as: "Someone had sex with me while I slept"; but what came out was: "Someone raped me while I slept."

That was just the beginning of my insights into what had happened. For a while longer I would still use politics to talk about it in a roundabout way. I wasn't ready yet to completely insert myself into the scene, but I was ready to start looking at it. All it took for me to feel like I could say it out loud was for it to be part of a conversation among students about rape, sexual assault and consent. I had never envisioned talking about it. But it felt as though speaking the words in this safe context was, in itself, enough to demonstrate the value of the consent workshops. In other words, saying it at this stage was a political tool rather than an acceptance that this was something that had a deep impact on my life.

Before they'd even been held, the consent workshops in Trinity had sparked a national debate. Some of the commentary cemented to me why they are needed. My eyes were opened, and I understood why I found it so hard to verbalise what had happened to me. Women are regularly shamed and blamed for being raped. It's engrained in us as a society. *What were you wearing? Were you flirting with him? Ah, but you had loads to drink, didn't you?*

So, on the same train journey, as we set out our plans for the workshops, I decided to write an article about consent for *The Irish Times*. Some commentators were effectively saying, "Trinity teaches men how not to be rapists", so I wrote the article as a response to this. Maybe it was too soon after I had accepted the fact I had been raped. Maybe it was all too raw. While I did not discuss the rape in the article, I spoke about not knowing how to say "no" when I didn't want to have sex. I had hoped to address more niche parts of the consent debate.

I was attacked online over the article. *She is a bike. She is a tramp. Her parents dragged her up. She had sex and now she is blaming other people because she was easy.* Writing this article left me feeling very unwell in the aftermath, exposed and vulnerable. I felt like a teenage girl being bullied and called names. I took to my bed for days. These nasty commentators missed the point of my article and they highlighted the exact reasons girls don't speak up about rape. The message is, there is a possibility that you will be attacked and shamed for it.

I regret that it took me so many years to speak up. I know now that a rapist is not usually some man who holds a knife to your throat and drags you down a lane. He is often a friend, a relative, someone in your friends' group or, in my case, someone who sneaks into your bedroom at night and rapes you while you sleep.

So much of this came to light during my time in Trinity. I felt safe in this space to begin to talk about being raped with my fellow students and I am thankful for the debate that started in Trinity on consent and consent workshops, because it has led me to face this. To face the fact that I was raped.

Since admitting out loud in 2015 that I had been raped, I have told a number of people, including Jordanne and my ma, but I would minimise its impact, deny myself some of the detail. My ma was devastated for me, but she and Jordanne gave me all the support and love they could. I thought I had dealt with it, now that it was out there. That was until Noeline Blackwell from the Rape Crisis Centre came before the Joint Oireachtas Committee on the Eighth Amendment in October 2017.

Noeline said something like, "Some women deny to themselves that they have been raped." That really struck a chord with me. *I think that might be me.* I know now I was in denial for a long time. Through every committee where rape was spoken about, I wanted to scream, but I stayed calm. Every time one of the TDs said that women should report rape the next morning, I felt like shouting out that there are women like me, almost a decade later, who still haven't reported it. Women like me who have spent years hating themselves for all the things society tells us we should have done differently.

Around the same time, George Hook's comments apportioning blame to rape victims made me question whether I was ready to talk about some of the most private aspects of my life. I watched as trolls and Twitterheads joined in on the victim blaming and it threw me into a spin. Was I to blame for everything that had ever happened to me?

But still I didn't speak out. Instead, throughout the conversations at the committee relating to rape, I could feel the shutters come down again. I didn't want to be touched by my partner or my kids. I wanted to be alone. But this time, I knew I didn't want to feel that level of loneliness and isolation again. Had I not given that man enough of my life already?

It was at that point, in December 2017, that I made the call to 1800 778 888, the Rape Crisis Centre's helpline.

Noeline Blackwell's words about denial were front and centre in my mind as I went to my first appointment at the RCC on 20 April 2018. *Maybe I should leave well enough alone,* I said to myself as I walked towards Leeson Street in the sun, the first bright day after a miserable, extended winter. *Maybe I'm only forcing this event in my past to become an issue by sitting in the Rape Crisis Centre as a client, as a victim.* My head knew that it was not my fault I was raped, but I wished my heart could catch up with it. I kept wondering if I should cancel the appointment. But then I was there. I rang the bell. I walked in.

The counsellor called me and I followed her up a flight of stairs. I spotted Noeline coming down. I would have to pass her. Should I say hello? Should I put my head down?

"Hello, Noeline."

"Hello, Lynn."

The counsellor was taken aback by this exchange. She didn't know that I have a public profile. She was concerned about my anonymity, or maybe that being recognised would upset me. It didn't.

I have had counselling for the best part of twenty years and I had managed to keep this topic out of the counselling room. I had completely denied it to myself. This was my first session, the first time I would give a blow-by-blow account of what had happened to me. I heard myself saying things I had never said out loud before.

"After I pushed him off me, he didn't move at first. He tried to soothe me. At this point I turned so that he was no longer inside me. I pretended to fall back asleep, so he would think I would never know." I felt weaker, reliving it all. It felt weak to pretend to sleep rather than shout.

About thirty minutes into the session, I admitted to the counsellor, and to myself, that I still blamed myself. At that point I began to cry. In all the years since the rape, those were the first tears that I had shed for myself, the first time I had told the story in all its truth. The first time I heard my self-blame out loud. It was also the first time I had explained what happened to me without having to consider how it might affect another person. When I told my ma, a friend or the kids in the last couple of years, I would always follow up by saying, "I am grand. This happened in my past, but I am OK." This time, though, I had the space around me to acknowledge it as the devastating event that it actually was.

I left the session feeling like I had just met a new side to myself. I usually walk at a fast pace but that day I strolled out of the appointment and slowly wandered around town with lots of questions in my head.

Is this really me?

Am I really a person who can deny such realities to herself for so long?

Can I really minimise rape just to cope?

Can I really still blame myself after everything I have learned about consent?

Is denial that powerful?

If I remember any new supressed details, will people believe me?

Have I hidden anything else in the corners of my brain?

The next two days were spent crying. I was surprised by this.

As I write these words, I have to wait another two weeks before I can go back. I have so much to explore.

I am not sure who this person is. I am not sure what I will find on this journey. The biggest sadness for me in the days after that first appointment were that I can't undo any of it. Now that I can feel this pain, I know it is reality. I was raped, I am affected by it and now that I have acknowledged it I can't undo it. I can't go back into denial.

I feel somewhat freer now that I have stopped blaming myself, I feel I have some power back. That does not mean I am not scared shitless about how others view this, how others view me. I still have a lot of work to do on myself in this area but I will be a work-in-progress until the day I die. That's OK by me.

CHAPTER 19:
LET'S SHAKE UP THE SEANAD

"Lynn, you should run for the Seanad."

I'm not sure how often I heard those words throughout my time as president of the Students' Union in Trinity College. At first, I thought people were joking; then I thought they were mad. I didn't feel I had the experience required. I would be out of my depth. I had somehow blocked out all of my lived experience and long history as a campaigner and addiction worker.

Somewhere along the line, I picked up the idea that politicians had to be a certain type of person: highly educated, wears a suit, a walking encyclopaedia of Irish history and politics. I wasn't any of those things. The politics I knew were learned on the streets of Killinarden and Bluebell, and in the lecture halls at Trinity. I didn't follow Irish politics in an in-depth way.

After a while, some of those conversations about running for the Seanad began to have an impact. I sat at home one evening mulling over the idea. I didn't sleep that night as my mind mapped out my political knowledge and questioned if I had enough to do this. The journey I had taken, which ran through my mind that sleepless night, led me to my decision to run.

✦✧✦

Back in 2001, An Cosán had invited a group of local representatives to talk to us during a week-long introduction to politics. Most of them I could not understand. But one man – Deputy Seán Crowe – seemed to say all the right things and in a language that was accessible to the young working-class mothers from West Tallaght. I was sixteen years old, and this introduction to politicians instilled in me a desire and a sense of duty to exercise my democratic right to vote. My parents always voted, though I couldn't tell you who for, as we never spoke about it. But what really spurred me on was learning that women had to fight for the vote, that women's voices were not always seen as worthy.

From then on, I always knew who was in power, I always voted, and I always paid attention to the budget. The budget was the stand-out moment for me every year in Irish politics, usually because of the sense of fear it generated – especially from 2008 onwards. I was an activist who knew very little about the history of our country and only knew about the state of our society for certain groups of people. I was on the ground helping individuals fight the fires of their everyday lives. I was one of the thousands of people trying to sweep up the debris of pain, deprivation and inequality during the years of austerity and this, in a way, politicised me. Though I had spent my whole life challenging the injustices that were, for the most part, the outcome of political decisions or due to lack of political intervention, I had never viewed myself as political.

I had no further interaction with politicians until 2009 when I was developing the addiction services in Bluebell. I had been on many protest marches by this time and was growing more aware of social class and who the political establishment was. John Curran was Minister for Drugs at the time and we found him to be very accessible and open to engagement. There's a picture of us with the minister at the launch of Drug Awareness Week in the canal communities. It was brief; we told him about what we were up to, got a picture and that was it.

Politics was something that was happening out there in the world, but it wasn't something I actively sought out. I didn't write to TDs or attend their clinics to ask questions. I was busy doing the everyday job of supporting people in their drug use and recovery. And protesting.

During the Brian Cowen recession era, I witnessed the very real effects of cutbacks on the communities of Bluebell and Tallaght. I brought Jordanne to a meeting about an upcoming protest against the budget cuts. She hadn't even turned ten but she seemed to get it more than I did. My head was always so focused on the delivery of the work in Bluebell, which is obviously important, but I knew there must be more I could do. I just didn't know what. At home that evening Jordanne came down the stairs and began chanting at me, to the tune of the Freddy Krueger song from *A Nightmare on Elm Street*: "1, 2, Cowen's coming for you! 3, 4, he's at your door! 5, 6, it's your children he picks! 7, 8, he's at your gate!"

Later that year she would chant this through a loudspeaker to thousands of protesters on O'Connell Street. She drew a picture of Brian Cowen on the body of Krueger and told the crowd, "This is the new stuff of children's nightmares. I'm more afraid of political decisions now than of a horror movie." In that moment, she inspired me to do more – not just to go along to protest meetings but to sit the *fuck up and pay attention. Jordanne was becoming much more tuned in than I was to the relationship between politics and the people.

She asked me what I spent my children's allowance on. I told her I pay life insurance and savings bonds for her and her sister and the remainder goes to the crèche. Her question made me think about what other mothers spend their allowance on. In most cases probably much more important things like rent and food. Her questions shifted my focus from the everyday tasks of keeping the Bluebell project going. It made me consider instead what it would mean on a broader level if Cowen cut the children's allowance. What exactly would that mean for the people I supported? What would it mean for families living in poverty? How could I even begin to become more than a support worker to the people I work for? How could I become an advocate for them?

I had learned during the years of austerity that the government had huge influence over our everyday lives. They could decide if Bluebell would have an addiction support worker after the next budget or not. I knew that at every Canals Task Force meeting, people were deciding which project or programme they would have to cut, or if they should instead opt to accept a lower wage. I knew that in some room, decisions were being made about our futures, about my job and about things like children's allowance.

It wasn't until I went to Trinity that I began to open up to other ways that I could effect change. The spark that was lit in me in An Cosán was reignited. I had side-lined delving deeper into politics because I was so consumed with the narrower areas of addiction, dynamics within communities and how disempowered people can overcome trauma on a personal level. I saw that I had failed to make the connection in any real way between the policy and the people.

I have always had heart, compassion, determination and the drive to change things. I want to help people, I want to help them heal and I want to empower them. I have always been willing to work hard and fight for what is right. But my biggest problem, up until this time, had been my inability to articulate myself.

As I lay in bed that night, I thought of all I had learned in Trinity and during my time in the Students' Union. I read over my political essays and I assessed my skill set. Then I abandoned all of this. I thought of my life and my pain. I thought of the unequal education system and I thought of all the homeless men I had watched wither away and die. I thought of my friends who are now dead and I thought of my peers who struggle daily with their mental health. I thought of all the women raising their babies alone, some struggling to survive and some fleeing violence. I thought of every one of my amazing friends who have experienced immeasurable trauma and obstacles in their life. Yet each of them gets up every day with a smile on their face and a fight in their belly. They laugh and cry together. They support each other, and me, with every blow we have faced and every death we have wrongly endured. They are amazing men and women. They are fighters in every way.

I do not have the political experience and knowledge of others, but I have something they don't. I have lived through some of the toughest shit and I have battled through inequality – in income, in housing, in education, in social supports, in health. I can amplify those voices that never get heard, our voices. I can remind the policy-makers of how their policies affect people. We would no longer be abstract statistics, numbers moved around the page of some white paper. We would be real people with real voices. I would run for politics and I would share the real, lived experiences of the people I have encountered and continue to encounter in my life.

I could be a voice for the people who fall into a bracket that keeps them completely ostracised and oppressed. I could help raise awareness of how people are dying because of their class. I decided it wasn't my Trinity degree or my ability to recite the constitution that would make me a good politician; it was my love and empathy for people from all walks of life and my belief in people from all social classes and their right to fulfil their potential. To begin to fulfil our potential we must first be noticed, be seen and be heard. I had a decision to make.

My ma called me the next morning.

"Well, have you made up your mind?"

"I have. I'm going to run for the Seanad."

Late into the next night, I sat in the window of my top floor apartment gazing at the big tree in my garden. My garden for the past while had been Front Square of Trinity College Dublin. I never in my life imagined I would be in such a position. I didn't even aspire to be in a position where I would be living with my daughters in this massive institution. I didn't aspire to it because it was not even on my horizon. I thought about the journey I had taken, just a year earlier, to become president of Trinity College Students' Union. That had been a powerful and worthwhile campaign and maybe, just maybe, we could do it again. So, after weeks of going back and forth in my mind as to whether I had something to offer Irish political life, I had decided to go for it. I was scared. I felt like people would laugh at me for thinking I could secure a seat but if you can't believe in yourself, then who will? I slept well for the first night in weeks, as finally the decision was made. Now I just had to figure out what happened next.

Within a couple of days of making the decision to run for the Seanad, Seb McAteer reached out to me to offer some advice on the campaign. Seb was working in an internship with Amnesty at the time and had just finished a degree in History and Politics in Trinity. I had met him once or twice in passing but this was our first real conversation. We sat at my kitchen table like the odd couple – Seb with his upper-class accent and floppy hair, me with my West Tallaght accent and tattoos – while Seb confidently told me what I would need to do. He was the perfect political nerd, as well as being sound and extremely intelligent. He knew all the first steps I needed to take and every time I went off on a tangent he had a natural talent for reining me back in, which is no easy task. I knew then and there that he was the campaign manager I needed. I just had to convince him. It took a day or two for him to come around to the idea and thankfully he did. Seb kept everything under control. I was still busy in my role as SU president, gearing up for a two-day activist festival that I was organising.

My first task was asking people to nominate me. I needed two nominees and eight supporting signatories. This made me feel sick. I was embarrassed and scared that people would think I wasn't worth it, that they would never attach their good names to my nomination form – apart maybe from Dr Fiona O'Reilly and Dr Austin O'Carroll of the Safety Net Services, who had known me for years, so I asked them first. I wanted my nomination list to be representative of my life and my career. I chose people who worked in addiction, homelessness and education in Trinity. I asked Professor Paul O'Grady, head of the Philosophy School and a well-respected academic. After I was elected as president of the SU he had taken the time to write me a beautiful email congratulating me on my success and he spoke very personally about education inequality. Still, I thought he would say no, and I was over the moon when he agreed to add his signature.

I then moved on to the legendary Áine Hyland. I had first met Áine when she'd agreed to sit on the board of trustees of the Students' Union. She blew me away from the second I interacted with her. She was full of knowledge, experience and fight. She has always been a passionate advocate of education equality and her many years in the sector had not eroded her ambitions to achieve it.

Over the course of that week I made my way to each of the nominators that I hoped would support me, and they did. I was thrilled with each and every signature.

When we sat down to plan out a campaign it was obvious just how much the odds were stacked against me. I felt inadequate when I first took to the stage with all the other candidates at the hustings in Trinity. When it came to my turn, I nervously stood up and walked towards the podium. I trembled in fear and I could feel my palms become sticky and clammy. I was worried I would faint; I was worried I would fall; but most of all I was worried that I was out of my depth. So I tried to be true. As my pal Gary Gannon always says to me: "Be Lynn Ruane. Be you." I began:

> So, people like me. I've been told: "We need more
> people like you in the Seanad." And before that I was

told, "We need more people like you in Trinity." But what does that mean? "People like me?"

My name is Lynn Ruane. I am a Trinity student, an activist and a lone parent. I believe in equality, I work hard, and I am the TCD Students' Union president.

So, what's different about me? There aren't many people like me in Trinity. There aren't many people like me in the Seanad. Is it my voice? My accent? My history? Where I am from? There aren't a lot of us, people with my accent in Trinity. There are some in the Dáil, and none in the Seanad. People with my accent usually don't have a voice. As a child, I loved to learn. I had high hopes and aspirations. But something happens to hope in children in working-class communities, and in no time, I was out robbing cars, drinking, and I ended up pregnant at fifteen. I was told I'd wasted my life. I was talked about in the past tense. But I was determined, and with the help of An Cosán, I was able to continue my education and I started a career in community and addiction work.

I went on to tell my story, from An Cosán through Bluebell and on to Trinity. Then I turned the very idea that this was a "story" on its head.

Last year, I was elected Students' Union president and I got a national platform. I've been on TV and radio and in the newspapers. I have become a story. The story is: "A single mother, from West Tallaght, who has managed not only to get into Trinity, but be elected TCDSU president."

Imagine what kind of world we would live in if that wasn't a story? If it wasn't a big deal? Although my journey has been long and hard and filled with obstacles to overcome, it is a success story, but a story that shouldn't be so exceptional that it captures so many headlines. We should and we can work towards a society in which people with the same social backgrounds as mine have equal opportunity to education and a better life. I shouldn't be a story. There shouldn't be a story about me. I want to create a society where it's so run-of-the-mill that *someone like me* would run for the TCDSU presidency, or the upper house of parliament, that nobody bats an eyelid.

There are walls around Trinity, and every educational institution in the country. I'm not talking about the walls that make us feel safe inside them, I am talking about the walls that make the people on the outside feel like they can't come in. Those walls aren't necessarily made of bricks and mortar. They are made of exclusion, of poverty, of social disadvantage. They are made of the same stuff that makes people tweet about my accent when they hear me on television. For some, these walls are made of massive childcare bills, or the fear of student debt. For some, it's the belief that they themselves hold that they can't come in. And for others, it's the fear that they will be kept out, found out and told to get out – so why bother trying?

I want to tear down the walls. I want everyone like me, who comes from an estate like mine, to feel they can access an education, to have a voice in the conversation, without having to fight. Well, maybe without having to fight so much. I think that's something that each and every Trinity graduate wants too. Trinity has instilled in all its graduates the value of a world-class education. I know that if you elect me a senator, I will fight for equal access to education. I know I can make a change in education and give others the opportunities I have fought for. Education is what gave me a voice. I want the voiceless to be heard. Please vote for me.

There – it was done. As the crowds applauded, I let out a breath of relief. I had done it, I had launched myself out there and asked for people to vote for me. I did not feel at this point as though I had done enough to be in with a chance to win, but I was proud that I had stood up on that stage and amplified my voice in front of the Trinity alumni. It was just as scary as the first time I had stood in front of a bunch of students and told them who I was and that I wanted to be their president. Public speaking was still relatively new to me.

I was also very aware that there were academics, researchers and successful business people in the room and I had yet to sit my final year. I was conscious that I was asking them to vote for a student to become their representative. I was asking them to place their trust in me. I hadn't studied law and my only experience of politics was those past six months in my post as president of the union. I had no idea how the Seanad even worked. When I said all of this out loud to friends I thought it sounded absolutely ridiculous that I would expect people to put a preference beside my name. I pushed past those thoughts and convinced myself that I learn best while on the job, I have always picked things up quickly, and were I to be elected, this would be no different.

Myself, Seb and many others worked over those couple of months to put me in with the best shot possible. Trinity alumni campaigned behind the scenes for me, contacting their friends and colleagues who had attended Trinity. Niall Ó Tuathail, the Galway West candidate for the Social Democrats, was busy campaigning for me in Galway, examining the register and cold calling homes from the phone book.

I had considered whether I would run for the Social Democrats. I could see they were growing a base of interesting, creative and innovative activists. I wondered whether they could be a party that I would join. I had never considered joining a party before. But in the end, I couldn't do it; it didn't feel right – not that they didn't feel right, it was simply that I didn't see myself in party politics. I like doing my own thing and I knew that if I was to pursue politics that I could still work closely with them and other like-minded politicians to get shit done. That appealed to me much more. I was supported throughout my campaign, personally and professionally, by Gary Gannon and Ann-Marie McNally. Every wobble I had they nudged me along.

All Seb's hard work and dedication led us to the exciting morning of the first count. My ma and my aunty Rita stayed with me that night, but I could not sleep. I was still living in Trinity and I would only have to walk less than one minute to the count in the exam hall, but I was up at the crack of dawn. I felt ill with the nerves. I just kept telling Seb and my family that it would be great to just do OK. Statistics from previous Seanad elections have shown a trend that first-time candidates rarely get more than a couple of hundred votes. It took many of the senators a few runs to get elected. What chance did I have? All we could really hope for was that I would do well enough to save face.

We all gathered in the exam hall to see the first boxes being opened. I had stood in this hall in 2012 on graduating from the Trinity Access Programme. It felt surreal. I was so full of hope in 2012 – hope that I could get a degree, hope that I wouldn't fail, hope that I could even stick it out. Here I was now, a short four years later, waiting to hear my name being announced.

It was a long day in the exam hall before the results of the first count came through. I couldn't believe my ears. I had received over eight hundred first preference votes, putting me in third place on the first count in a three-seat constituency. I was in the game. I could actually do this.

It didn't look like I was going to be put out of my misery any time soon. We had been in that hall all day and only one count had been completed. David Norris was elected, reaching the quota on that first count as expected. We had never been aiming for his seat. Sean Barrett had only one term under his belt, and we reckoned his seat was the most vulnerable, though with his background in business and economics, he represented a different cohort than mine. The only other likelihood was that Senator Ivana Bacik would be in trouble because of the collapse in support for Labour after their term in government with Fine Gael. I was conscious, however, that Labour's poor results in the general election might not be repeated on this panel. Ivana has a long history with Trinity, is well liked and still lectures there.

The count was adjourned for the night. I walked home with my family, bursting with excitement. I couldn't let my head rest. I thought a lot about my da; every time I do well at something I feel his absence much more. I lay in bed imagining what it would be like to win, what I would say after they read out my name. I could picture my ma's face and I knew that, like me, she would want to tell Da. I visualised myself as a senator. Visualisation is something I have done my whole life. I used to imagine I was a famous singer, a famous footballer or a female version of David Attenborough. Maybe I wouldn't have to visualise anymore; maybe I could actually become a senator.

I bounced up the next morning, too full of beans to even notice I hadn't slept. We had another long day ahead and the cameras were following me. For the past few months we had been part of *Inside Trinity*, a documentary by Loose Horse Productions to be aired later in the year. I had grown used to their presence and had to watch myself; I have a loose mouth as it is.

My best memory from the second day of the count is watching my ma and my aunty Rita become masters of the count. They had never been in a count centre before but by midday on that day they were hanging over the barriers with their score sheets in their hands. These two five-feet-tall women from Finglas with no history in politics were keeping count and catching mistakes. They were amazing. Paul Gannon, Gary's younger brother, manoeuvred around the room with his clipboard, making sure all my counters were at their stations. He seemed excited to be in this role. Clearly he enjoys elections.

As we ended that day it was even clearer; I had as good a chance as two other candidates. Ivana had won the second seat. Myself, Averil Power and the sitting senator Sean Barrett were all hovering around the same numbers in the race for the final seat. I was worn out but we would have to hang in there another day. We left the count hall and went home again.

As we woke on 27 April, we knew that would be the final day, the end of the count, and I would know my fate.

I observed everything around me; I always do. I take in each face and I wonder about them. That day was no different. I sat on the ground and breathed right down into my belly, to try to calm myself. The room was filled with the college security, the academics, the students and my family and friends. It was a great, diverse mix. The security men were eager to see me elected as many of them came from similar communities to my own. I was buzzing off the energy in the room. The last few hours were nail-biting as it became clear it was going to be down to a tiny number of votes between me and the incumbent. I paced the room, which was becoming more difficult as it was now full of people, people who wanted to see something. Little did I realise, they wanted to see me being elected. Before the very last count I went up to Sean, gave him a little hug and wished him well.

Finally, we arrived at the last count, all the counters had finished and the piles looked similar in size. I could see some of the younger counters bouncing a little on their feet with excitement. I could almost feel the electricity in the room. I stood close to my ma.

Then it happened. The Returning Officer took to the podium to announce who had taken the final seat. Her voice began to break and I wondered if she was about to cry as she said the words: Lynn Ruane. *That's me; that's my name.* The place erupted, the students, the security, the staff, my friends. Seb and my ma bounced on top of me. I, Lynn Ruane, had been elected. I cried in the arms of my mother, in complete disbelief. I was conscious of my joy being Sean's disappointment and I tried to calm myself so I could go shake his hand. He was so gracious and said a few words to introduce me as the new Trinity panel senator.

I tried to speak but I broke down. All I wanted was my da. I wished he could see that I had turned out OK in the end. That I had done him proud. I would have given anything in the world to share that moment with him.

CHAPTER 20:
IN THE CHAMBER

The government had not yet formed so there was a gap of a few weeks between the Seanad election and the first sitting. During those weeks, I wandered around a lot. I would stroll from building to building, familiarising myself with the layout. I would sit on a bench outside Leinster House and just stare at the building. *Do I work here? Really?* I was scared. Not that anybody else would notice this.

Apart, that is, from Harry McGee, political correspondent for *The Irish Times*. He would always sit down beside me to chat. He would show interest in my views and talk about life in Tallaght. I didn't feel so alone when Harry was in Leinster House. He became a familiar face and, most importantly, a friend. He would tell me who was who and give me the lowdown on the politics of the government parties. Without knowing it, Harry played a huge role in helping me to settle in to a place I was so frightened of.

I had no clue what was expected of me when I started in my new position. Being an independent meant I had no party telling me the rules of the Seanad. *When do I speak? How do I submit a commencement matter? Where do I see what legislation is coming up?* I had so many questions and I felt I was out of my depth. Luckily, Seb was always a few steps ahead of me and was busy figuring everything out. He came on board as my assistant and is always one hundred per cent as invested as I am in the work we do. It would have taken so much longer to be on the ball in there without his steady leadership of our new office.

David Norris contacted me early on after the election. He wanted to develop a super-group, made up of five university senators and all the independents. This would have been quite a large technical group, placing us further up the list of speakers. Groups speak by size, meaning that, with the current numbers, Fine Gael go first and Fianna Fáil second. The proposed group would speak before Sinn Féin and Labour. David Norris is an intelligent, impressive man, he has been there a long time and knows how the system works, but I was not eager to form this super-group. I was so new and some of the men in this group had long political careers. I worried that I would be lost in this group of men. I needed to learn the ropes and I wanted to feel confident in my position. I was keen on battling past all these political experts. Besides, I wanted to be part of something new, something different.

On the National University of Ireland panel, Alice Mary Higgins had been elected and I wondered if she felt the same. I made contact with her and, thankfully, she did. We sat down to air our concerns about the technical groupings. We went through the list of new senators and chatted about how exciting it would be to set up a new group. At this stage it may have been expected that we would be part of a group with the other university-elected senators, as had been the case in previous years. As we sat together that morning, I felt a positive vibe from Alice Mary as we looked at the backgrounds of our colleagues. First, we looked at John Dolan, CEO of the Disability Federation, and Frances Black, who had created the Rise Foundation, which works with families of people who experience addiction. Like myself, John and Frances, Alice Mary Higgins has a long history of advocacy, through organisations like the National Women's

Council, Older and Bolder and others. There was also Grace O'Sullivan from the Green Party, who had previously been a long-time environmental activist with Greenpeace. It was clear we had the potential to build an exciting group of activists with strong connections to social justice and to civil society.

Now all Alice Mary and I needed to do was to convince our new senator friends to work with us, not only for technical reasons or speaking rights, but for a stronger voice for our shared causes. It did not take much for everyone to agree, and some weeks later, after the Taoiseach announced his eleven nominees, we also approached Colette Kelleher, who has worked in the COPE Foundation, the Simon Community and, at the time of election, was the CEO of the Alzheimer's Society of Ireland.

Very quickly, we six became a team. Our aim is to involve civil society in the work that we do. There are so many activists, community groups and NGOs doing amazing work so we try to utilise their knowledge to inform our work. With a lot of crossover in our interests, there was so much we could do to support each other.

Alice Mary became not only the leader of the group but also a friend and teacher to me. I have no idea how she fits so much in her head and knows so many things about so many different areas of society. She amazes me. Our group has had many wins in the Seanad and we have improved many areas of legislation, including the Public Health Alcohol Bill, Data Protection Bill, the Heritage Bill and the Domestic Violence Bill. Every single senator and their assistants in the Civil Engagement Group works tirelessly in their role and I have learned so much from each of them. I am proud to work alongside them and I hope we can continue all the important work together for as long as possible. We are more than a technical group for the purposes of speaking; we are a team of five women and one man who work bloody hard to get things done.

In the run-up to the first sitting of the Seanad, I had a recurring dream. I had bought a classy and expensive blue skirt suit on Grafton Street. I hung it up in my office. Then, when the day of my maiden speech arrived, I put on the blue suit, entered the Seanad chamber and took my seat. My name was called to speak, but when I looked down, my beautiful new suit had turned into a pair of fleecy Mickey Mouse pyjamas. Everyone turned to stare at me as I raced back to my office to change. But every time I re-entered the chamber, it happened again.

When I analysed what the dream meant, I acknowledged that, for the first time in my life, I truly felt out of place and like I didn't belong. And if I stuck out so much, then people would ridicule me.

I decided again to return to Gary Gannon's advice: "Be Lynn Ruane." So, I went out shopping with a friend, Chekov Feeney, an interesting character who seemed to enjoy shopping more than I did. He helped me choose a dress – one which left a lot of my tattoos on display. My tattoos tell my life story and might tell you as much about me as these chapters do. So, with my new dress, skin on show, tattoos there for all to see, I entered the chamber as me. Yes, I still stuck out like a sore thumb, but they had to accept me as I am, because I am good enough.

On that first day, the Seanad was buzzing with people, families everywhere. I was shaking the hands of other excited families there to watch their loved ones' first day in the chamber and all I wanted to do was run home and tell my ma that I was not cut out for this. I hadn't invited my own family because I couldn't have escaped the emotion of Da's absence. I couldn't have looked at my ma in the public gallery knowing that my father should be sitting in the chair beside her.

Once I had settled in, I was determined to make my mark. During my first year in the Seanad, I was delighted to see three amendments I put to the house pass. My first was an amendment to the government's

Adoption (Amendment) Bill 2016, which passed with majority support in the Seanad. When I read this legislation, I was instantly drawn to a line which, in certain cases, allowed for the consent of the parents of a child in care to be dispensed with so that the child could be put up for adoption. I accept there could be a small number of cases where this may be required, but once it is in legislation then at any time it could be used more liberally. We are still hearing the awful stories of Irish women who were locked away from their loved ones, with their pregnancies concealed, and forced to put their children up for adoption. This is not our history; it's our present – many of those women and their children are still alive, dealing with the pain of what this state did to them.

I also felt very strongly about safeguarding working-class women in this legislation. There was a huge increase in the number of kids from minority and disadvantaged communities who ended up in care during the years of cuts to communities, family resource centres and support projects. My amendment, I hope, creates that safeguard. It sets out a simple instruction, that before the High Court can make an adoption order, the Child and Family Agency must be satisfied that the parents were offered or referred to the relevant supports. Because of my amendment, the legislation will now require the Child and Family Agency to be satisfied that every reasonable effort of support has been offered to the birth parents of a child before that child can be adopted by foster parents without the consent of the birth parents. In practice, this can mean referring the parents to housing authorities, addiction support or family resource supports, or whatever is appropriate for the family's specific circumstances. This does not impact those children being taken into foster care for their own safety. It is a simple instruction to direct the parents towards whatever supports they may need.

My first year in the chamber also brought another great success – an amendment to the Mediation Bill to improve safeguards for domestic violence victims in mediation processes. The policy intention of the amendment was to better safeguard the rights of victims of domestic abuse who may feel pressure to enter into the mediation process with an abuser. This important amendment was pulled together in a very short space of time after a similar one had failed in the Dáil. We felt a little worried about pushing the amendment as it would eat into the next bill, which was Colette Kelleher's Family Reunification Bill and supported by our Civil Engagement Group. I pushed it anyway and risked annoying others, and luckily it worked out, as did the Family Reunification Bill.

Not long after this, another amendment was brought forward by myself and Frances Black, this one relating to the Domestic Violence Bill. Our amendment allows for implementation of a mechanism for out-of-hours emergency barring orders. Initially, I was delighted when our amendment was passed, but it didn't make it through committee stage in the Dáil. The Domestic Violence Bill was important to many people across both houses of the Oireachtas, but I have to commend the work of Alice Mary Higgins, Colette Kelleher and others in making the convincing and much-needed case for coercion and control to be listed as forms of domestic violence.

I am proud of the amendments I have secured, which I believe to be valuable work in supporting women and families.

As in all areas of life, I soon discovered that, to achieve things as an independent senator, relationships are important. To be effective, we must be able to converse and negotiate our positions across the political divide. Because of the make-up of both the Dáil and Seanad, Fianna Fáil supported many of our amendments to pass. I can nearly always rely on Sinn Féin, Labour and the Independents for support, but unfortunately that isn't enough to beat the government – unless we get Fianna Fáil onside, it is much harder to get amendments over the line. On occasion, government will accept your amendment, and will sometimes ask for time to redraft it to better fit the bill. If an amendment is redrafted, the government resubmit it as their own, which is OK with me. It may no longer have my name on it, but it achieves what I intended it to achieve. My politics don't always align with the politics of Fianna Fáil but we do often agree on particular topics, and, like other parties, they had been very supportive of my efforts in the chamber. There would always be crossover but we have different political agendas.

Apart from personally getting on with members of other parties, even when our differences are clear, I knew it was important to build political alliances to push for key amendments. There is a wealth of expertise across all political parties and I want to be able to tap into that, regardless of political beliefs. Of course, sometimes I oppose government legislation outright but that is almost always a losing battle, as they have the majority. So, for now, I see my time better spent trying to improve the legislation, where possible. Such good working relationships are of great benefit in equality-proofing and gender-proofing legislation, for instance. That will be necessary until the Dáil and all government departments are as diverse as the society that they represent. Then we can move more towards agenda-setting to protect minority groups and vulnerable sectors of society rather than slightly influencing policies. That's where the real work of change begins.

Such professional relationships are also built outside the Seanad chamber. One example of this was a trip to Taiwan, on the invitation of the Taiwanese Foreign Affairs department. The primary focus of that trip was to build closer relations between Ireland and Taiwan, with the aim of increasing trade. On the flight over, I sat with John Curran and James Browne, both Fianna Fáil TDs. We were joined on the trip by James Buu, an official from the Taipei office in Dublin. James and the Taiwanese representative Simon Tu had filled us in about our trip, the ministers we would meet and the places we would visit.

I blushed at the thought of my friends seeing me on that flight – legs outstretched, warm scented hand towel, a glass of red wine to hand. I knew they would be happy for me but I was embarrassed about the luxury I was travelling in. A year into my role as a senator, I still felt like a fraud. Cultures collided: wearing my Adidas runners and Nike tracksuit, I ordered a posh cheese board. I thought of my brother's infectious laugh as he slagged my ma about the cheese board she had prepared last Christmas. For the first time in my life I was leaving the country for such a big trip without financial help from my mother or brother, and I wondered how I could ever repay them for all they have done for me. I missed Jordanne and Jaelynne. I had not left them for more than four days in several years.

On a personal level, I was excited to use this trip to Taiwan to broaden my knowledge of world politics. I would never take such opportunities for granted or come to expect them to be a normal part of life. None of this is normal to me and I am in awe of every new opportunity that comes my way. I want to learn as much about the world, politics and other cultures as I can and I will savour every moment of the life I am living.

In a way, I am thankful for the lack of confidence I have in these new situations. I use it to drive myself. I use it as an opportunity to learn and step up to the mark. My biggest fear in life is allowing anything to stand in my way as I strive to access my full potential. The moment I become complacent will be a sad day, so I will continue to wake up every day and remind myself who I am and what I can do with my life.

I had spent the previous few weeks learning all about Taiwan: its culture, its history and its politics. I spent hours researching policy areas of the Taiwanese government. I attempted to learn some basic pleasantries such as "hello" and "thank you" in Mandarin.

I stumbled across something called the Sun Flower Movement, motivated by the student movement in Taiwan. The students had occupied the Taiwanese legislature – a first for the Taiwanese government. I have always been an advocate for students connecting with what happens outside their university buildings. I love watching people power in action.

Still, I felt out of my depth in this international relations exercise. I sought ways to feel like I deserved to sit at the table and have these conversations. I turned my focus to what I do know: education, foreign direct investment and innovation. I gave myself a crash course in research and development in Taiwan. I didn't know much about IT, which was daunting as it is possibly their biggest area of innovation. I took in as much as I could and hoped that I could engage positively and constructively on the trip.

A week later, I was back on the plane, exhausted but fulfilled after a fascinating, amazing visit to Taiwan. As the flight took off, I wondered to myself, as I have done many times since I became a senator: how the hell did I get here? A senator, me? How? I have not stood still long enough since I was voted in to look at my journey here or to even appreciate just how significant it is.

In my work and throughout my education I have always aimed to use whatever platform is available to me to address inequality, usually related to social class. Trinity and the Seanad have provided me with the platforms, and Tallaght provided me with grit and resourcefulness; I do not take any of these for granted.

Outside the walls of Leinster House I have been given opportunities that I never would have even dreamt of. I have been on *The Late Late Show*, stood on the stage at the Fringe as part of the amazing theatre piece *Riot*, advocated for reproductive rights in the Olympia and spoken on homelessness in the Abbey Theatre. I have met many amazing people and I have been especially encouraged and inspired by the young people I have met around the country when I am invited to speak in their youth clubs, Youthreach groups and in Mountjoy Prison. I have been humbled by the numbers of letters I have received from people around the country wishing me well, sharing their own life stories and thanking me for inspiring them.

I used to party at the Electric Picnic but now I have been honoured to be invited to speak there on issues such as the Eighth Amendment and mental health. I have shared a stage with my pal, the working-class hero Grace Dyas, and the powerful Mairead Healy at Body & Soul. Trinity alumni in London and in Northern Ireland have made me feel welcome as their guest and speaker at their events. I have stood in the Seanad chamber and won amendments to government legislation and I introduced my own legislation on drug decriminalisation.

Not so long ago, I would only have been able to name three Irish presidents: Mary Robinson, Mary McAleese and Michael D. Higgins. Now I can say I have shared a platform with Mary Robinson, greeted Mary McAleese and heard Michael D. Higgins say to my ma that she must be extremely proud of me.

CHAPTER 21:
THE CAGE YOU LIVE IN

I was still president of the Students' Union when I was approached by the street artist Joe Caslin. At that time, he was best known for his mural on George's Street during the marriage referendum. He seemed a little nervous chatting to me. He explained his idea for his new piece, "The Volunteers", which would be made up of four parts. He asked me to be part of the first installation, on the theme of addiction, and of course I jumped at the chance. I was in the Seanad before the piece was ready to be installed.

I couldn't believe my ears when Joe told me that the piece would be erected on the façade of the provost's offices in Front Square. Coincidentally I had published a bill on drug decriminalisation the same week. I had spent months preparing the bill alongside experts in the field, with a huge amount of input from Seb. The bill was drafted by Niall Neligan of DIT with support on its content from Niamh Eastwood, Executive Director of Release, and Damian Barrett, who was part of the UK delegation to the UN Commission on Narcotic Drugs. Aodhán Ó Ríordán and I had co-sponsored the bill and within a week there was a giant picture of me on the walls of Trinity.

In the picture, I am a volunteer in a 1916 bomb-carrying jacket, but replacing the bombs in the pockets is a copy of the Controlled Drugs and Harm Reduction Bill. Alongside me is Fiona O'Reilly, portraying a nurse attempting to pull the medical institutions into a twenty-first-century approach to drug use, and my good friend Rachael Keogh. The doctor is represented by a man who shall remain unnamed, although David Norris would jokingly suggest it is him. I can assure you it is not.

Lust for Life, a movement for mental health and wellbeing, came on board to support the piece. I was so excited to have addiction spoken about respectfully and openly and for Trinity to allow the conversation happen on their walls and display it across their historic buildings.

At the time I was publishing the bill, Lust for Life and others asked me why I care so much about the topic of drugs, and why I believe we must decriminalise addiction. I can only explain it through my life's experience. Most, if not all, of my volunteerism, my activism, my career in addiction and now my political work have been underpinned by my lived experiences. Drug use and the impacts of problematic drug use have been central in my search for more: more for myself and my community, more understanding, more empathy, more resources, more services and more connection. After what I would call a lucky escape from the grasp of drug addiction, I moved on to a career in the treatment of addiction and addressing the wider inequalities in society that create an environment in which drug abuse seems more attractive than reality. What starts out as temporary pain relief winds up bringing more pain, until reality and non-reality become equally painful. When I began setting up and developing drug services in Bluebell, I was conscious never to sell the false mantra: "Get clean and things will be better". When a person becomes drug-free, they also become friend-free, time-free and free from a sense of belonging.

For people on the outside looking in, the perception is often that there are two choices: either you take drugs or you decide not to take drugs. However, it isn't always a choice and free will is questionable. Maybe free will is a luxury. Or maybe we can only truly access free will when our basic human needs are met. Being socially responsible relies heavily on a foundation of safety, connectedness and a good standard of living.

Over the many years that I have worked and lived in communities destroyed by the heroin epidemic, I became aware that social class and addiction were killing us. I came to realise that not everyone was living like we were; not everyone was struggling to survive. Johann Hari, in his book *Chasing the Scream*, talks about how, for each traumatic event that happens to a child, they are up to four times more likely to grow up and experience addiction. When I think of this statistic, I think of the people I have worked with and how they often experienced trauma on a weekly basis. You do the maths on the likelihood of them ending up in addiction.

If we can accept that environment and early development have a role to play in addiction, then the only logical step is to redirect expenditure away from prosecution and prison and invest in communities and young people. We must move towards addressing the cause rather than putting plasters on the effect. It seems obvious that we should aim to build communities that can flourish and succeed, where individuals don't feel so disconnected and alone. Instead we spend millions on what fragmented societies produce instead of fixing what isn't working. I believe that most people can agree on the following two premises: problem drug use is harmful and prohibition has not worked. But we fail to reach a new conclusion.

I have worked with people between the ages of fourteen and eighty. My approach has been to take each person as they come. I recognise the story and life they have each lived and accept that recovery looks a little different for each of them. Hari writes that "addiction is an adaptation. It's not you – it's the cage you live in." I remember reading this and realising that there is no master key to set everyone free. There is no one-size-fits-all approach. The current system of criminalisation, shaming and stigmatisation must be abandoned to create a system that is holistic, diverse and accepting.

In all my years in this field I have attempted to create an environment for people to move at their own pace, to find their course of harm reduction or recovery, a path with which they were comfortable. Over time it became clear to me that the workers and the services on the ground aren't enough. We can develop programmes and facilitate individuals, but without changing society's perceptions of a person in addiction, how will they ever feel good enough? How will people ever feel like they belong if they open a newspaper and read a headline that calls them a zombie – a non-human, absent of consciousness? Why would any person caught up in addiction want to integrate into a society that labels them zombies and imprisons them for their addiction?

"The Volunteers" mural by Joe Caslin was about opening up those conversations. For me it is about challenging perceptions, addressing oppressive policy and raising awareness of a group of people that society excludes. I may now be political but for me this art piece, my Controlled Drugs and Harm Reduction Bill and my continued involvement with addiction services is not about politics. It's about my friends, family and community, who continue to deal with the impact of addiction and all that it brings. Drug abuse is a symptom of society's failings. It is time we wake up and stop blaming and shaming the individual.

In April 2018 I presented my case for drug decriminalisation to the working group set up by the Minister of State at the Department of Health with responsibility for Health Promotion and the National Drugs Strategy. In the room were experts in their fields, from retired judges, the DPP, government officials, doctors, the gardaí and one person representing service users. Everyone in the room had knowledge but also vested interests. I enjoyed the rigorous debate, but my fear is that people see too many obstacles that no one is willing to remove. I hope the group in its consultations and deliberations identify solutions and move towards a health-led approach to drug use, not a punitive one.

Change is a process of education. We cannot progress if we do not open up our minds and allow ourselves to go on that education journey. Social class is without a doubt in my mind the most important area where policy-makers and decision-makers need to open their minds to greater understanding.

Take risk as an example. People talk about taking risks in their lives. I once heard a girl from a well-off family speak about taking risks in life to pursue the thing that makes you happy. She spoke about changing jobs and dropping out of her degree to travel the world. This is all positive and, yes, we must pursue what is good for our souls and what makes us happy. But taking risks when you have a safety net is completely different from earning less than minimum wage, parenting alone and having no second-level education. You are not in a position to take risks. You are merely surviving and your options for pursuing happiness are limited by your need to provide the basics. In lower socio-economic classes, we take risks *with* our lives, not *in* our lives.

Ever since I was a teenager, every few weeks for years I would receive letters from lads in prison and it always struck me that those letters read like they were written by the teenagers they were supposed to be. So many sentences would begin with "When I get out I am going to . . ." – go back to school, join Youthreach, stop robbing, get a job, make it up to Ma. This always broke my heart as I quickly learnt that the aspirations they had as prisoners always fell by the wayside when they were back in the environments where the opposite of those aspirations was the norm.

I always held onto the young men's words in those letters as a clear sign of the role that environment plays. I knew something drastic had to change in the prison system and society if those young men would ever have the chance to fulfil their very simple goals. Those young boys blamed themselves for all their failings, and their parents blamed themselves, but something bigger is at play, something they cannot be blamed for, which is an unjust society. What happened to me, to the young men, to those struggling parents, is bigger than any individual. A young man in a cell decides all he wants to do is go back to school and get in no more trouble. But then what happens? Why doesn't he go back to school? The idea of him returning to school is based on his individual choice, but that is not met with a wider collective effort to address the problems of class. When you return to a household where there is not much money or education, where maybe your older siblings or a parent are in active addiction, your reality reminds you very quickly that school appears to be the least important thing in life. Finding ways to distract yourself from the shite around you is more achievable with a bag of cans and a joint than it is in a history class. So, these young men – and women – land back in reality and find a way to escape it again – as did I, almost every day, for years.

In 2017 I was invited to speak at Alexandra College in Dublin 6. It was a lovely evening and all the speakers were inspiring and entertaining. One woman, a past pupil of the school, spoke about her successful career and how she has maintained the friendships with the ten best friends that she made while at the school. They are also successful and scattered around the world.

I began to think about friends that I grew up with. So many of my childhood friends have died, while others have experienced addiction or mental health issues, and many have had to fight for everything they have achieved. Of course, many have done well but it hasn't always been easy, and we have all experienced more than our share of death. It really upset me that we live twenty minutes from Dublin 6, yet we are not reaching our full potential in the same way.

From the moment my friend Jenny died, when I was thirteen, our lives fell like dominos. Bernie, Tracy, John, Dotty, Curly, and many more, are all dead. We all started these lives together, we were all acting out together, we were all fighting, loving and laughing together, and I will never fully come to terms with the fact that I am one of the few left to tell the story. I get to tell my side, but they don't. Behind each death is their own story, their own loving family and their own struggles. Every death pushes me to fight for a wider understanding that social class kills.

It would take me a long time to find the words to verbalise this. Throughout my teenage years and beyond, my anger would continue to drive my decision-making. It is as though death would bring more and more of us together and it would drive bigger wedges between us and the adults in our lives. It seemed as though they didn't understand what we were going through.

Even now, my biggest fear in life is death. The phone rings late at night or a knock comes at the door, and I hope it's not a death. I open Facebook every morning with caution: *RIP, thoughts and prayers with the Farrell family today, the Killeen family, the Wade family, the Kinghorne family, the Ryan family, the Kelly family, the Maughan family,* and so on. Jenny died and the rest followed. Bernie, Tracy, John, Dotty, Curly, Nick, Tomo, Bobby, William, Git, Tommy, Kevin … the list goes on and on.

The list. That's not what they are. They aren't a list. We've seen everything from murder to suicide to overdose. We shed a tear when we hear their funeral songs, we remember them and the stories we shared, but it is as though we are locked in, always waiting for who is next. Someone is always next. I remember where I was when I heard the news of each death. I began to recognise the process.

For the first few deaths, I was floored. I would drink and cry myself to sleep. Then I began to expect death, so I would grieve but I would get on with my day. I hate this about myself. What am I? I feel like I have died inside each time this happens.

Grief didn't reveal this power I have to compartmentalise death and my daily duties so that I can continue my day after the death of a friend. It changed me. It made me expect death and it changed how I dealt with it. I wanted to give my friends' deaths the reactions they deserved — tears, screams, howls of pain — but no, I would get on with my day. I have learned to live in this pain; I know it so well. We have all grown so used to it. It numbs us.

I remember where I was when I was told John was dead. I was with Tracy. It was her twenty-first birthday. John died alone in a prison cell. Teenage life lost again. We sat in Tracy's sitting room sharing stories of John. Tracy was protective of him.

My brother phoned one day and I knew by his greeting that someone else was dead. This time, it was my friend Dotty. I felt the pain in my gut and I hung up the phone. Then I walked into the Hamilton Building and gave a talk to hundreds of potential mature applicants to the Trinity Access Programme. I talked to them about education and its importance and the transformative power it would have on their lives. I left out the fact that they would still be surrounded by pain and hardship in their communities. I left the lecture hall and then I repeated my brother's words to myself: Dotty is dead.

I remember sitting on the number 27 bus home that day, trying to go through my head for memories of Dotty. Every time someone dies I am afraid I won't be able to remember them. I smiled to myself as I remembered his little grin when I woke up with no eyebrows in his sitting room. Dotty was such a messer, but in moments like this I wish I had a scrap book of every experience I had with him and with others, especially when I know I will never make any new memories with them.

I remember the day of another friend's death. He was a giant. A big, complex giant, full of flaws and positives in equal measure — anger, sharp wit and, when you got close enough to him, a softness and insecurity that didn't match the version of himself he put out in the world. It was late and I was woken up by a panicked call from another friend, Aoife. Our friend had been in a bad car crash and it looked like he wouldn't make it. I bounced out of the bed and drove quickly to his friend's house. I banged frantically on the friend's door and got him to Tallaght hospital. We were too late. He was gone and we could not go in to say goodbye.

I got back into bed at four in the morning and woke to my alarm three hours later. I gave my kids their breakfast and dropped them to school, not yet mentioning to Jordanne that our friend was gone. They had an odd relationship; she was so tiny and he was so large but she had his attention every time she gave out to him about something. She would always tell him he needed to behave better and look after himself.

After dropping off the kids, I sat through a day's training on crack cocaine in Sophia Housing in Cork Street, as though it was any ordinary day. As though the night before was some normal event. I looked around at the faces in the room and I wanted to scream at them that our friend was dead and it was awful. But I didn't.

I remember the death of Tracy on 18 November 2004. I was sitting on the blue sofa in my parents' house when my phone buzzed with the text: Tracy was dead. I flung the phone across the room with the fright.

Twelve years later, to the day, Tracy's best pal Bernie would follow her. Tracy and Bernie were inseparable. Although I am not religious, I often hope that I am wrong and that they are together. Laughing, singing and most likely ripping the absolute piss out of someone.

Bernie's death in 2016 revealed to me that I can learn of death and then stand in the Seanad chamber and not mention it. I can cry all the way to work and then talk about canal boat licences. Inside, all I want to do is tell all the other senators to shut up, to stop taking pops at each other. I want them to know and understand that my childhood friends are dying.

Then there were the two phone calls I received from the Maughan family, one in 2015, one a year later. The Maughans are a Traveller family from my community. They are an important part of Tallaght, especially Killinarden, and are actively involved in the community and well respected. Joe, the father, founded the Sacred Heart Football Club and worked for years lobbying for the club to be given its own grounds – which eventually it was. He dedicated his life to generations of kids who came through the club.

In April 2015, I received a call to say that Joe and Nel's son William had gone missing. William and I had been friends for years and he had his ups and downs, but for the most part all he ever wanted to do was find a girl to marry and work hard like his father. He had been living on a site in Gormanston. He had decided he wanted to come home to Tallaght to work, and to get away from a gang he was living beside. He had called his ma to collect him, but by the time she arrived at the site, William and his girlfriend Ana had both vanished. I went straight up to the family home to see if I could do something.

Over the coming days I phoned my friends in the homeless sector to check the PASS system to see if William and Ana had stayed in any of the hostels. I didn't really know what else to do. I had no idea why they had just vanished. The family knew instantly that something bad had happened. To cut a long story short, we know now that William and Ana were murdered, though their bodies have not been found. The Maughan family have been strong, vocal and relentless in pursuing the killer, and it would appear that many people know who is responsible.

A year later, I received a call to say that the grave of William's brother Bobby had been vandalised. Bobby had died of meningitis a few years earlier. He was my friend and a great character. My fondest memory of Bobby was when he woke me up at seven o'clock one morning, banging on my ma's hall door, begging me to take him to the nuns. He wanted to take a pledge to stay off alcohol and, of course, as he had a strong Christian faith, this pledge would only be significant if there were nuns as witnesses. So off we went in search of the nuns.

Somebody had dug up Bobby's grave. Nel, Joe and all the family were understandably distraught. This was no random attack. They were being threatened by somebody who wanted to silence the Maughan family in their pursuit of justice. Travellers are a Christian community who take huge pride in the burial sites of their loved ones, so to pick the grave as a form of attack was hard-hitting and ruthless.

As a senator, I had hoped to be able to create change for those I love, for my community. I want them to stop dying. But when it comes to circumstances like this, I am helpless. I can't bring William's body home; I can't stop the escalation of gang violence. I want to, I try to, but, let's be honest, the best I can do is tell our stories in the hope that others will do something.

I cannot now or ever will allow myself to believe that violence and deliberately hurting someone else is something that any of us are OK with, and for the most part we all grew up to be non-violent adults.

We are being killed by class. Homelessness, addiction, risky behaviours and mental health are not just statistics to me, they are not the stories you read in the paper, they are my friends.

Death is inevitable and we all know it is coming to every one of us. We all experience loss at different stages of our lives and it does not always come in the form of a loved one passing away. Sometimes we feel loss when addiction or mental health has changed the relationship between us and a loved one, or sometimes we feel loss when our life's journey takes a different path from those around us.

Loss is everywhere and I have come to know it well. It is almost as familiar as an old friend. From the loss of a goldfish at five years old to the loss of a father at twenty-eight, I have learned to understand it, know it and expect it, but I have never learned how not to be shaped by it.

Throughout my first year in politics, which coincided with the final year in my degree, class was at the fore of my mind. I attempted to look at class through moral and ethical philosophy. I hoped it would help me to better understand "people like me" and how our class shapes us and influences us. When we unpack class we usually revert to sociological concepts. It is important to examine how class is produced if we are to attempt an assessment of its relation to morality.

Is the class system immoral? I believe it is. Whether it be Karl Marx or Pierre Bourdieu, we do not need to look too far for concepts of class. Several different theorists refer to a variety of different concepts of societal structure. However, I found Andrew Sayer's theories, in his book *The Moral Significance of Class*, the most relatable.

To me, it's also important to recognise that it's not just the "working class", it's the forgotten class: the homeless, the voiceless, the addicts, the young men in prison, and anyone else who has possibly never worked in their life. There are children born every day into intergenerational poverty and unemployment. There are families that have had three generations of addiction in the one household. Are they the working class? How do we define the working class? So many families have never benefitted from a wage or the positive experience of working and integrating with co-workers and all the positives that these social interactions can have on a person's professional and personal development. If the truth be told, we have various layers of class and they impact us differently and sometimes we move between them but mostly we exist side-by-side.

Ultimately, it did not matter how many books I read, philosophers I turned to or documentaries I watched; I have never fully settled on a theory of class. I think I am too close to it to have a theory. Instead my view is that the class we are born into is complete luck, moral luck even. However, luck plays no part in the fact that the class system is maintained.

Some of my friends still experience addiction or are involved in criminality. I will not abandon them, because they are the reason I am here. I will continue to fight for them as much as I fight for everything else that I do as a senator. Society often champions people like me for "becoming something" that they see as worthy of applause. But I want to be clear: I don't want to become something different. I want to flourish in my own community. I don't want to leave it and move to a nice house in some Dublin 6 location. So how do we achieve this? How do people like me flourish in communities like mine and who is going to help us achieve this? How do I translate what happens in my everyday life to the Seanad floor, to raise awareness of what is happening to people like me?

My story is my story, yet I couch it in political terms and tell it through tales of class and sociological concepts. There are two reasons for this. One is that I am scared to share and show my pain. Sharing life through a narrative like this helps me cope with the telling of my story. Second, I am intertwined completely with my class, my gender and my experience. Everything is an educational journey and that includes the telling of my life. My story is about "people like me" and we are "people like you".

I received a Christmas card in 2017 from a friend who has been a source of support to me over the last couple of years. We got to know each other because he is a big supporter of TAP. In his card he wished me well and said I was helping to change Irish society. I hope this is true, I hope I can play a part in changing Irish society, as it is not enough just to change our individual circumstances. As long as politics is a place where I can effect change, I will look to stay there.

CHAPTER 22:
ONE BRICK AT A TIME

Something beautiful has happened since I was elected to the Seanad; I have arrived fully in the world as a woman. I never truly connected with the power of my gender and I have always felt part of a class struggle much more than any struggles I may have experienced as a woman. So, in the centenary year of women's suffrage in Ireland, I can't help but feel excited for my future in my new skin, my female skin.

When I was younger I wanted to be a boy. I wanted to walk like a boy, talk like a boy and be with the boys, and I did everything I could to achieve this. I wanted to do what they did and go the places they went. My role models were male, the posters on my walls were all men and my respect for people tilted towards men. I believed men were better at their jobs. When I needed advice, I sought it from men.

I have no idea why this was the case. Maybe I had always subtly received these messages. I was surrounded by strong women, but working-class women are often silently strong. They don't talk about gender or misogyny and they often do not see themselves as any different from their male friends and family members. I believe that this is because we share similar struggles – with problematic drug and alcohol use, low levels of education and high levels of income inequality. Many families have multiple tragic deaths in one household and our streets are filled with trauma. When we are firefighting at that level, recognising the impact of our gender is often lost. It was to me anyway.

That week-long event on politics at An Cosán, where I first learned that women didn't always have the vote, was my first real inkling of the impact of gender inequality. I remember walking down the hallways of An Cosán and gazing at the black-and-white pictures of women in the early 1900s, fighting for our right to be heard, to have our vote count. I vowed in that moment always to vote, a promise that I kept, though it took me many more years to understand just how much women were locked out of public life.

As I have said many times, I went to Trinity to learn the language of power, a language I had no access to. Everything I went to Trinity for I got, and so much more. I finally tapped into the language and power of my gender, of who I am as a woman. My views on inequality and the unjust society were cemented and reinforced, but I also evolved as a woman.

My feminism is here to stay. It is a feminism I did not know was sitting there underneath my childhood desires to be a boy. My feminism has allowed me to replace all those childhood memories that airbrushed women out of my sight. I can now see the women that were always around me. The women who, with very little income, managed to ensure their babies were warm, fed and in school on time – often managing this alone – or in tough or violent households. I now see the woman who, even in the depth of addiction, never missed a parent–teacher meeting. I see the woman who made sure her kids were at every single one of their football games through rain, hail and snow, and who stood strong at the sideline cheerleading her kids alone, not a father in sight. I see the woman whose son was murdered but who still volunteers in the local services. I see the woman who lost six kids to heroin offering comfort to her neighbours when they experience the same. I have always been surrounded by warrior women, feminists like me who didn't know that that is what they were. Never complaining, never knowing that the injustices they have faced are not faced by everyone, and always remaining strong in their silence.

Is my mother a feminist? Ma is the unsung hero of my life. She has been a strong, consistent source of support and love. She has worked hard her whole life, but I can honestly say I have never heard her complain. She gets up, does her day's work, goes to the gym in the evening and then watches TV for an hour before bed. As well as raising me and my brother, she has helped me rear my children, she has let us live with her rent-free, and she has championed me every step of the way. Even when my da was alive, my ma was the one who painted, changed the plug fuses and put the flat packs together.

In her forties, Ma took a diploma in business management and was the production manager in Uchiya Ireland. She employed half of the estate and lots of my friends.

Everyone loves my ma. She is the least judgemental person I know. She has a whopper sense of humour but she knows when it's important to lay down the law.

She nursed the man of her dreams through years of illness and lost him in 2013 when she was only in her early fifties. I would love for her to find happiness again. Every time I say to her, "Ma, would you not meet someone new?" her response is, "It wouldn't be fair, I would only ever compare them to your da".

I wish we had been friends growing up. I wish I hadn't fucked her over, I wish I had got to know her better. The anger that controlled my life at that time blocked me from recognising who my parents always were and the lovely life that we had. My ma remained true to her word no matter how horrible I was to her. She supported me one hundred per cent.

As I grew older and began to understand the importance of agency and autonomy, I finally realised that choice is one of the most important forms of support a mother can give. It would take years to give my mother the respect she deserves. I try to make up for it now.

My favourite thing to do now is to take my ma to fancy events, to watch her get dressed up and enjoy a free glass of wine in a green room. At a friend's fiftieth birthday recently, she sat on a bar stool, tapping her feet to the music. She leaned in and said, "This is my favourite night so far." This means so much to me, not just because of everything I put her through, but because enjoying a night out without my da is a big thing for her. She misses him so much.

I recently took her to the annual An Cosán fundraiser in the Shelbourne on International Women's Day. She ordered a new dress for the occasion. We were meant to head to Áras an Uachtaráin afterwards but instead, tipsy on wine, we arrived at the women's march in town in evening dresses. I was proud to march beside my ma. As we stood on the steps to the Custom House, an anti-choice protester barged his way to the steps and began shouting at the crowd. He had a placard with "Murder" written on it. As women from the crowd tried to cover his sign, I made my way off the steps, pulled it from his hands and threw it out of reach, behind the railings of the Custom House.

I looked at my ma and caught a glimpse of the worried look on her face. She obviously still has memories of me as a very con- frontational young woman. I am sure she was worried I would end up scrapping on the steps of the Custom House. She gave me a relieved smile when she knew that now I stand up for myself and for others, but the violence inside my soul has subsided. I don't need to shout and fight anymore, not in the unhealthy way I once did. My actions don't stem from hurt. Everything I do now, I do out of love, out of passion and out of ambition. I have a different approach to life now. It's one of vision and education.

My daughters thankfully know their value, worth and power and struggling in silence will hopefully never be an issue for them. I truly believe ending intergenerational poverty and low education attainment begins by educating women – mothers and daughters. My new-found sense of feminism goes beyond thinking about gender and has begun to seep into my work in the Seanad. I feel comfortable in a space where I can attempt to represent groups from lower socioeconomic backgrounds as well as fighting for women from across social divides. I have witnessed my politics and my feminism evolve in parallel. When I speak, I speak from everything I am as a Tallaght woman, but my voice has gained in strength and articulation through Trinity. When I speak in the Seanad or amend legislation, it is for an often-silent majority; when I speak, the people of my past, present and future merge into one. My work has become about addressing the inequalities that I saw all around me in my past.

Politics is a better place with women in there fighting for women. I am honoured to be part of that. Working alongside women from all parties and none has really shown me the power of women when we unite. Of course, women from different classes have different struggles so we must ensure progression for all. Being a woman can leave you at a disadvantage, but being a woman from a lower socio-economic class can leave you completely out of the picture. We must work effortlessly to bring all women with us – Traveller women, migrant women, women with disabilities, LGBTQ+ women and women of all social classes and sectors of society. We are stronger together.

Nowhere was this more evident than in the committee on the Eighth Amendment. I spent three months on this committee; it felt like the biggest piece of work I had done to date. This committee reinforced my belief in the power of educating people. I learned more from listening to the voices of those who spoke to the committee than I had learned in my whole life.

I feel honoured that I witnessed the likes of Senator Ned O'Sullivan take in what he was hearing in a spirit of openness and

217

compassion. I have huge respect for him and others who went on that journey. I felt a strong sense of solidarity amongst the women on this committee. I felt we could achieve great things when we work together rather than against each other.

As I drove to work on the morning of the vote, 13 December 2017, I sang Bob Marley's "Redemption Song" at the top of my voice, tears rolling down my cheeks. I felt so emotional about the vote, which ultimately recommended a "repeal simpliciter" and access to abortion for up to twelve weeks' gestation, without restriction.

During the repeal campaign, the weeks go so fast. Every second person I meet asks, "How's the campaign going, Lynn?" I usually respond, "I'm trying not to think about it". This is not true. It is all I think about. What if it doesn't pass? What will that look like for the women of Ireland? What if it's really as close as they are all saying? I spend the final weeks touring Dublin, Portmarnock, Coolock, Cork Street and more, talking to communities and preparing canvassers for the conversations they will have on doorsteps. I worry that I might not be doing enough, but I can't fit more time into my day. Over the course of three weekends I canvass alongside the Dublin South West crew, and they are growing in numbers. I am glad to take a back seat here: to just be Lynn, not a senator. I just go where the hard-working and dedicated canvass leaders tell me to go.

The day before the result I worry we haven't had enough time, even though I also want it to be over. It's silly, really, when I think about it. Women have had this amendment hanging over them since 1983, and I wasn't even born. Ireland was ready, the generations of women and families before me were ready – it was me who wasn't ready.

In a last push I step onto a mini bus headed for Roscommon to support the local campaigns of Boyle, Leitrim and Longford. I nearly didn't make it. Alice Mary Higgins wasn't going to tell me where the bus was going from or what time. She had been all over the west canvassing, just like Colette Kelleher had been in Cork, and she felt that I was needed more in Tallaght. I assured her the campaign team in Tallaght was strong and big, and I really wanted to leave Dublin at least once during the campaign. She wasn't giving in, though, until Teresa Newman said, "You know Lynn really wants to go on the bus" – Teresa knew I had spent the afternoon texting people to ask if they had organised a bus to Roscommon.

The next morning, I arrive on Bachelors Walk, getting more and more excited about our canvass as I watch a diverse group of people arriving to help out. Then Alice Mary arrives and, with a big embrace, says, "I am so glad you're coming".

As we arrive in each county that day I become more confident that we are going to win this referendum. As we stand outside shops in Boyle, we get a simple nod. People may refuse a leaflet or badge, but they nod in our direction. We have been fed a line for months about the silent no, but now I begin to think it is a silent yes.

We soon move on to Leitrim and, as I walk through a small green area, I sit down on a bench and chat to the locals – all the conversations are positive. By the end of our time in Carrick-on-Shannon, the town is erupting with the noise of beeping cars, honking trucks and 'Yes' being shouted from the windows of vans and taxis – the melody of an ice-cream van playing in the background. The No campaigners are a little further down the road and it is much quieter at their end, with the odd beep every few minutes. I somewhat admire their staying there and sticking it out; I would be distraught standing there if the support was in their favour.

We move on to the bridge that joins Roscommon and Leitrim, and hang our Together for Yes banners over the bridge. We wave the county flag high in response to more beeps as drivers make it known that they intend to be on the right side of history. People like Colm O'Gorman, Ruth Coppinger, Clare Daly and others are confident that Ireland is ready for this. Ruth says that politicians are behind on this issue, not the people. I should have listened and taken comfort in their confidence but I was too anxious.

We finish the day off in Longford and the street we arrive on is filled with No posters, but then we meet a group of Longford campaigners lining the street with banners, doling out leaflets and cheers. The campaigns in these small towns and rural areas deserve huge commendation; they are small but dedicated groups that cover huge amounts of space.

The energy is high as we make our way back to Dublin. I lay my head on Alice Mary's shoulder. She looks at me and says, "I am so glad we spent the last day of the campaign together." So am I.

I open my eyes on the morning of 25 May and we are itching to get out and vote. The sun is shining and there is an excitement in the air. We quickly walk to where my boyfriend's polling station is. He looks at me and says, "I have never walked to vote with such purpose." As soon as we're done, I'm eager to go get my ma. She can't concentrate on her work so she is happy when I call to take her out to vote. As we head to the voting booth we drive past my sister-in-law, Laura, and my nephew, Caiden, who are full of smiles as they make their way back home having cast their yes votes. Ma and I are buzzing to be voting together, and Jordanne and Jaelynne are slightly unhappy that they aren't old enough to do the same. Jordanne gets plenty of texts throughout the day from friends and family to let her know that they cast their votes for her, including her uncle Jay and her da.

As the day goes on, I notice people around Tallaght updating their Facebook statuses to say they voted yes and I feel a huge sense of pride in my friends, family and community. Everyone saying yes. Adrenalin runs through my body and I can't sit still, so I decide to meet up with some of the Dublin South West campaign team who are out reminding people to vote on their way home from work. As we stand together, banner in hand at the Spawell roundabout, I again find myself listening to an orchestra of honking horns and cheers of support from the passing traffic.

My spirits are so lifted by all of this that instead of going home, I go to Donnybrook to meet friends for a quick drink and a chat. When I arrive I can feel the excitement, nervousness and tiredness of Tara Flynn, Roisín Ingle and Sinéad Gleeson. When Anna Cosgrave arrives, she looks scared enough for us all. Our conversation turns to the 'what ifs', but we reassure each other by talking about all of the positive experiences we've had on the campaign trail. Tara is almost tearful when she says, "Lynn, is Ireland going to welcome us home tomorrow?" This sentence stuck with me all night. Imagine Ireland didn't welcome Tara home, or all the other people who have had to travel.

Colm O'Gorman is having none of this worry. He keeps insisting that we will win this referendum by 65 per cent or more. We all look at him as if he is mad but we also want to believe him. I can't stay here any longer so I go home, my fear about the exit polls taking over. I ring Alice Mary on my way and she is still walking up and down canals and Luas stops, making sure those enjoying a few drinks in the sun have voted. She does this until the polling stations close.

I'm not long in the door when the exit polls come in. There it is: 68 per cent. A landside for Repeal! The *Irish Times* exit poll comes in first, followed by RTÉ's, which shows a similar result. Jaelynne leaps off the sofa and begins to dance like she's never danced before: "That's my victory dance, Ma!"

I think to myself that there's no way both polls could get it so wrong, but I have to see those boxes opening in Citywest the next morning all the same. From the Committee on the Eighth Amendment to the day of the vote, everything has been a team effort. The whole country has been a team: Seb and Mairead Enright made sure I was ready for every committee meeting, Jaelynne canvassed everyone from my hairdresser to my nail technician, and Jordanne campaigned relentlessly both online and off-line. Everyone got us here. Every jumper Anna sold, every conversation Amnesty started, every march led by the Abortion Rights Campaign, every rally the Coalition and ROSA had. Every single conversation at kitchen tables around the country got us here.

I float around the RDS for the afternoon hugging everyone, high on a combination of relief and excitement. It all hits me right in the face as I stand onstage that evening in Dublin Castle looking out at thousands of happy faces, banners flying high. I stand still, take a breath and say to myself, "We have choice. I have choice."

I can't help but feel pride as a woman. As we celebrate the women who fought for our suffrage, I have begun to take stock of how far we have come and I am eager to map the way forward, together. What are our values as women? Do we value ourselves? How can we ensure that all women feel the value that I now feel today? I know my worth, but there are many women who still feel they are worthless. As a woman, a feminist and a citizen, am I doing enough? Is it enough to find the gender gaps at the top while thousands of women are still at the bottom? I don't feel it is, so I will strive to focus on those women who are ignored, as I once was. Was it enough to win the vote in 1918 if still today large cohorts of women cannot participate in public life? Let's remember the women of the early 1900s by fighting together to remove the barriers to women's participation.

Dorothy Day once said:

> People say, what is the sense of our small effort? They cannot see that we must lay one brick at a time, take one step at a time. A pebble cast into a pond causes ripples that spread in all directions. Each one of our thoughts, words and deeds is like that. No one has a right to sit down and feel hopeless. There is too much work to do.

I want to be one of those bricks. I want to become part of the foundations of equality for women.

CHAPTER 23:
FLOURISHING

When I was growing up, I was fixated on the age of thirty-two. I think it was the age my ma was before I found out about my da. I was convinced if I could make it to thirty-two I would be safe. I was right.

As I turned thirty-two, my personal life began to flourish. I was in the final year of my degree, Jordanne was starting the Trinity Access Programme, Jaelynne was becoming the most powerful young feminist I know and I was elected to the Seanad. I was much more centred and the kids were benefitting from the new space I was in. I was so much more certain of myself and I was becoming stronger as a woman. Being thirty-two was turning out to be all that I hoped it would be. I even allowed myself to love again.

I had just left the Fringe Festival where I was the surprise guest on the amazing show *Riot*. It was the first time I had heard Emmet Kirwan's spoken-word piece *Heartbreak*, part of the show. It made me cry. How could this man capture so many of my thoughts in a poem? It was as though he was retelling my life. He didn't know anything about me, yet I thought he knew all of me. His poem wasn't about me, but it could have been. It was about working-class young mums like me. Jordanne would later play the role of that young woman in the short film, *Heartbreak*. As I left the Fringe I went to meet with Amo (Anne-Marie McNally of the Social Democrats), who was having a couple of drinks with her campaign team in a bar on Dame Street.

After an hour or so a young man walked in. Rónán. We had met before so I said hello and we chatted away. As we talked, I realised we were staring into each other's eyes a little longer than we should have been. I got a bit freaked out. I felt connected to him, to the gentleness in his manner. I skipped ahead a few years and ran through our lives. He was twenty-five. He was too young. He had no kids, and I didn't want any more. He is gentle and I am loud. I would petrify him. I had to save myself from a future heartache. I visualised myself breaking his heart or him leaving me because he wanted a family. I hadn't so much as kissed Rónán and, in my mind, we had already had a life together and a painful break-up. So I stood up and declared I was going home. I went home to protect us both from this made-up story in my head.

The next day, I couldn't stop thinking about Rónán. His nice smart look, his fuzzy dark hair, but mostly his gentle eyes. He seemed too innocent for me. Life has battered me somewhat and I felt that any boyfriend I had would have to be as hardened as me. Maybe I would be too rough and feisty for Rónán. Obviously, I shouldn't do his thinking for him and convince myself of things that I have no clue of, but I was scared of heartbreak and rejection.

I sat down for breakfast the next day with Katriona O'Sullivan, another woman I regard as a working-class warrior woman. I chatted to her about Rónán as, coincidentally, she sits on the board of One Family with him. She encouraged me to let go of my preconceived ideas and text him. She gave me his number, so I did.

We texted back and forth for hours but it was the following week at the March for Choice before we would meet again. I was like a giddy child. I didn't have to convince myself to go on a date with him. It was natural and I wanted to. It wasn't long before we were spending every day together and I fell in love for the first time in my adult life.

There had been brief relationships in my twenties that I had thought might have been love, but with Rónán in my life I knew how love should really feel. The equality in it. Not one of us giving more than the other; both of us wanting to be around each other in equal measures. I couldn't stop touching him, holding his hand, stroking his face. The impulse to be in his arms was like nothing I had ever felt.

At Da's funeral, I had said that I would never settle for less than my parents had. Well, I think I found it. Maybe it does exist. Maybe we have it. With Rónán, I am not competing with anything else; he is in this with me. He is smart and compassionate, which is why he is so suited to the career he has chosen – building social enterprises with the objective of improving people's lives. I never feel unsafe in his presence and I absolutely love the fact that drugs, criminality and death haven't featured in his life as they have in mine. He understands it all though – he grew up in Clondalkin and runs community initiatives in Ballyfermot.

In Rónán, I have found the most beautiful human being to call my partner. To me he is perfect, we fit perfectly, and I have softened in his embrace and healed a little more with his love. I have not felt loneliness since he came into my life. I am often much more emotional than him and he always creates the space for me to express myself. Not that I need someone else to facilitate me in expressing myself, but Rónán is the first man in many years who encourages it and doesn't fight back against it or make it about him. I can be me in the relationship, he can be him. It is the nicest space I have ever been in with a man. I'm more mature now, I have succeeded in my education and all that I have achieved has been as a strong, independent, single woman, so I am no longer afraid that I am trying to take cover in a man's confidence. I have my own, and I believe that this is what he loves about me. I no longer have to pretend to have a soft side, it's now there for him to see. For all to see.

In the years since my da died, we have all tried to find out how we would fit together in his absence. For a while, I took my eye off the ball with Jordanne. That year, 2013, she was heartbroken and grieving as much as I was but I was consumed with my own sorrow. Jordanne was slowly going into her own little shell. She had it extra hard as her dad had possibly his worst relapse to date that year. Alan wasn't in a very good place and he made a lot of bad choices, which resulted in him going to prison for a number of years.

So, Jordanne lost two male figures in one year and this took its toll on her mental health. She had been feeling anxious that year, which is to be expected with all that she was going through, but I had not really expected for her to become as depressed as she became. It was hard to take and I was scared. After months of anxiety and severe sadness, she dipped into a space where suicide ideation came to the fore of her thinking. I was terrified when I first heard her speak those dreaded words:

"I do not want to feel anymore. I want to die."

In the end, two factors took Jordanne out of that space. First, we went to Pietà House; and second, the most amazing opportunity came her way when she was offered the lead in a film about suicide.

I spotted a Facebook post about a film by Frank Berry. Inspired by an article written by Dr Tony Bates, it was set in Tallaght and addressed the difficult topic of cluster suicides. Auditions were being held in the Killinarden Community Centre the next day and Jordanne eagerly went along without a nervous thought in her head. They were instantly impressed with her and she was hired straight away to play the lead role in *I Used to Live Here*.

The time and patience Da had put into watching all of Jordanne's performances would come to good use. Between her productions in the Joneses' and my da's encouragement, she was well prepared to pursue her love of acting. I also really believe this role was therapeutic for her and allowed her to play out the depths of her despair in an artistic way.

Every weekend for months Jordanne dedicated her life to the film. She was missing her dad and I was missing mine, but she pushed on through. This opportunity couldn't have come at a better time and she flourished. All the energy inside was being channelled through this role. You could say she played out her grief on screen. The raw talent and honesty she had was instantly felt by anyone in her presence. I was and am in awe of her. She showed no fear, just emotion, and she was putting it on display through her acting.

She got every ounce of recognition she deserved. The day of the screening was such a wonderful moment for her, and for us. The Ruanes and the Joneses all sat together in the IMC in the Square, as proud as punch of Jordanne. We would boast about her every opportunity we could. Jordanne herself was always modest, more reserved and less of a show-off than me.

Another amazing recognition of her talent came when she was nominated for an Irish Film and Theatre Award for best female lead. Ma and I sat in the Round Room of the Mansion House on the night of the awards ceremony, feeling like we were dreaming. Jordanne wore a beautiful gold dress. I looked at her, her sallow skin, her dark hair, her gentle presence, and I knew that all she really wanted was for her da and granda to be there, more than she wanted any IFTA. I wish she could have had that too and I know her da and mine would have given anything if they could have been there. She didn't win that time around but there was a rousing round of applause when her face came on the screen.

She was excelling professionally, had been signed up to the Lisa Richards Agency and was receiving positive reviews and awards. She received a scholarship for Bow Street and I thought to myself: we are set. She would feel empowered by this and the sorrow she felt would hopefully be equalled by the amazing opportunities she is getting. She never let an opportunity pass. She took on every new role and every new experience, no matter how difficult she found things. Her amazing talent to act and to follow her dreams was stronger than any pain. Jordanne is beautifully complex and equally as talented. She has no idea how special she is.

Our lives are so intrinsically linked that often our life choices work in tandem with one another. Jordanne's courage triggers my bravery and my determination aids hers. Jaelynne is our constant source of certainty. Unlike us, she is steady in herself. She has her own vision for life and she is confident in who she is. Or more confident than we are. Jaelynne can't be forced into situations that she doesn't want to be in and she puts herself first more than we do. She brings me and her sister back to earth more often than not. She is a realist and she is loyal; I am an idealist but forceful; and Jordanne is creative but passive and gentle. We are a mixed bag and for the most part we embrace that.

In times of anxiety or change Jordanne likes to be on her own; maybe even needs to be on her own. Sometimes I manage this well, but sometimes I throw fuel on the fire, pushing and pushing with questions: "What is wrong?" "Why have you changed so suddenly?" This aggravates the situation and I should know better. Anger grips Jordanne so I know things are bad. I would later learn how to respond better to Jordanne, not continually pick at her and push her to be OK just so I would be OK. I learned that it wasn't really anger but, in a sense, an emotional tiredness, and I kept disturbing the rest she needed.

Only three times in Jordanne's whole life have I seen her react this way to my constant questioning about how she's feeling. When I see it, I know she has hit breaking point. She would clearly demand that I leave her alone, but my fear wouldn't allow me to give her space. I needed her to tell me she was OK. I would want her to take that hurt and launch it at me with full physical force. I would not be thinking rationally, but in those moments I would have two thoughts: 1) I must have failed as a mother and I deserve whatever she gives me right now; and 2) maybe she can get all this sadness out, she can punch and kick me all she likes until she empties it all out. Maybe it would help. She has so much self-control and really just wanted a few days to gather herself – it was me who was making the situation worse.

This anger was never part of who she was. Looking at it now, it was never anger – it was pain. She was in pain. And it was on those three occasions that I heard those words: "I want to die." The first time I heard those words was on that occasion in 2013.

By January 2017, Jordanne was growing more and more distant from me. She was lying wide awake for half of the night for weeks and sleep deprivation was kicking in. She was studying for hours on end, terrified of the Leaving Cert. Her whole life, she has built structures and timetables. When she was eight I found pages in her wardrobe reading: *7.00 wake up, 7.03 brush teeth* . . . and so on. She often committed herself to unrealistic schedules and wound up feeling a huge sense of failure if she didn't get through all the tasks she had set herself. Her hard work and commitment never translated fully in her exam results. She never felt she was good enough and teachers' comments that she needed to work harder or study more, as you can imagine, added to her feeling that she was stupid and not good enough. This is not the fault of the teachers as they have been conditioned somewhat to look at results. The education system often wrongly assumes that exam results are a reflection of how much study you do. This could not have been further from the truth for Jordanne. She did work hard; in fact she worked too hard.

Her school experience was saved by an amazing teacher. Vaughan Byrne was a young teacher in Killinarden Community School. Jordanne got through school because of his teaching style and his rapport with the kids. He was interested in them and expanded their knowledge beyond the curriculum. He was that one good adult she so desperately needed during some of her toughest years.

Even so, this period led to one of the darkest times in Jordanne's life. Even I couldn't enter her world and negotiate with her. She was on self-imposed lockdown and I was frightened beyond words. I was sure

I was about to lose my daughter to suicide, so much so I couldn't sleep. I was on high alert and every noise in the night made me jump. If I heard something fall I would jump to my feet and run to her room, always panicked that I would open the door to find my daughter hanging. I couldn't escape this awful imagery in my mind, not even as I slept.

At the end of January, I was booked to speak at the Education World Forum in London. The night before the trip, I dreamt that I heard a noise out the back. I found Jordanne on the ground at the back door underneath the washing line. Her eyes were wide open and the tears were completely still on her face, as if they were frozen. I took her face in my hands and turned her head towards me. I was horrified to realise that her head was detached from her body. I kneeled in the back garden, with my daughter's head in my hands as she began to cry. "I am sorry Mam, I am sorry."

My hands are shaking as I write this. It was so real, it did not feel like a dream.

The next morning, I reluctantly packed my bag and headed for the airport. As I sat waiting to board, I texted my ma, Rónán and my friend Katriona, saying: "I don't want to go. I have a bad feeling about Jordanne." They all rang me and I told them that I couldn't stop my tears coming. "I think Jordanne wants to die." I told them about my dream. In fact, it wasn't really a dream, was it? She was, in real life, moving further and further away from me. Unlike the other times I was concerned about her, this time it felt more real. It felt like life and death. I felt helpless.

By now I was sitting on the plane and that was when fate stepped in. The flight was delayed due to fog in London; we could be on the plane for an hour. I was still in floods of tears as I jumped up and asked to be let off. The cabin crew told me I wouldn't be able to get back on the flight. I didn't care. I needed to get to Jordanne.

I burst through the front door to find Jordanne on the sofa. She began to cry and rock back and forth, her knees held up to her chest.

She was frightened. She looked me in the eye and said, "Mam, you asked me the other day to promise you that I wouldn't hurt myself. Well, I am sorry, but I can't make that promise." I held her in my arms and, just like I had promised my da years earlier, I assured her I would find a way to fix this.

After many years of holistically trying to support Jordanne through some tough times in her life, I pushed past my fear of doctors and brought her to the GP. There are obviously amazing doctors, but I have always been concerned about people being medicated unnecessarily. However, Jordanne has been in and out of counselling from a very young age. She is always proactive in caring for her health and engages positively with counselling. She went to a local boxing club for many years to help channel some of her energy and she generally reached out when she needed to most. Her actions are always positive, even during her scariest times, never turning to alcohol or drugs or engaging in negative behaviours. Unlike me as a teenager, she has resourced herself well. We put plans in place after her visit to the GP. For one thing, I began to change how I responded to her. Her darkest days were always made either worse or better by how I responded. I didn't always get it right.

The next six months were a mixture of ups and downs. I began to see huge improvements in her thinking and in her interactions with the world. She has always worked hard in her acting roles and this has been a constant positive in her life. However, the summer of 2017 saw Jordanne dip again. She lost her step-mam; she was, and still is, devastated by this loss. She has two young brothers and a little sister and her heart broke not only for her relationship with her step-mam but also for her siblings and her dad. Jordanne and her siblings all look so alike and Jordanne has some lovely memories of spending time with her dad, his partner and the kids.

Jordanne and her aunt had the heart-breaking task of visiting Alan to tell him the awful news that the mother of his babies, the woman he loves, was gone. Jordanne insisted on this. She told him: "Dad, we need you. Me and the kids need you. Please don't do anything stupid." Jordanne was petrified of losing her da too. It didn't matter how many times I assured her that her da would want now, more than ever, to get back home to them all. She was so scared he would soon be gone too.

In the middle of all of this, she sat her Leaving Cert. It was only after it was finished that the impact of her loss became obvious. One day in July, we were packing a lunch to head off to Glendalough for the day. To my surprise, Jordanne had agreed to come along with me, Jaelynne and Rónán. We were almost ready to leave when Jordanne's mood quickly changed. She retreated into her familiar pod of self-protection. I reverted to my pushing: "What's wrong? It's not fair on your sister, she was looking forward to you coming." I felt like I was losing her again. This time, after she said those words "I want to die", I drove her straight to the hospital. After hours in A&E, Jordanne had a very positive experience with the psychiatrist on duty. She was referred to Child and Adolescent Mental Health Services at the Lucena Clinic in Tallaght.

Jordanne's first appointment with the mental health assessment team in the Lucena Clinic was scheduled for October 2017, at a time when I was processing a lot of buried trauma from having been raped. That morning we decided to walk and leave the car at home. We talked the whole way down to the clinic, mostly about Jordanne's first few weeks in college. Her biggest goals were to do well and, more importantly, to fit in as who she is, not as someone she was trying to be. The apple doesn't fall far from the tree so Jordanne has a philosopher's streak, and we went deeper and deeper into conversation. We discussed identity. Are we true to ourselves, are we trying to reinvent ourselves or are we on a constant voyage to discover all the hidden layers of who we are? Like me, Jordanne questions her worth and she does this while never treating herself as worthless. I told her that, even though sometimes she doesn't feel as though she is good enough, she has the skill of self-preservation rather than self-destruction, and that is to be admired.

We arrived at the Lucena Clinic. In the waiting room were two other young people with their guardians. The room was silent. Jordanne whispered to me, "Ma, this is wrong. Everyone here is probably struggling like me or searching for help and answers. But we can't even look each other in the eye." She made an effort to smile at the other people in the room, then very loudly started to talk about everything that came into her head. Her voice broke the eerie silence and people began to shift a little in their seats.

Jordanne reached out to hold my hand and laid her head on my shoulder. As always, she gives me comfort in her public displays of love for me. I am always aware of our dependence on each other. She depends on me to facilitate the structure and accept all that she brings to me; and I depend on her to remind me that I am not alone and that she is not going anywhere, no matter how old she gets. If I was to explore it a little more, maybe we dip over into a co-dependent type of mother–daughter relationship, but for the most part it's a positive reliance.

Finally, we were called. The team went back and forth between me and Jordanne, exploring our lives from the beginning. Jordanne was born in the millennium year on a bank holiday Monday in August. She was a healthy baby, with dark hair and sallow skin. She suffered terribly with chronic bronchitis, often resulting in trips to A&E. I thought I must be doing something wrong, yet I was protecting her from all I thought could have caused her chest problems. I had never smoked during pregnancy and our home was smoke-free. I would never bring her into a smoker's home. She was eventually diagnosed with asthma but as she got a little older it all went away.

I told them how she walked on her tip-toes until she was nearly ten. How she spent a lot of time on her own, with only a pencil or a paintbrush to keep her company. When she was six, her dad first went to prison and she slept with a photo of him and her. There were Winnie-the-Pooh figurines on the frame. Once I fell asleep before I got a chance to take it off her. She held the frame so tightly that, when she woke the next morning, the shape of Winnie-the-Pooh's honeypot was imprinted on her face. She would look forward to visiting her dad but her anxiety would reach such high levels knowing she would have to leave him again that she would vomit all the way home. I was only twenty and to be honest I was making it up as I went along. I was trying to help and support her while also ensuring she maintained her relationship with her dad.

I was never afraid to ask for guidance and this has stood to Jordanne. I was always so concerned about failing her that I would look to organisations and counsellors who might be able to help. I told the mental health team how, through all the ups and downs of Jordanne's life, she remained this quiet, polite and well-behaved kid. She would never have stood out to teachers as a little girl who needed support.

As Jordanne and I walked the team through her life we began to recognise things about her that we hadn't previously. We made connections where we hadn't seen them before. In his book *The Philosopher and the Wolf*, Mark Rowlands talks about the stories we tell ourselves. The story I told myself was that Jordanne is a little quiet and likes to be on her own sometimes. She cleans a lot to have control because she couldn't control other aspects of her life where there was old trauma. I told myself that Jordanne's personality, quirks included, were all caused by external things out of Jordanne's control. Which is only partly true.

The story Jordanne told herself was that she is not good enough, that she lets people down, that she has to try harder and that she doesn't really fit in, that mammy being angry must mean she has done something wrong and that daddy struggling to stay clean must mean he doesn't love her enough. The stories we tell ourselves build a narrative of our lives that is not always accurate; now, at last, I was beginning to gain some insight into my daughter's story.

After four hours of mapping her life, our lives, from pregnancy and birth to the present, we began to move towards a diagnosis that made more sense than anything I could have imagined: Jordanne has Asperger's Syndrome. It is mild, but it explains a lot.

And so it is 2018 and Jordanne has yet again proven to me that she is stronger than anyone I have ever met. She is eighteen this year – an adult. Throughout it all – the lows of her undiagnosed Asperger's and the highs of her burgeoning acting career – she kept her sense of self. She opened up when she needed to and she always sought out the answers that would move her in the right direction. I watch her now in the Trinity Access Programme and she is excelling. She works hard and I will never get bored of saying, "Jordanne is the lead in a film. Yeah, it's out this year." To think, when she was younger, I tried to tell her to pick another dream, something more achievable. She knew what she wanted, she knew what was inside of her. Not only is she an amazing actress and activist but after a rough few years in secondary school she now realises what an amazing student she is too. When she rings me and tells me about her essays or excellent results, I take a big breath of relief.

Jaelynne has always been so full of energy and questions. She likes to engage at an intellectual level. At eleven years of age, she can pick out sexism more quickly than anyone I know. It's like a feminist super-power. She is the most loving human I know and if she could spend all her time with me, she would.

I watch her with all her little cousins. All boys on her dad's side. She is so maternal and loving. She wants to sit and show me photos of them on her phone and tell me all about what they did that day. She is more maternal with her cousins than I had the time to be with her.

The day Jaelynne was born I had promised her the world, but then I had to leave her for eight hours a day to get her that world. I was working over forty hours a week, pursuing my career in Bluebell, and then in Trinity, and she was at home with a childminder or in a crèche, just wanting her mammy. I didn't balance this right. It's hard when you're doing so much of it on your own. I feel I missed out on spending some time with her and I think she clings to me now in case I leave her again for long periods of time.

I tell Jaelynne a million times a day that I love her. I often say "I'm sorry" for no reason. Her standard response is, "Yeah, Mam, you told me that already." I hope she does know I am sorry that I couldn't be at home more and I hope when she is a young woman she will understand why. Knowing Jaelynne, I think she already does. I feel I need to make it up to her for working so hard, and maybe there are plenty of reasons to say sorry.

Throughout her little life so far, I have buried my da, I had to move home after being raped in my own bed, and I struggled with bouts of depression and loneliness. I wasn't a fun mammy. I was practical and driven and a little shouty – the kids would say a lot shouty. I rationed my fun side to when the three of us went on holidays or to concerts. I couldn't be the fun parent, the strict parent and the hard-working parent all at once. There was no time to be silly.

I promised my girls the world. They didn't want the world; they wanted me. They wanted me to be happy and they wanted me to have fun with them but, for me, being happy was harder than pursuing a better life for them. I thought if I got us a better life and better opportunities, our happiness would follow. It did follow, but I can't undo their childhoods. I can't go back and stay with them when they were sick instead of having them minded so I didn't miss an exam. I can't go back and read the bedtime stories that I never read. I know, for Jaelynne, that this is what she wants. She looks to me now for it. She wants to be minded and she wants whatever affection is going.

Jaelynne is intelligent, forgiving and loves her family. She is witty like her dad and argumentative like me. When I look at her, I know

236

her. She is hard on the outside but behind her armour is a pure sensitivity. She is a force but, like me, she needs to be needed, needs to be part of something bigger than herself. She will battle against you all day but battle for you until the end. I recognise her, because she demonstrates so much of who I was. I watch her dote over babies and remember my attempt to save a sparrow. I watch her be strong when I know she just wants someone to hold her. She reminds me of who I was before everything came crashing down. I know I need to mind her and entertain her so the boredom doesn't set in. I know I need to fill her with love so she doesn't search for it in places where she doesn't belong. She will have a path paved for her, the path that I couldn't find. I was pulled towards the void; she will pull away from it. Her creativity and intelligence won't take her to the depths I plunged to; instead they will take her to the heights she deserves.

I have not felt safe and secure for major parts of my life but Jaelynne gives me a security that no one else does. She is consistent and I never feel judged or less of a person in her company. She is my rock.

I hope my daughters both understand my choices for them. My biggest fear in life, apart from death, is that they hold those choices against me, or that they feel I made the wrong decisions for them. I try to talk to them as much as I can about our lives, our past and my own faults and flaws. I ask Jaelynne all the time if she needs to chat about anything or if there is anything about me she would change if she could. She has only twice responded to this, once saying I should stop shouting so much (which I have) and the second time that I should give her more hugs (she never has enough hugs).

At eleven years old, she talks a lot about feminism. She recently blew me away when she did an audition for a Roddy Doyle film. She was so scared but she pushed past her own fears and did it anyway. Both of my daughters have played parts in RTÉ's *Rebellion* and its sequel, due out in 2018. Jordanne stood on the stage in the Olympia at the Repeal gig to speak about bodily autonomy while my ma and Jaelynne cheered on from the crowd.

I talked about creating structure for Jordanne in the face of her Asperger's diagnosis, but the reality is, my daughters created the structure, set the foundations and erected the scaffolding that was necessary for us to live. Jaelynne is moving towards her teens and Jordanne towards adulthood. They have both lifted me back up when I just wanted to sit down and give up. If I achieve anything in this world I want it to be that they experience life more positively than I did when I was their age. Like any mother, I just want for them to be happy and to find what it is they want to do in life.

EPILOGUE:
BITE OF LIFE

I sit on my own in Dún Laoghaire, staring out to sea. I belong here, at this moment, alone. I have been writing this book for some time and am nearing the end. I walk through each chapter, especially the hard ones: the rape, the deaths, the sadness and the hardship. I stroll past and stare at the empty suits of armour I have left behind. Now I am armourless, I am raw. It doesn't feel good. I have no protection from the world. I want to step back into each coat of armour, but I can't. Instead I have to meet this part of myself. I am alone. I walked the journey alone and now no one is here waiting on me, expecting me to stumble from the pages of this book, naked, skinless and sad. Nothing is on the other side, apart from the sea. That's all I can imagine right now. The sea and its strong pull, inhaling me.

I think to myself, I should never have written this book, because now I know the trauma. It's not just the story I tell; it's the life that has moulded me. It is me. I want to run back through each and every page and tell that girl she is not to blame. I want to tell her she is good and she is worth more. I want to tell her that she has internalised every single bad thing that has happened in her world, but that these things are not her fault. I want to give her a hug and fill her with love, because little does she know that when she gets to the end of the book she will step out from its pages, confused and sore.

I am so open right now and have been for months. This book, Jordanne's diagnosis, Jaelynne's love and Rónán's presence in my life took me to a whole other level of what love, compassion and companionship mean, and I want it. I am creating something new with my family. I want it, but I am on shaky grounds. I stand here now, in this place in my life, with no shell, feeling like jelly, wanting to feel OK, but also needing to stay out in the open to make this new transition.

At times I want to put back on the war clothing, my warrior steel. I want love, compassion, understanding and gentleness. It is not from others I want it but from myself; I want to forgive myself. It is as though I was seven and I fast forwarded through lots of pain, and writing this book spit me out at the end without warning, without protection from its pages. No one was there to catch me. Instead I have to feel what I am feeling. What the book has brought me is a necessary pain, because now, unlike then, I have acquired better skills and supports to look at it.

I look at Jordanne and Jaelynne now and I want to travel back and do my time with them all over again, with this new sense of emotion and feeling. That's pointless though because I know I resourced myself in the best way possible, in a way that was needed to get us to this point. I am sensitive and vulnerable now. I have no idea where I am going or what I am meant to be.

As I neared the end of this book, I began to look for different employment. I was worried this political world wasn't for me. Yet, I know that I don't know what world I am meant to be in. I have no idea who I am.

Every few years I dissect the pieces of myself, and for that moment in time I am not whole. I did it after I found out about my da; I did it after Jenny died; I did it when I got pregnant; I did it at An Cosán; I did it when I decided to go to Trinity; I did it after I was raped. But this is the first time in years I have left myself again. I have left myself to find myself. The book instigated three months' transition through my deepest thoughts. Exploring what I needed to shed to be a better person. A better mother. The person I am now knows that who I was wasn't good enough. Yet who I was, was all I was capable of at the time. Each and every one of my transitional periods produces a new best version of myself.

It's another day. I sit in the Bite of Life café in Dublin, with my couscous salad and green tea, writing. The voice in my head says, "It's a long way from green tea and couscous you were reared, Lynn Ruane."

Jordanne has joined me after her session with Grace Dyas and Theatre Club. She is excited to be working on their new theatre piece, *Not at Home*, which captures the real lives and experiences of women who have had to travel for abortion. *Not at Home* is the perfect opportunity for her to combine her acting and her activism for the cause of advancing women's rights, particularly the right to access abortion in Ireland, which she feels so passionate about.

I notice she is holding a copy of Rachael Keogh's book, *Dying to Survive*. After many years of her trying to absorb and understand her own father's addiction, I wonder if reading this book is the best thing for her. She misses her dad and hates the hold addiction takes on people. She has begun to understand its power and I imagine she must feel helpless and powerless.

I point at Rachael's book. "I'm not sure you should read that yet. Will you be OK with it?"

She looks me in the eye. "Ma, I can't avoid stuff just because it's sad, just because I might be able to relate to some of it."

Unlike me, Jordanne allows the feelings of trauma and injustices to sit with her, to sit within her. She has the power to stop and say, "You know what? This is not OK. This is not how things should be."

I couldn't have done that at her age. I would acknowledge something bad happening but it's as though sitting with this trauma for longer than two minutes would plunge me back into a life I had barely escaped from. And where would that leave my kids? All I need to do is to keep moving forward, ploughing my way through to the other side, to a life that is stable and secure, a life where my kids have opportunities.

So, I sit in the café, after weeks of writing about myself, dissecting myself and reliving my life, and I still feel like I have failed in so many areas of their lives. Is it enough for them to turn out well and then claim to have been a good mother? What is it to be a mother? It is as though my goal as a mother was to create the space for them to have more than me. More positive experiences, travel the world, go to university – and for the love of these things, not because they feel they have to prove something to the world.

I wanted my daughters to be intelligent, well-rounded, empowered, assertive, compassionate and empathetic young women. I succeeded and they are all of those things. But I felt like the future of my daughters, and their daughters, relied on me achieving change. When they look at our lives, will they see the absence of a family, a family sitting around the dinner table talking about their day? Will they miss the mundane things that didn't happen often enough?

I look at Jordanne sitting quietly beside me, seventeen years old, artistic, intelligent, successful, and I wonder at how she could be my daughter. I think of Jaelynne, eleven years old, a strong, principled, feminist warrior, and I wonder at how she could be my daughter.

"Mam, are you going to work again?"

"Mam, will you please put the laptop down and listen to me?"

"Mam, I don't feel well. Will you stay with me? Please don't go to that meeting."

"Mam, Mam, Mam."

I didn't always put them first in those moments. Essays to finish, amendments to submit. I didn't have time for sick children. They want me, but I am in the dream. The dream of change, the dream of waving them off to college, the dream of watching them flourish and change the generations to come after us.

Turns out that them loving me is important; how they see me is important. But instead they see a woman who struggled, who fought, who often wore that fight on her face in an angry grimace. And yes, they have seen a mother who brings them to cool places, showed them as many countries as she could. But I believe they would have preferred to see a mammy who was more playful, more forgiving, who shouted less, who was a little more present. I wasn't those things and I look back now, older and wiser, and wish I could have found a way to be both. I try to be both now and I attempt daily to right some of the wrongs or harm I may have caused. I have found a way to be a little more comfortable in my own skin while also striving for success. I thought I could show them the worst of me and the best of me and that would be enough. I thought I could show them the world and they would forgive me my flaws. I hope they can, I hope they do and I hope they see me, because I love them more than life.

Jordanne lifts her face from her book and I ask her if she has read the acknowledgements. I tell her that her dad wanted to call her Roy if she was a boy. She turns the pages to the acknowledgements of Rachael Keogh's book and I point to the name Roy Murphy. I tell her that Rachael and her dad shared a friend, and that friend was Roy. Roy died before I got a chance to meet him but, if she had been a boy, she would have been named after him.

"It's a small world, Jordanne, and we are all connected," I tell her. "Some of us are here to tell our stories. Others will never get the chance."

She sees the tears in my eyes and asks me to read what I have written. In a quivering tone I begin to read, trying my hardest not to start sobbing uncontrollably like a child. I am afraid that if I start to cry I won't be able to stop. As I read each line, I begin to notice that the anger, the rage, the trauma, whatever it is that I have been carrying, is no longer the mask that I wear. If you wear a mask for long enough, you assume its identity, and it becomes difficult to know if the mask is you or just the side of you to which you give your energies so you can get through life. The mask I wore to get us here – tough, angry, take no shit – is slipping and behind it now is a vulnerable woman who hopes her children can see through it.

Jordanne watches me as I read. When it gets too much, she reaches her hands out to me, my beautiful JJ; she wraps her arms around me and she whispers: "I needed to hear that, just as much as you needed to write it. I love you, Mam. Me and Jaelynne, we both love you."

As I move through the months of transition after I have written my final chapter, I have become stronger and the armour looks less attractive. I find peace sitting next to Rónán in bed reading; or chatting to my brother on the phone; or taking my mother out on the town; or reading over an essay for Jordanne, knowing what Harvard referencing is; or listening to Jaelynne call out sexism everywhere she goes; or when my nephew Caiden walks into the room and I hear, "Aunty Lynn". When I see Caiden, I am guaranteed to be asked a question that I sometimes have to google. He is such a bright kid with a real interest in history, which was never my forte. His mind is hungry for knowledge. One of my favourite memories of 2018 was watching Caiden engage in forty minutes of conversation with Alice Mary Higgins on peace and neutrality. They barely took a breath. I love to watch my brother commit himself to Caiden the way my da committed himself to Jay – never missing a training session or a football match or a chance to boast about what a great player Caiden is. Their little family is held together by my sister in-law, who likes to sneak down to ours to have a glass of wine and watch some crap TV – our house full of women a much-needed respite from the boys.

Even with the new appreciation for all that is in front of me, I am still not sure of my place in this society, but I know where I belong. It's with my family. I also know where my heart is. It is with my community and my friends, the ones who are here and the ones who are not. My duty is to those who have experienced the traumas of a class system that they never should have.

I have done it all because of my family and for my community. If I can hold that thought close to my heart, my intentions will only ever be good.

I am not just a politician, I am a woman, a mother, a friend and a partner. They are intertwined and often they have an impact on each other. My political life is enhanced and often inspired by my private life. I may never be the type of politician that people imagine I should be. I will always be a friend to those whom society often want to ostracise and label. I will always be part of my Tallaght community and that brings with it situations that not everyone in the political world will understand. I can feel love, more now than I ever did. Love for every single person who entered my life. Some stayed, some left and some taught me valuable lessons, and each and every experience that I have had has been used as fuel to drive me forward.

I refuse to feel insulted anymore when someone says, in a negative way, "people like you". I love people like me. In fact, I love people like you, too. Even with your differences, your views and your experiences. You are people like me. The only differences are our circumstances and our outcomes. At the core of our humanity, we are people like each other. Let's come together.

Gill Books
Hume Avenue
Park West
Dublin 12
www.gillbooks.ie

Gill Books is an imprint of M.H. Gill & Co.

978 07171 8018 9

All family photos courtesy of Lynn Ruane

Print origination by Carole Lynch
Edited by Brian Langan
Printed by CPI Group (UK) Ltd, Croydon, CRO 4YY

This book is typeset in Bembo.

The author and publisher have made every effort to trace
all copyright holders, but if any have been inadvertently
overlooked we would be pleased to make the necessary
arrangement at the first opportunity.

The paper used in this book comes from the wood pulp of
managed forests. For every tree felled, at least one tree is planted,
thereby renewing natural resources.

A CIP catalogue record for this book is available
from the British Library.

5 4 3 2